Dietary Guidelines

Dietary Guidelines

Written by the
Dietary Committee
Texas Children's Hospital
Houston, Texas

Edited by
Evelyn J. Lorenzen, Ph.D., M.D., Chairman

Gulf Publishing Company Book Division
Houston, London, Paris, Tokyo

Dedicated
to ALL infants and children entrusted to our care in
Texas Children's Hospital

Library of Congress
Catalog Number 78-53194

ISBN 0-87201-176-3

Foreword

Dietary Guidelines has been compiled by a committee of extremely knowledgeable individuals with varied abilities and backgrounds. They have brought together a vast amount of basic information concerning nutrition and related fields for use in multiphasic applications, from normal nutrition to conditions amenable to dietary therapy.

The importance of treating every patient on an individualized basis has been emphasized, thus allowing for each person's normal, specific, or abnormal needs. The information uniquely focuses on infants and children and brings together much scattered material: It emphasizes the requirements of *growing* subjects, the varying growth and maintenance needs of different body tissues and functions, and, in turn, compares these needs to those of adults.

The comparative nutrient composition tables of the various milk-based, soybean-based, and special formulas—as well as the tube feedings alone—are exceedingly helpful and time-saving to anyone who manages the feeding of infants and children. The information is well documented, well organized, and practical.

This book should be an invaluable aid and reference for practicing physicians, residents, interns, medical students, clinical and therapeutic dietitians, nurses, and other paramedical personnel. It is not only of value to Texas Children's Hospital, but can be used to advantage by other institutions as well.

Russell J. Blattner, M.D.
Physician in Chief
Texas Children's Hospital

Dietary Committee of Texas Children's Hospital

Evelyn J. Lorenzen, M.D., Ph.D., Chairman
Clin. Assoc. Prof. Ped., BCM, UTH
Private practice, Ped.

Arthur L. Beaudet, M.D.
Chief, Genetics and Birth Defects Clinic, TCH
Asst. Prof. Ped. and I.M., BCM

George D. Ferry, M.D.
Director of Clinical Nutrition and Gastroenterology,
Clin. Asst. Prof. Ped., BCM

Robert S. Zeller, M.D.
Chief, Neurology Service, TCH
Asst. Prof. Ped., BCM

Russell J. Blattner, M.D., ex officio
Physician in Chief, T.C.H.
Prof. and Dept. Chairman, Ped., BCM

Earl J. Brewer, Jr., M.D.
President, Medical Staff, TCH
Chief, Dept. of Rheumatology, TCH
Clin. Assoc. Prof., Ped., BCM

Miss Opal M. Benage, R.N.
Associate Administrator, Nursing Service, TCH

Mrs. Carolyn Roe, R.N.
Associate Director, Nursing Service, TCH

Mr. Kevin J. O'Donnell
Assistant Administrator, TCH

Mrs. Martha S. McLaughlin, R.D.
Assistant Director, Professional
Dietetic Services, TCH

Mr. Joseph Bergaila
Director, Food Service Department

Mrs. Sally Betts, R.D.
Clinical Dietitian, TCH

Mrs. Lynne Corder, R.D.
Clinical Dietitian, TCH

Miss Nancy Law, R.D.
Clinical Dietician, TCH

Guest Contributors

Leighton Hill, M.D.
Chief, Renal-Metabolic Service, TCH
Prof. Ped., BCM

Paul Rambeau, Ph.D.
Former Head, Nutrition Laboratory, NASA
Food and Drug Administration
Washington, D.C.

William J. Klish, M.D.
Asst. Prof. Dept. Ped.
Nutrition and Gastroenterology, BCM

Joseph Rogers, M.D.
Fellow, Dept. of Ped.
Nutrition and Gastroenterology, BCM

BCM = Baylor College of Medicine
UTH = University of Texas at Houston
TCH = Texas Children's Hospital
NASA = National Aeronautics and Space Administration

We wish to acknowledge the following companies for their helpful information in compiling some of our tables.
Mead Johnson Laboratories
Ross Laboratories
Eaton Laboratories
Syntex Laboratories
Loma Linda
Wyeth Laboratories
Doyle Pharmaceuticals
Gerber Company
Cutter Laboratories

Preface

Texas Children's Hospital (TCH), in the Medical Center Complex of Houston, Texas, functions for the care and treatment solely of infants and children from birth to nineteen years. The upper age limit was extended from fifteen to nineteen in 1972. Patients beyond the age of nineteen are handled by the joint facilities of St. Luke's Episcopal Hospital (SLEH). These two hospitals are operated in conjunction with a third, the Texas Heart Institute (THI).

The need arose for dietary and nutritional guidelines to serve the specialized age group of Texas Children's Hospital, providing a concise, pertinent and facile source of information pertaining strictly to pediatric dietary management.

Nutrition is a basic part of total care in health or any altered state. It is impossible to plan a specific diet for each individual disease or disease complex, and the goals of diet therapy must change as newer knowledge and data are accumulated. Many of these views have changed drastically over the past two decades. While much is known regarding the nutritional needs of the healthy, normal individual, relatively little regarding nutrition per se and nutritional requirements in disease, especially in the area of metabolic disorders, is known.

A diet manual is obsolete as soon as it is printed, since no set diet can apply to more than a specific individual under specified circumstances. The astute clinical dietitian is capable of making individual adjustments for each patient based upon current information and guidelines. Necessary knowledge involves specific composition of individual foods, specific breakdown of individual nutrients and the mode of metabolism, if known. The utilization of this knowledge for a particular patient and his or her specific needs is genuine diet therapy in its practical application.

The pediatric age group differs from all other age groups by the constant growth and development of its subjects. This factor must always be taken into consideration in addition to the nutritional needs for maintenance, activity, normal losses (skin, urine, feces), abnormal losses (fever, burns), tissue repair, disease states, etc.

It is hoped that *Dietary Guidelines* will aid the physician in planning and ordering a normal diet for any age, as well as a modification or special diet used in the treatment of any condition amenable to diet. We trust the interns and residents will find it a valuable teaching aid.

It is also hoped that, with the participation of the dietitian, working along with the physician or surgeon and nurse as a team toward the total care of the patient, the highest standards of service and understanding may be achieved.

Dietary Guidelines has been written as a project of the Dietary Committee of Texas Children's Hospital. It represents considerable time and effort on the part of the individual members of the committee. Genuine appreciation and gratitude is hereby expressed to: all members of the committee, those individuals with personal contributions bearing their names, all of the dietitians who have worked so long and faithfully on the various diets, calculations, tables and revisions; Mrs. Nelda Steel, Mrs. Ruby Selby, and Mrs. Joan Robbins, for their valuable secretarial assistance; Mr. Robert Park, TCH Librarian, who aided greatly in obtaining numerous references; NASA and Paul Rambeau, Ph.D., for the analyses of the hospital diets; Mr. Newell E. France, Executive Director of TCH, SLEH and THI, Mr. Ralph Ux, Associate Director-Staff Services, and Mr. Kevin J. O'Donnell, Assistant Administrator, for their continued help, support and encouragement during the long period of preparation; Miss Opal Benage, R.N., Associate Administrator—Nursing Service, and Mrs. Carolyn Roe, R.N., Associate Director of Nursing, for their support and assistance; and Mrs. Evelyn Lawrence, for consulting assistance in the publication of this material.

In addition to the present committee members, special thanks and appreciation are extended to Miss Ann Caskey, R.D., formerly of TCH and a member of the committee, now engaged in graduate work at Oklahoma State University, Stillwater; Mrs. Faye Martin Walker, R.D., formerly of TCH and a member of the committee, now affiliated with M & IC and Family Planning, Houston, Texas; and Miss Elaine Potts, R.D., Research Dietitian, Clinical Research Center, TCH, for their contributions and suggestions.

All have given so generously and graciously of their time and knowledge.

Evelyn J. Lorenzen, M.D., Ph.D.
Chairman, Dietary Committee

Contents

Foreword V
Preface VII

Dietary Procedures, 1

Physician's Diet Order Sheet, 1; New Admissions/Diet Changes, 1; Nourishment (Between Meals), 3; Diet Instructions, 3; Caloric Intake or Dietary Analysis Requests, 3; Infant Intake Pattern, 5

Diets for Infants, 6

Infant Feeding, 6; Ingredient List of Infant Formulas, 6; Nutrient Composition of Infant Formulas, 7; Modular Formula, 14

Normal Diets, 21

Basic Principles, 21; A Guide to Good Eating—Daily Recommendations, 23; Recommended Daily Dietary Allowances, N.R.C., 1974, 24; Recommended Daily Food Intake Patterns for Children, 27; Recommended Dietary Allowances for Infants Expressed in Relation to Energy Needs (amounts per 100 kcal), 30

Standard Hospital Diets, 32

Regular House Diet, 32; Chopped Diet, 33; Soft Diet, 34; Dental Soft Diet, 36; Liquid Diet, 37; Clear Liquid Diet, 37; Polycose (Glucose Polymer), 38; Lytren, 40; Full Liquid Diet, 41; T & A Diets, 42

Tube Feedings, 45

Basic Principles, 45; Blenderized Feedings, 45; Protein (approximately 15%), 45; Carbohydrate (approximately 50%), 45; Fats (approximately 35%), 46; Commercially Prepared Tube Feedings, 46; Nutrient Composition of Tube, Elemental and Supplementary Feedings, 47; Indications for Tube Feeding, 48; Elemental Diets, 50; Ingredient List of Tube Feedings and Supplemental Feedings, 53

Total Parenteral Nutrition (TPN), 56

Indications, 56; Principles of TPN Infusion, 57; Metabolic Variables To Be Monitored, 58; Major Complications, 59; Guidelines for Intralipid Use, 61

Therapeutic Hospital Diets, 63

Generalized Gastrointestinal Disorders, 63; Specific Gastrointestinal Disorders, 64; Minimum Residue Diet (Surgical Soft), 64; Low Residue Diet, 66; Carbohydrate Intolerance and Enzyme Deficiencies, 68; Milk Free Diet, 70; Celiac Disease, 71; Gluten Restricted Diet, 73; Gluten-Free Commercial Products, 74; Low Sucrose Diet, 77; Sodium Restricted Diet, 78; Salt Consumption of Infants, 81; Sodium and Potassium Values Special Solutions and Products, 84; 250 Milligram

Sodium Diet (11 mEq), 85; 500 Milligram Sodium Infant Diet, 88; 500 Milligram Sodium Diet (22 mEq), 89; 800 Milligram Sodium Diet (35 mEq), 92; 1000 Milligram Sodium Diet (44 mEq), 96; 1500 Milligram Sodium Diet (65 mEq), 100; 2000 Milligram Sodium Diet (87 mEq), 103; Conversion of Milliequivalents and Milligrams of Sodium Chloride, 107; Potassium-Restricted Diet, 107; Protein Diets, 109; Exchange Lists for Protein Restricted Diets, 111; Renal Solute Load, 117; Acid Ash and Alkaline Ash Diets, 118; High Calorie Diet, 119; Low-Calorie Diet, 121; The Ketogenic Diet, 123; Dietary Therapy of Inborn Errors of Metabolism, 126; Dietary Management of Childhood Diabetes Mellitus, 130; Childhood Diabetes, 131; Galactosemia, 137; Galactose-Free Diet, 139; Phenylketonuria, 142; Dietary Management of Phenylketonuria, 144; Phenylalanine Content of Gerber Baby Foods, 148; Phenylalanine Exchange List Vegetables, 150; Phenylalanine Contents of Food (Gerber's), 156; Maple Syrup Urine Disease (MSUD), 157; Glycogen Storage Diseases, 159; The Homocystinurias, 160

Appendix, 162

More Common Carbohydrates in Foods per 100 gm., 162; Less Common Carbohydrates in Foods, per 100 gm., 167; Metric Equivalents, 168; Exchange Lists for Meal Planning, 169; Test Diets, 175; VMA (Vanillymandelic Acid) Test Diet, 177; Low Tyramine Diet, 177

Index, 178

Chapter 1

Dietary Procedures

I. Physician's Diet Order Sheet
All physicians are required to complete the Physician's Diet Order Sheet, Form PS 209 within 24 hours after ordering the admitting diet for new admissions to Texas Children's Hospital. Any change of diet should be ordered under *Dietary Changes.* (see example, Figure 1.)

A. *For Infants*

1. *List specific formula desired by brand name, number of feedings, ounces per feeding and calories per ounce.*

2. List solid foods or supplements requested, giving number of feedings per day.

B. *For Older Children*

1. Check diet desired or write specific order if a special diet is requested in the allotted space; i.e., 1000 mg. Sodium.

II. New Admissions/Diet Changes

A. Diet orders for patients admitted to Texas Children's Hospital, through the Admitting Office, will be handled by the Professional Dietetic Staff. Staff physicians will list their standing diet orders with the Professional Dietetic Staff; if a staff physician does not have a standing diet order, his/her patient will receive a regular house diet for their first meal.
(Note: This policy does not pertain to Emergency Admissions)

B. Diet changes, for each meal, are transcribed in ink, on the unit Diet Check List, then transposed to the Nursing Care Plan. The first copy of the Diet Check List is tubed to the General Diet Office (H-4) for Lunch by 9:30 A.M. and for Dinner by 1:30 P.M.

Diet changes after 4:00 P.M. will not become effective until the following meal. This rule applies to breakfast and luncheon meals,

TEXAS CHILDREN'S HOSPITAL

PHYSICIAN DIET ORDER

ADDRESSOGRAPH

ADMITTING DIET ORDER (to be entered within 24 hrs. after admission)

Date/Time ____________________ Physician's Signature ______________________________

☑ Check appropriate diet, or when applicable, write specific diet in OTHER section.

☐ Formula (birth to 1 year) ☐ Breast Fed

_________/_________/_______q______hrs or on demand_______

Brand Kcal/oz. oz.

☐ Strained: check foods desired:

☐ Cereal ☐ Fruit ☐ Meat ☐ Vegetable ☐ Egg Yolk ☐ Juice

☐ Chopped (1 to 3 years)

☐ Regular (3 to 19 years)

☐ Soft

☐ Full Liquid

☐ Clear Liquid

☐ NPO

☐ 1 Gram Sodium (Cardiac Diet)

☐ 2 Gram Sodium

☐ Regular, No milk or milk products

☐ Regular, no added salt (3 - 5 gm Na)

☐ Juvenile Diabetic (no concentrated sweets)

OTHER____

FOOD ALLERGIES/OR INTOLERANCES (list each)_________________________________

DIET CHANGES (Specify as above)

Date/Time	Physician's Signature

PHYSICIAN DIET ORDER SHEET over

Figure 1. Physician's Diet Order form.

also. The only exceptions are changing liquid diet to soft diet or N.P.O. diet to resume diet.

Breakfast changes — call before 6:30 P.M.
Luncheon changes — call before 11:00 A.M.

After the check list for the next meal is off the floor, diet changes must be telephoned to the General Diet Office (Extension 2004).

III. Nourishment (In-between Meal)

In-between meal nourishments are routinely distributed to patients in Texas Children's Hospital by Nursing Service personnel. Special foods are provided by the Dietary Department for children on modified diets if they request in-between nourishments. These include fresh fruit, popsicles, low sodium peanut butter, low sodium bread and low sodium crackers. Nursing Service orders unit supplies for nourishments daily on Form PS 87. The order must be received by the General Diet Office by 9:30 A.M.

IV. Meals are routinely served at the following times:

Breakfast	6:45 A.M.
Lunch	11:15 A.M.
Dinner	4:15 P.M.

V. Diet Instructions

A. *In-patients*
Any physician desiring his or her patient to receive discharge dietary counseling or instruction regarding either regular or therapeutic diets, should make such request at least twenty-four hours (24) prior to the time of discharge. Requests should be kept to a minimum on week-ends, when the Professional Dietetic Staff is also at a minimum.

B. *Out Patients*
Out-Patient diet instructions are done by the Therapeutic Dietitian by appointment only. The physician is requested to write the diet order on his office prescription form. This prescription should be brought by the patient at the scheduled instruction time. A nominal fee is charged for the consultation.

VI. Caloric Intake or Dietary Analysis Requests

Any physician desiring a caloric intake record for his or her patient should request such by written order twenty-four (24) hours prior to the period of observation. Caloric intake records will be taken for a period of three (3) days unless otherwise specified. A complete dietary analysis (for 24 hours) may be obtained after written request and specifying the individual nutrients to be included.

TEXAS CHILDREN'S HOSPITAL
INFANT DIETARY INTAKE PATTERN

Patient ______________ Height ______________

Age ______________ Weight ______________

Date ______________

The following foods that are checked have been introduced into this child's eating pattern.

STRAINED		JUNIOR
____	Beef	____
____	Chicken	____
____	Lamb	____
____	Veal	____
____	Turkey	____
____	Ham	____
____	Liver	

Others (specify)
____
____
____
____

STRAINED		JUNIOR
____	Carrots	____
____	Green Beans	____
____	Spinach	____
____	Squash	____
____	Beets	
____	Green Peas	

Others (specify)
____
____
____
____
____

STRAINED		JUNIOR
____	Applesauce	____
____	Peaches	____
____	Pears	____
____	Apricots	
____	Pears/Pineapple	
____	Plums	
____	Prunes	
____	Apple Juice	
____	Orange Juice	

Others (specify)
____
____

STRAINED

____ Barley Cereal
____ High Protein Cereal
____ Mixed Cereal
____ Oatmeal
____ Rice

Others (specify)
____
____

SPECIAL PROBLEMS:

EATING PATTERN PRIOR TO HOSPITAL ADMISSION

BREAKFAST	LUNCH	DINNER

Favorite Foods	Foods That Are Refused	Known Allergies	Questionable Intolerance

____
Dietitian

Figure 2. Infant Dietary Intake Pattern form.

VII. Infant Intake Pattern

If a physician desires a twenty-four (24) hour intake record for a child under one year of age, a written order is requested for same. The dietitian will complete Form TC 0-70 (Infant Intake Pattern, Figure 2) and place the original copy in the patient's chart; the carbon copy is filed in the dietitian's office.

VIII. Selective Computerized Menu

Selective computerized menus are distributed daily to pediatric patients on Regular, Soft, Chopped and most modified diets. Menus are printed a day in advance for the above diets. Name, room number and diet type are also printed on each Selective Menu.

Diet Clerks distribute the menus daily, with the exception of a few diets not coded in the computer (i.e., gluten free, galactose free).

IX. Formula Room

The Formula Room, 4 B 014, is operated by the staff of the Professional Dietetic Services. Formula Room Technicians prepare and distribute pre-packaged and specially prepared products daily to designated nursing units.

The Formula Room is open daily 9:00 A.M. to 5:45 P.M. Any specially prepared formula ordered after hours will be prepared by the Nursing Supervisor on duty in Texas Children's Hospital.

X. A Therapeutic Dietary Products Center, operated by the Women's Auxiliary of Texas Children's Hospital, provides therapeutic infant formulas and specially prepared products used in the treatment of many diseases amenable by diet. The Center is located in the Snack Bar, second floor (street level). The Snack Bar is open Monday through Friday from 8:30 A.M. - 7:00 P.M. and on week-ends, 9:00 A.M. - 5:00 P.M. Their telephone number is 521-2255.

The Snack Bar is closed on holidays.

Chapter 2

Diets for Infants

Infant Feeding

Practically every formula manufactured for the feeding of infants and children is available at Texas Children's Hospital. The detailed nutrient composition of milk-based, soy-based and special formulas is provided in Table I. In ordering a diet or formula for an infant, the physician simply uses the Physician's Diet Order Sheet and lists the brand, kilocalories/oz. and frequency of feeding. Sources of protein, carbohydrate and fat are found in Table II.

For ease of preparation, proportions for various dilutions of the concentrated liquid formulas are listed in Table III and those for the powdered formulas in Table IV. Complete ingredient lists for each formula are found below.

Because of the wide divergence of opinion regarding the introduction of solid foods in the infant's diet, no pre-planned diet is available but a choice that allows each physician to simply check the specific solid foods that he or she wishes the particular patient to have.

Any special diet may likewise be ordered in the appropriate area or any dietary change should be indicated on the Diet Order Sheet. In this way, one sheet reveals the diet or foods that the patient has been or is presently receiving. Any food allergies or intolerances are also listed on this sheet.

Ingredient List of Infant Formulas
Texas Children's Hospital

Bremil Skimmed grade A milk; water; sucrose; soy and coconut oils; lecithin; calcium carrageenan; sodium ascorbate; dl-methionine; ferrous sulfate; d-alpha-tocopheryl acetate; niacinamide; dl-calcium pantothenate; vitamin A palmitate; cupric sulfate; riboflavin; thiamine hydrochloride; pyridoxine hydrochloride; crystalline vitamin D_3; folic acid; potassium iodide; vitamin B_{12}.

Table I

Nutrient Composition of Infant Formulas

per 100 mls.	COMPANY	DILUTION	KILOCALORIES per 100 mls./per oz.	PROTEIN (gms.)	FAT (gms.)	CARBOHYDRATE (gms.)	VITAMIN A (I.U.)	VITAMIN D (I.U.)	VITAMIN E (I.U.)	ASCORBIC ACID (mgs.)	VITAMIN B_1 (mcgs.)	VITAMIN B_2 (mcgs.)	NIACIN (mcgs.)	VITAMIN B_6 (mcgs.)	SODIUM (mEq./mgs.)	POTASSIUM (mEq./mgs.)	CHLORIDE (mEq./mgs.)	CALCIUM (mEq./mgs.)	PHOSPHORUS (mEq./mgs.)	IRON (mgs.)	RENAL SOLUTE * (per liter)	INTESTINAL SOLUTE ** (per liter)
MILK-BASED																						
ENFAMIL	Mead Johnson	a 1:2	44.0/13.2	1.0	2.4	4.6	110	27	0.8	3.4	34	41	550	27	0.8/18	1.2/46	0.8/28	1.8/36	2.0/31	0.10	85	
ENFAMIL	Mead Johnson	b 1:1	67.3/20.2	1.5	3.7	7.0	169	42	1.3	5.3	53	63	846	42	1.2/28	1.8/70	1.2/43	2.7/55	3.0/47 d	0.15	128	293
ENFAMIL	Mead Johnson	c 1½:1	80.4/24.1	1.8	4.4	8.4	203	50	1.6	6.4	64	76	1015	50	1.4/34	2.2/84	1.4/52	3.2/66	3.6/56	0.18	153	
SIMILAC	Ross	a 1:2	43.9/13.2	1.2	2.3	4.5	163	26	1.0	3.6	42	65	460	26	0.9/21	1.4/54	1.1/38	2.2/45	2.3/36	tr	102	
SIMILAC	Ross	b 1:1	67.6/20.3	1.6	3.6	7.2	250	40	1.5	5.5	65	100	700	40	1.0/22	1.7/68	1.6/56	2.9/58	2.8/43 e	tr	134	293
SIMILAC	Ross	c 1½:1	81.1/24.3	2.2	4.3	8.5	300	48	1.8	6.6	78	120	840	48	1.4/32	2.5/96	1.9/69	4.0/83	4.3/66	tr	183	
SIMILAC	Ross	f R/F	92.1/27.6	2.5	4.8	9.6	338	54	2.0	7.4	90	140	940	54	1.5/35	2.9/114	2.1/76	4.6/93	4.8/74	tr	208	424
SIMILAC 60/40	Ross	g .66:2	44.3/13.3	1.0	2.3	4.9	163	26	0.7	3.6	42	65	475	20	0.5/10	1.0/38	0.8/30	1.3/26	0.8/13	0.17	80	
SIMILAC 60/40	Ross	h 1:2	68.3/20.5	1.6	3.5	7.6	250	40	1.0	5.5	65	100	730	30	0.7/16	1.5/58	1.3/46	2.0/40	1.3/20	0.26	126	427
SIMILAC 60/40	Ross	i 1¼:2	81.8/24.5	1.9	4.2	9.1	300	48	1.2	6.6	78	120	876	36	0.8/19	1.8/70	1.6/55	2.4/48	1.5/24	0.31	150	
SIMILAC ADVANCE	Ross	b 1:1	56.1/16.8	2.8	2.0	6.2	240	40	0.8	5.0	75	90	1000	60	1.5/35	3.1/120	2.8/100	4.0/80	3.9/60	1.80	234	
SKIM MILK	Ross	f R/F	34.5/10.4	3.5	0.1	4.9	170	40	0.5	5.5	70	100	1140	40	2.3/52	4.4/171	3.2/114	6.5/130	6.1/95	tr	299	291
SMA	Wyeth	a 1:2	43.5/13.1	1.0	2.3	4.7	172	27	0.7	3.8	46	69	653	27	0.5/10	0.9/36	0.7/24	1.4/29	1.4/21	0.83	78	
SMA	Wyeth	b 1:1	67.2/20.2	1.5	3.6	7.2	264	42	1.0	5.8	71	106	1004	42	0.7/15	1.4/56	1.0/37	2.2/44	2.1/33	1.27	117	300
SMA	Wyeth	c 1½:1	80.3/24.1	1.8	4.3	8.6	317	50	1.2	7.0	85	127	1205	50	0.8/18	1.7/67	1.2/44	2.6/53	2.6/40	1.52	140	
SOY-BASED																						
CHO-FREE	Syntex	b 1:1	39.2/11.6	1.9	3.5	j 6.4/0.02	211	42	1.1	5.5	53	106	740	43	1.6/37	2.3/90	1.0/37	4.3/85	4.1/64	0.85	157 j	509
ISOMIL	Ross	a 1:2	43.5/13.1	1.3	2.3	4.4	163	26	1.0	3.6	26	39	585	26	0.8/20	1.2/46	1.0/34	2.3/46	2.1/33	0.78	104	
ISOMIL	Ross	b 1:1	67.6/20.3	2.0	3.6	6.8	250	40	1.5	5.5	40	60	900	40	1.3/30	1.8/71	1.5/53	3.5/70	3.2/50	1.20	160	215
ISOMIL	Ross	c 1½:1	81.1/24.3	2.4	4.3	8.2	300	48	1.8	6.6	48	72	1080	48	1.6/36	2.2/85	1.8/64	4.2/84	3.9/60	1.40	193	
MULL-SOY	Syntex	a 1:2	42.3/12.7	2.0	2.3	3.4	137	27	0.7	3.6	34	69	618	28	1.0/23	2.3/90	1.0/35	4.2/85	3.6/55	0.55	157	
MULL-SOY	Syntex	b 1:1	65.6/19.7	3.1	3.6	5.2	211	42	1.1	5.5	53	106	951	43	1.6/36	3.6/139	1.5/54	6.5/130	5.5/85	0.85	244	236
MULL-SOY	Syntex	c 1½:1	78.3/23.5	3.7	4.3	6.2	253	50	1.3	6.6	64	127	1141	52	1.9/43	4.3/167	1.8/65	7.8/156	6.6/102	1.00	291	
NEO-MULL-SOY	Syntex	a 1:2	42.3/12.7	1.2	2.3	4.2	137	27	0.7	3.6	34	69	481	28	1.0/24	1.5/59	0.7/24	2.8/55	2.7/42	0.55	100	
NEO-MULL-SOY	Syntex	b 1:1	64.7/19.3	1.9	3.5	6.4	211	42	1.1	5.5	53	106	740	43	1.6/37	2.3/90	1.0/37	4.3/85	4.1/64	0.85	157	253
NEO-MULL-SOY	Syntex	c 1½:1	77.8/23.3	2.3	4.2	7.7	253	50	1.3	6.6	64	127	888	52	1.9/44	2.8/108	1.2/44	5.2/102	5.0/77	1.02	190	
NURSOY	Wyeth	a 1:2	44.3/13.3	1.5	2.3	4.4	172	27	0.7	3.8	46	69	653	27	0.6/13	1.2/48	0.7/24	2.1/41	1.9/29	0.83	111	
NURSOY	Wyeth	b 1:1	68.8/20.6	2.3	3.6	6.8	264	42	1.0	5.8	71	106	1004	42	0.9/20	1.9/74	1.0/37	3.2/63	2.8/44	1.27	169	
NURSOY	Wyeth	c 1½:1	82.7/24.8	2.8	4.3	8.2	317	50	1.2	7.0	85	127	1205	50	1.1/24	2.3/89	1.2/44	3.8/76	3.4/53	1.52	206	
PROSOBEE	Mead Johnson	a 1:2	43.8/13.1	1.6	2.2	4.4	137	27	0.7	3.6	41	69	550	34	1.2/27	1.2/48	0.8/27	2.5/51	2.3/35	0.83	123	
PROSOBEE	Mead Johnson	b 1:1	67.8/20.3	2.5	3.4	6.8	211	42	1.0	5.5	63	106	846	53	1.8/42	1.9/74	1.2/42	3.9/79	3.4/53	1.27	192	252
PROSOBEE	Mead Johnson	c 1½:1	81.7/24.5	3.0	4.1	8.2	253	50	1.2	6.6	76	127	1015	64	2.2/50	2.3/89	1.4/50	4.7/95	4.1/64	1.52	230	
SOYALAC	Loma Linda	a 1:2	45.7/13.7	1.4	2.5	4.4	137	27	0.3	3.4	27	41	550	27	0.9/21	1.3/50	0.7/24	1.8/37	1.2/18	0.69	109	
SOYALAC	Loma Linda	b 1:1	69.8/20.9	2.2	3.8	6.7	211	42	0.5	5.3	42	63	846	42	1.4/32	2.0/77	1.0/37	2.8/57	1.8/28	1.06	169	203
SOYALAC	Loma Linda	c 1½:1	83.8/25.1	2.6	4.6	8.0	253	50	0.6	6.4	50	76	1015	50	1.7/38	2.4/92	1.2/44	3.4/68	2.2/34	1.27	201	
I-SOYALAC	Loma Linda	a 1:2	43.3/13.0	1.4	2.5	4.4	137	27	0.3	4.1	34	41	550	27	0.9/21	1.2/49	‡	2.0/41	2.2/34	1.03		
I-SOYALAC	Loma Linda	b 1:1	66.7/20.0	2.1	3.8	6.7	211	42	0.5	6.3	53	63	846	42	1.4/33	1.9/75	‡	3.1/63	3.4/53	1.59		
I-SOYALAC	Loma Linda	c 1½:1	80.0/24.0	2.5	4.6	8.0	253	50	0.6	7.6	64	76	1015	50	1.7/40	2.3/90	‡	3.8/76	4.1/64	1.91		
SPECIAL																						
LOFENOLAC	Mead Johnson	h 1:2	67.5/20.3	2.3	2.7	8.5	211	42	1.1	5.5	63	106	846	53	1.4/32	1.8/69	1.4/48	3.1/63	3.1/48	1.27	177	362
MEAT BASE †	Gerber	a 1:2	43.3/13.0	1.9	2.1	4.1	116	31	0.4	3.8	39	65	476	57	0.5/12	0.7/25	0.4/13	3.3/65	2.8/44	0.90	123	
MEAT BASE	Gerber	b 1:1	66.7/20.0	2.9	3.3	6.3	178	47	0.6	5.9	60	100	733	87	0.8/18	1.0/38	0.6/20	5.0/100	4.3/67	1.40	189	174
MEAT BASE	Gerber	k 1½:1	79.9/24.0	3.5	4.0	7.6	214	56	0.7	7.1	72	120	880	104	1.0/22	1.2/46	0.7/24	6.0/120	5.2/80	1.70	227	
NUTRAMIGEN	Mead Johnson	g .66:2	43.3/13.0	1.4	1.7	5.6	137	27	0.7	3.6	41	70	550	34	0.9/21	1.2/45	0.9/31	2.0/41	2.0/31	0.83	110	
NUTRAMIGEN	Mead Johnson	h 1:2	66.6/20.0	2.2	2.6	8.6	211	42	1.1	5.5	63	106	846	53	1.4/32	1.8/69	1.4/48	3.1/63	3.1/48	1.27	171	468
NUTRAMIGEN	Mead Johnson	i 1¼:2	79.5/23.9	2.6	3.1	10.3	253	50	1.3	6.6	76	127	1015	64	1.7/38	2.2/83	1.7/58	3.7/76	3.7/58	1.52	204	
PORTAGEN	Mead Johnson	g .66:2	45.7/13.7	1.6	2.1	5.1	183	18	0.7	3.6	69	83	824	89	0.9/21	1.4/55	1.0/38	2.0/41	2.0/31	0.83	124	
PORTAGEN	Mead Johnson	h 1:2	70.5/21.2	2.4	3.3	7.8	282	28	1.1	5.6	106	127	1268	137	1.4/32	2.2/85	1.6/58	3.1/63	3.1/48	1.27	189	346
PORTAGEN	Mead Johnson	i 1¼:2	85.2/25.6	2.9	4.0	9.4	338	34	1.3	6.7	127	152	1522	164	1.7/38	2.6/102	1.9/70	3.7/76	3.7/58	1.52	227	
PREGESTIMIL	Mead Johnson	g .66:2	44.6/13.4	1.4	1.8	5.7	137	27	0.7	3.6	41	69	550	34	0.9/21	1.2/45	0.9/31	2.0/41	2.0/31	0.83	110	
PREGESTIMIL	Mead Johnson	h 1:2	69.2/20.8	2.2	2.8	8.8	211	42	1.1	5.5	63	106	846	53	1.4/32	1.8/69	1.4/48	3.1/63	3.1/48	1.27	171	715
PREGESTIMIL	Mead Johnson	i 1¼:2	83.4/25.0	2.6	3.4	10.6	253	50	1.3	6.6	76	127	1015	64	1.7/38	2.2/83	1.7/58	3.7/76	3.7/58	1.52	204	
PROBANA	Mead Johnson	g .66:2	43.8/13.1	2.7	1.4	5.1	344	69	0.7	3.6	41	69	550	34	1.8/40	2.0/79	1.8/65	3.8/75	3.8/59 l		210	
PROBANA	Mead Johnson	h 1:2	68.2/20.5	4.2	2.2	7.9	529	106	1.1	5.5	63	106	846	53	2.7/61	3.1/122	2.8/100	5.8/116	5.8/90 l		325	653
PROBANA	Mead Johnson	i 1¼:2	81.4/24.4	5.0	2.6	9.5	635	127	1.3	6.6	76	127	1015	64	3.2/73	3.7/146	3.4/120	7.0/139	7.0/108 l		388	
HUMAN MILK ●■			71.0/21.0	1.2	3.3	7.0	189	00.4	0.6	4.3	16	36	147	10	0.7/15	1.4/55	1.2/43	1.6/33	0.6/15	0.15	10	
COW'S MILK ●■★			69.0/20.0	3.3	3.7	4.8	156	02.4	0.1	1.1	44	175	94	64	2.5/58	3.5/138	2.9/103	6.2/125	3.7/96	0.10	28	

a 1:2 indicates 1 part of formula concentrate to 2 parts of water.
b 1:1 indicates 1 part of formula concentrate to 1 part of water.
c 1½:1 indicates 1½ parts of formula concentrate to 1 part of water.
d Enfamil with Iron contains 1.27 mgs. iron per 100 mls.
e Similac with Iron contains 1.27 mgs. iron per 100 mls.
f Prepackaged--for hospital use only, in 4 oz. or 8 oz. bottles.
g 0.66:2 indicates 2 teaspoons formula powder to 2 ounces of water.
h 1:2 indicates 1 scoop (1 Tablespoon) formula powder to 2 ounces of water.
i 1¼:2 indicates 3 3/4 teaspoons formula powder to 2 ounces of water.
j When diluted with an equal volume of 12.8% carbohydrate solution, the yield is 19.3 kilocalories per ounce and 6.4 grams of carbohydrate per 100 mls.
k 1:1½ indicates 1 part of formula concentrate to 1½ parts of water.
l Add 6.8 mgs. Iron/liter from some other source.
* 1 gram dietary protein yields approximately 5.7 mOsmols urea.
** Values by Texas Children's Hospital Laboratory.
† Meat Base (Gerber) now in 15 oz. can and standard dilution (20 kilocal/oz) is 1:1.
‡ Chloride values unavailable.

ADDENDUM

SOYALAC, I-SOYALAC, and NEO-MULL-SOY are now packaged in 14-oz. lead-free cans.

● Macy, Icie G., Harriet J. Kelly and Ralph E. Sloan, The Composition of Milks, Committee on Maternal and Child Feeding of the Food and Nutrition Board, National Research Council, Pub. 254, 1953.

■ Kon, S.K., Milk and Milk Products in Human Nutrition, Food and Agriculture Organization of the United Nations, Rome, 1972.

★ Hartman, Arthur M. and Leslie P. Dryden, Vitamins in Milk and Milk Products, Published by American Dairy Science Association, U.S.D.A., 1965.

Table II

Sources of Protein, Carbohydrate and Fat in Infant Formulas

Product	Protein Source	Carbohydrate Source	Fat Source
Bremil	Skimmed, grade A milk	Lactose, sucrose	Soy oil, coconut oil
Enfamil	Skimmed, non-fat milk	Lactose (70%) Milk Lactose (30%)	Soy oil (80%) Coconut oil (20%)
Similac	Skim, non-fat milk	Lactose	Corn oil (40%) Soy oil (20%) Coconut oil (20%)
Similac w/iron	Skim, non-fat milk	Lactose	Corn oil (40%) Soy oil (20%) Coconut oil (20%)
Similac 60/40	Demineralized whey solids, CaNa Caseinate	Lactose	Coconut oil, corn oil
SMA	Skim, non-fat milk, electrodialyzed whey	Lactose	Coconut oil, soy oil, oleo, safflower oil
CHO-Free	Soy protein isolate	*	Soy oil
Isomil	Soy protein isolate	Sucrose, corn syrup solids, modified cornstarch	Coconut oil, corn oil, soy
Mullsoy	Soy flour	Sucrose	Soy oil
Neo-Mullsoy	Soy protein isolate	Sucrose	Soy oil
Nursoy	Soy protein isolate	Sucrose, corn syrup solids	Coconut oil, soy oil, oleo, safflower oil
ProSobee	Soy protein isolate	Sucrose (60%), corn syrup solids (40%)*	13.5 Soy oil
Soyalac	Soybean solids	Sucrose (60%), dextrose, dextrins-maltose	Soy oil
i-Soyalac	Soy protein isolate	Sugar, Tapioca starch	Soy oil
Meat Base Formula	Beef hearts	Sucrose, Modified tapioca starch	Sesame oil
Lofenalac	Enz. hydrolyzed casein**	Corn syrup solids (80%)**, Modified tapioca starch (15%)	Corn oil
Lonolac***	Casein	Lactose (100%)	Coconut oil
Nutramigen	Enz. hydrolyzed casein	Sucrose (69) Modified tapioca starch (31)	Corn oil
Portagen LF (Lactose Free)	Sodium Caseinate	Sucrose (25%) Corn syrup solids (75%)	Corn oil (13%), MCT (87%)
Pregestimil	Enz. hydrolyzed casein	Dextrose, modified tapioca starch	Corn oil, MCT
Probana	Skim, non-fat milk, whole milk curd, Enz. hydrolyzed casein	Lactose (25%), Dextrose (45%) Banana Powder (30%)***	Corn oil, butterfat
Advance	Non-fat milk solids, soy protein isolate	Lactose, corn syrup	Corn oil, soy

*Carbohydrate must be added separately
**Low in phenylalanine
***Not classed as standard formula for infant feeding

Table III

Dilutions for Concentrated Liquid Formulas*
Texas Children's Hospital

Calories Per Ounce	For 2 Ounces Formula	For 8 Ounces Formula	For 12 Ounces Formula	For 16 Ounces Formula	For 20 Ounces Formula	For 24 Ounces Formula	For 26 Ounces Formula	For 32 Ounces Formula
30 Calories	45 ccs Base 15 ccs Water	180 ccs Base 60 ccs Water	270 ccs Base 90 ccs Water	360 ccs Base 120 ccs Water	450 ccs Base 150 ccs Water	540 ccs Base 180 ccs Water	585 ccs Base 195 ccs Water	720 ccs Base 240 ccs Water
27 Calories	40 ccs Base 20 ccs Water	163 ccs Base 77 ccs Water	243 ccs Base 117 ccs Water	324 ccs Base 156 ccs Water	405 ccs Base 195 ccs Water	486 ccs Base 234 ccs Water	526 ccs Base 254 ccs Water	648 ccs Base 312 ccs Water
24 Calories	36 ccs Base 24 ccs Water	144 ccs Base 96 ccs Water	216 ccs Base 144 ccs Water	288 ccs Base 192 ccs Water	360 ccs Base 240 ccs Water	433 ccs Base 287 ccs Water	468 ccs Base 312 ccs Water	577 ccs Base 383 ccs Water
20 Calories	30 ccs Base 30 ccs Water	120 ccs Base 120 ccs Water	180 ccs Base 180 ccs Water	240 ccs Base 240 ccs Water	300 ccs Base 300 ccs Water	360 ccs Base 360 ccs Water	390 ccs Base 390 ccs Water	480 ccs Base 480 ccs Water
18 Calories	28 ccs Base 32 ccs Water	108 ccs Base 132 ccs Water	163 ccs Base 197 ccs Water	216 ccs Base 264 ccs Water	270 ccs Base 330 ccs Water	324 ccs Base 396 ccs Water	351 ccs Base 429 ccs Water	433 ccs Base 527 ccs Water
15 Calories	23 ccs Base 37 ccs Water	90 ccs Base 150 ccs Water	135 ccs Base 225 ccs Water	180 ccs Base 300 ccs Water	225 ccs Base 375 ccs Water	270 ccs Base 450 ccs Water	293 ccs Base 487 ccs Water	360 ccs Base 600 ccs Water
13 Calories	20 ccs Base 40 ccs Water	78 ccs Base 162 ccs Water	118 ccs Base 242 ccs Water	156 ccs Base 324 ccs Water	195 ccs Base 405 ccs Water	234 ccs Base 486 ccs Water	254 ccs Base 526 ccs Water	313 ccs Base 647 ccs Water
10 Calories	15 ccs Base 45 ccs Water	60 ccs Base 180 ccs Water	90 ccs Base 270 ccs Water	120 ccs Base 360 ccs Water	150 ccs Base 450 ccs Water	180 ccs Base 540 ccs Water	195 ccs Base 585 ccs Water	240 ccs Base 720 ccs Water
5 Calories	8 ccs Base 52 ccs Water	30 ccs Base 210 ccs Water	45 ccs Base 315 ccs Water	60 ccs Base 420 ccs Water	75 ccs Base 525 ccs Water	90 ccs Base 630 ccs Water	98 ccs Base 682 ccs Water	120 ccs Base 840 ccs Water

***Base** refers to concentrated liquid of infant formulas. These dilutions are not to be used for CHO-Free (Syntex) since carbohydrate must be added to this formula.

Table IV

Dilutions for Powdered Infant Formulas*
Texas Children's Hospital

Calories Per Ounce	For 2 Ounces Formula	For 8 Ounces Formula	For 12 Ounces Formula	For 16 Ounces Formula	For 20 Ounces Formula	For 24 Ounces Formula	For 32 Ounces Formula
30 Calories	1 tablespoon 1½ teaspoons	¼ cup 2 tablespoons	½ cup 1 tablespoon	¾ cup	¾ cup 3 tablespoons	1 cup 2 tablespoons	1½ cups
27 Calories	1 tablespoon 1 teaspoon	¼ cup 1 tablespoon 1¼ teaspoons	½ cup ¼ teaspoon	½ cup 2 tablespoons 2½ teaspoons	¾ cup 1 tablespoon 1½ teaspoons	1 cup ½ teaspoon	1¼ cups 1 tablespoon 1¾ teaspoons
24 Calories	1 tablespoon ½ teaspoon	¼ cup 2½ teaspoons	¼ cup 3 tablespoons ½ teaspoon	½ cup 1 tablespoon 1¾ teaspoons	¾ cup	¾ cup 2 tablespoons 1¼ teaspoons	1 cup 3 tablespoons ½ teaspoon
20 Calories	1 tablespoon	¼ cup	¼ cup 2 tablespoons	½ cup	½ cup 2 tablespoons	¾ cup	1 cup
18 Calories	2¾ teaspoons	3 tablespoons 1¾ teaspoons	¼ cup 1 tablespoon 1¼ teaspoons	¼ cup 3 tablespoons ½ teaspoon	½ cup 1 tablespoon	½ cup 2 tablespoons 2½ teaspoons	¾ cup 2 tablespoons 1¼ teaspoons
15 Calories	2¼ teaspoons	3 tablespoons	¼ cup 1½ teaspoons	¼ cup 2 tablespoons	¼ cup 3 tablespoons 1½ teaspoons	½ cup 1 tablespoon	¾ cup
13 Calories	2 teaspoons	2 tablespoons 1¾ teaspoons	3 tablespoons 2¾ teaspoons	¼ cup 1 tablespoon ½ teaspoon	¼ cup 2 tablespoons 1½ teaspoons	¼ cup 3 tablespoons 2½ teaspoons	½ cup 2 tablespoons 1¼ teaspoons
10 Calories	1½ teaspoons	2 tablespoons	3 tablespoons	¼ cup	¼ cup 1 tablespoon	¼ cup 2 tablespoons	½ cup
5 Calories	¾ teaspoon	1 tablespoon	1 tablespoon 1½ teaspoons	2 tablespoons	2½ tablespoons 1½ teaspoons	3 tablespoons	¼ cup

*The amounts listed in this chart indicate the measurements of powdered formula to use. Water is to be added to bring the volume of the formula to the amount needed. This allows for the volume of the dry powder.

CHO-Free

Water; soy oil; soy protein isolate; potassium citrate; tri-calcium phosphate; lecithin; dibasic magnesium phosphate; salt; dl-methionine; calcium carrageenan; potassium iodide; cupric sulfate; manganese sulfate; sodium iron pyrophosphate; zinc sulfate; ascorbic acid; choline chloride; vitamin A palmitate; vitamin D_3 crystalline; d-alpha tocopheryl acetate; thiamine hydrochloride; riboflavin; pyridoxine hydrochloride; niacin; vitamin B_{12}; dl-calcium pantothenate; inositol.

Enfamil

Nonfat dry milk; lactose; soy and coconut oils; soy lecithin; vitamins (vitamin A palmitate, calciferol, sodium ascorbate, tocopheryl acetate, thiamine hydrochloride, riboflavin, niacinamide, pyridoxine hydrochloride, calcium pantothenate, choline bitartrate and vitamin B_{12}) and minerals (ferrous sulfate, cupric sulfate and sodium iodide).

Isomil

Water; sucrose; corn syrup solids; soy protein isolate; corn oil; coconut oil; corn starch; calcium phosphate; potassium citrate; mono- and diglycerides; potassium chloride; soy phospholipids; magnesium chloride; calcium carbonate; ascorbic acid; dl-methionine; carrageenan; sodium chloride; choline chloride; ferrous sulfate; zinc sulfate; niacin;calcium pantothenate; vitamin A palmitate; cupric sulfate; vitamin D_3 concentrate; riboflavin; thiamine; pyridoxine; potassium iodide; phytonadione (vitamin K_1); biotin; folic acid; vitamin B_{12}; alpha-tocopheryl acetate.

Lofenalac

Corn syrup solids; specially processed casein hydrolysate (an enzymic digest of casein containing amino acids and small peptides, processed to remove most of the phenylalanine); corn oil; arrowroot starch; sugar; amino acids (l-tyrosine, l-trytophan, and l-methionine); minerals (calcium gluconate, monobasic potassium phosphate, calcium hydroxide, dibasic potassium phosphate, potassium chloride, magnesium oxide, zinc sulfate, cupric sulfate, sodium iodide and ferrous sulfate); and vitamins (vitamin A palmitate, calciferol, d-alpha-tocopheryl acetate, sodium ascorbate, thiamine hydrochloride, riboflavin, niacinamide, pyridoxine hydrochloride, calcium pantothenate, cyanocobalamin, folic acid, biotin, and choline chloride).

Lonalac

Lactose; casein; coconut oil; monobasic calcium phosphate; potassium carbonate; calcium hydroxide; calcium chloride; calcium carbonate; potassium chloride; magnesium oxide; vitamin A palmitate; thiamine hydrochloride; riboflavin; niacinamide; artificial color; flavoring.

Meat-Base

Beef hearts; water; cane sugar; sesame oil; modified tapioca starch; tricalcium phosphate; calcium citrate; sodium ascorbate; ferrous sulfate; tocopheryl acetate; vitamin A palmitate; thiamine hydrochloride; vitamin A; pyridoxine hydrochloride and phytonadione (vitamin K_1).

Mull-Soy

Water; soy flour; soy oil; sugar (sucrose); invert sucrose; glyceryl monostearate; tricalcium phosphate; salt; calcium hydroxide dl-methionine; sodium iron pyrophosphate; manganese sulfate monohydrate; citric acid; potassium iodide; vitamin A palmitate; vitamin D_3 crystalline; sodium ascorbate; niacin; d-alpha-tocopheryl acetate; dl-calcium pantothenate; pyridoxine hydrochloride; thiamine hydrochloride; riboflavin; vitamin B_{12}.

Neo-Mull-Soy Water; sucrose; soy oil; soy protein isolate; tapioca starch; potassium citrate; tricalcium phosphate; dibasic magnesium phosphate; lecithin; salt; sodium ascorbate; carrageenan; l-methionine; sodium iron pyrophosphate; choline chloride; niacinamide; manganese sulfate; zinc sulfate; dl-alpha-tocopheryl acetate; d-calcium pantothenate; vitamin A palmitate; riboflavin; cupric sulfate; thiamine hydrochloride; pyridoxine hydrochloride; vitamin D_3; potassium iodide; vitamin B_{12}.

Nutramigen Sugar; casein enzymically hydrolyzed and charcoal-treated to reduce allergenicity; tapioca starch; corn oil; dibasic calcium phosphate; potassium chloride; calcium hydroxide; magnesium oxide; hydrochloric acid as needed to adjust pH; vitamin A palmitate; calciferol; sodium ascorbate; thiamine hydrochloride; riboflavin; niacinamide; ferrous sulfate; sodium iodide; d-alpha-tocopheryl acetate; pyridoxine hydrochloride; cyanocobalamin; folic acid; calcium pantothenate; zinc sulfate; cupric sulfate; biotin; choline chloride.

Nursoy Water; corn syrup solids; sucrose; soy protein isolate; oleo; coconut oil; oleic (safflower) oil; soybean oil; soy lecithin; l-methionine; calcium carrageenan; potassium citrate; dibasic calcium phosphate; sodium chloride; calcium chloride; magnesium chloride; calcium hydroxide; calcium carbonate; monobasic sodium phosphate; ferrous sulfate; zinc sulfate; manganese sulfate; cupric sulfate; potassium iodide; ascorbic acid; choline chloride; d-alpha tocopheryl acetate; niacinamide; calcium pantothenate; riboflavin; vitamin A palmitate; thiamine hydrochloride; pyridoxine hydrochloride; beta-carotene; phytonadione; folic acid; biotin; activated 7-dehydrocholesterol; cyanocobalamin.

Portagen Corn syrup solids; sugar; medium chain triglycerides (fractionated coconut oil); sodium caseinate; corn oil; lecithin; vitamin A palmitate; calciferol; d-alpha-tocopheryl acetate; sodium ascorbate; thiamine hydrochloride; riboflavin; niacinamide; pyridoxine hydrochloride; calicum pantothenate; cyanocobalamin; folic acid; phytonadione (K_1); biotin; choline bitartrate; inositol; calcium citrate; dicalcium phosphate; ferrous citrate; sodium iodide; potassium chloride; potassium citrate; cupric sulfate; magnesium phosphate; manganese sulfate; zinc sulphate.

Pregestimil Dextrose; casein enzymically hydrolyzed and charcoal treated to reduce allergenicity; tapioca starch; medium chain triglycerides (fractionated coconut oil); corn oil; dibasic calcium phosphate; potassium citrate; calcium hydroxide; potassium chloride; magnesium oxide; hydrochloric acid as needed to adjust pH; vitamin A palmitate; calciferol; sodium ascorbate; thiamine hydrochloride; riboflavin; niacinamide; ferrous sulfate; sodium iodide; d-alpha-tocopheryl acetate; pyridoxine hydrochloride; cyanocobalamin; inositol; phytonadione (K_1); folic acid; calcium pantothenate; cupric sulfate; zinc sulfate; manganese sulfate; biotin; choline chloride.

Probana

Protein milk powder (whole milk curd and non-fat dry milk with added lactic acid and sodium lactate); an enzymic casein hydrolysate; banana powder; dextrose; vitamin A palmitate; calciferol;and d-alpha-tocopheryl acetate.

ProSobee

Water; sugar; soy oil; corn syrup solids; soy protein isolate; potassium citrate; tricalcium phosphate; lecithin; guar gum; salt; dibasic magnesium phosphate; dl-methionine; carrageenan; vitamin A palmitate; calciferol; sodium ascorbate; thiamine hydrochloride; riboflavin; niacinamide; sodium iron pyrophosphate; potassium iodide; pyridoxine hydrochloride; cyanocobalamin; calcium pantothenate; choline chloride; inositol; cupric sulfate; manganese sulfate; zinc sulfate.

Similac

Nonfat milk; lactose; coconut, soy and corn oils; mono- and diglycerides; soy lecithin; carrageenan; ascorbic acid; niacin; vitamin A palmitate; vitamin D_3 concentrate; thiamine; pyridoxine; riboflavin; alpha-tocopheryl acetate; cupric sulfate; cyanocobalamin.

Similac with Iron

Nonfat milk; lactose; coconut, soy and corn oils; mono- and diglycerides; soy lecithin; carrageenan; ascorbic acid; ferrous sulfate; vitamin A palmitate; potassium citrate; niacin; vitamin D_3 concentrate; thiamine; riboflavin; pyridoxine; and alpha-tocopheryl acetate; cupric sulfate; cyanocobalamin.

Similac PM 60/40

Partially demineralized whey; partially demineralized non-fat milk; corn oil; lactose; coconut oil; potassium citrate; lecithin; calcium citrate; sodium citrate; magnesium chloride; monoglycerides; calcium chloride; ascorbic acid; polysorbate 80; ferrous sulfate; zinc sulfate; vitamin A palmitate; niacin; copper gluconate; calcium pantothenate; vitamin D_3; alpha-tocopheryl acetate; thiamine; riboflavin; pyridoxine; manganese chloride; folic acid.

Skim Milk Infant Formula

A fortified skimmed-milk feeding especially prepared for infants, made from skimmed milk to which has been added lactose; carrageenan; ascorbic acid; vitamin A palmitate; niacin; vitamin D_3; cupric sulfate; alpha-tocopheryl acetate; pyridoxine; thiamine; folic acid; potassium iodide;and vitamin B_{12}.

SMA

Nonfat milk; water (liquid formula only); demineralized (electrodialyzed) whey; lactose; oleo; coconut, and oleic (safflower) and soybean oils; soy lecithin; calcium carrageenan (liquid formulas only); potassium bicarbonate and chloride; calcium citrate and chloride; sodium citrate and bicarbonate; ferrous, zinc and cupric sulfates; potassium iodide; ascorbic acid; d-alpha-tocopheryl acetate; niacinamide; vitamin A palmitate; calcium pantothenate; thiamine hydrochloride; riboflavin; pyridoxine hydrochloride; beta carotene; folic acid; activated 7-dehydrocholesterol; cyanocobalamin.

Soyalac Water; soybean solids; corn syrup; soybean oil; sugar; calcium carbonate; sodium citrate; soybean lecithin; salt; calcium citrate; 1-methionine; ferrous sulfate; vitamin C (ascorbic acid); niacin; vitamin A palmitate; calcium pantothenate; vitamin D (ergocalciferol); vitamin B_1 (thiamine hydrochloride); vitamin B_2 (riboflavin); potassium iodide; vitamin B_6 (pyridoxine hydrochloride); vitamin B_{12} (cyanocobalamin).

i-Soyalac Water; sugar; soybean oil; soy protein isolate; tapioca starch; dibasic calcium phosphate; soybean lecithin; potassium citrate; potassium chloride; calcium carbonate; salt; 1-methionine; magnesium phosphate; ascorbic acid; ferrous sulfate; zinc sulfate; vitamin A palmitate; biotin; choline chloride; manganese sulfate; alpha-tocopherol acetate; calcium pantothenate; cupric sulfate; niacin; riboflavin; pyridoxine hydrochloride; vitamin D_2; thiamine hydrochloride; potassium iodide; folic acid; vitamin B_{12}.

Modular Formula

William J. Klish, M.D.

The basic modular components of an infant formula are protein, fat, carbohydrate, minerals, vitamins and water. With existing commercial infant formulas, the physician cannot change simply one of these components of the diet when a new formula is substituted but is obliged to change several of them. As our understanding of chronic diarrheal disease increases, it is becoming obvious that infants can develop complex intestinal intolerances. Carbohydrate malabsorption can present simply as an intolerance to lactose or as an intolerance to all carbohydrates including glucose. A fermentative diarrhea results if the ingested sugar is not altered to correspond to the ability of the intestine to absorb it. Chronic diarrhea may lead to a depletion of the bile acid pool (personal observation) causing maldigestion of long chain fats. Specific protein hypersensitivity may go undetected because of the overlap of symptoms associated with other nutrient intolerances. In order to allow rational adjustments of a single component in an infant's formula according to specific requirements, a method was developed to package the protein and mineral modules separately. Infants with chronic diarrhea and failure to thrive constitute approximately 3% of our hospital admissions. Many of these infants must receive total parenteral nutrition in order to overcome their intestinal absorptive defects and to be able to tolerate formulas of normal caloric content without developing dehydrating diarrhea. Other children can be rehabilitated without resorting to total parenteral nutrition by structuring this modular formula so that the nutrients will challenge their intestines sequentially.

Modular Formula is composed of protein in the form of calcium sodium caseinate and electrolytes. This core formula is packaged in powdered form with an enclosed 1-tablespoon measuring scoop which aids in preparation and helps to prevent the use of excess minerals. The core is usually used in a concentration of 3 gm of core mix per 100 ml of water which provides 2.2 gm of protein and essentially the same minerals as found in most commercial formulas (Table VI).

To this core the physician may add fat of any nature and in any quantity that he considers desirable. The kinds of fat we most frequently use because of their availability are corn oil, if long-chain triglycerides are desired, or fractionated coconut oil, as a source of medium-chain triglycerides. Since fractionated coconut oil is deficient in linoleic acid, 3 ml of safflower oil are added to each liter of formula to supply this essential fatty acid. The final concentration of fat is generally 3.5 to 4.5 gm per 100 ml (see Table VII).

The type and amount of carbohydrate to be added are determined by the gastrointestinal tolerance of the individual patient. Final concentrations

Table V

Method of Preparation of Modular Formula

1. Assemble necessary ingredients and sterile equipment.
2. Measure 12 ounces of warm sterile water (from sterile hot water heater), then cool.
   DO NOT USE HOT OR COLD WATER
3. Pour ½ of the water into a sterile blender.
4. Add measured amount of Baylor Core mix. Begin blending.
5. Slowly add measured amount of MCT Oil to mixture while blending (add only if needed in formula).
6. Add glucose water if needed in the formula.
7. Add enough remaining sterile water to make the total volume 12 ounces. Continue blending until well mixed.
8. Let foam settle. Pour 3 ounces each into four bottles. Label and date each bottle.

Do not autoclave formula

Do not use sterile water in 4 oz bottles (it will not dissolve the formula properly.

% Modular Formula	% Fat	% Carbohydrate	Amount Modular Formula	Amount MCT Oil	Amount 10% Dextrose Water
1% Baylor Core (0.7% Protein)			1¾ teaspoons		
2% Baylor Core (1.5% Protein)			1 tablespoon + ½ teaspoon		
3% Baylor Core (2.2% Protein)			1 tablespoon + 2¼ teaspoons		
	1% MCT			¾ teaspoon	
	2% MCT			1½ teaspoons	
	3% MCT			2½ teaspoons	
	4% MCT			1 tablespoon + ¼ teaspoon	
		1% CHO			36 cc 10% dextrose water
		2% CHO			72 cc 10% dextrose water
		3% CHO			108 cc 10% dextrose water
		4% CHO			144 cc 10% dextrose water
		5% CHO			180 cc 10% dextrose water
		6% CHO			216 cc 10% dextrose water
		7% CHO			252 cc 10% dextrose water

Table VI

Composition of Modular Formula, Human Milk and Milk Base Formulas

	Modular Formula (usual concentration)	Human Milk	Milk Base Formulas* (range)
Protein (g per 100 ml)	2.2	1.4	1.51— 3.6
Calcium (mg per 100 ml)	42.00	34.0	44.0 —100.0
Phosphorus (mg per 100 ml)	32.00	14.0	33.0 — 80.0
Sodium (mEq/L)	8.0	7.0	7.0 — 17.0
Potassium (mEq/L)	20.0	13.0	14.0 — 32.0
Chloride (mEq/L)	22.0	11.0	10.0 — 29.0
Magnesium (mg per 100 ml)	4.0	4.0	4.0 — 8.5
Iron (mg per 100 ml)	0.62	0.05	Trace— 1.8
Copper (mg per 100 ml)	0.08	0.04	0.04— 0.10
Zinc (mg per 100 ml)	0.32	0.30	0.20— 0.42
Iodine (mg per 100 ml)	0.03	0.03	0.04— 0.10

*Include Similac (Ross), Enfamil (Mead-Johnson), SMA (Wyeth), and Similac Advance (Ross)

Table VII

Standard Composition of Modular Formula

Quantity per Liter			Grams per 100 ccs			Calories per 100 ccs
Modular Core (a)	Fat (b)	Cho (c)	Protein	Fat	CHO	
10 gms	....	....	0.7	...	...	2.8
20 gms	....	....	1.5	...	...	6.0
30 gms	....	....	2.2	...	...	8.8
30 gms	15 ccs	....	2.2	1.4	...	21.4
30 gms	30 ccs	....	2.2	2.8	...	34.0
30 gms	45 ccs	....	2.2	4.2	...	46.6
30 gms	45 ccs	10 gms	2.2	4.2	1.0	50.6
30 gms	45 ccs	20 gms	2.2	4.2	2.0	54.6
30 gms	45 ccs	30 gms	2.2	4.2	3.0	58.6
30 gms	45 ccs	40 gms	2.2	4.2	4.0	62.6
30 gms	45 ccs	50 gms	2.2	4.2	5.0	66.6
30 gms	45 ccs	70 gms	2.2	4.2	7.0	74.6

(a) 1 tablespoon of Modular Formula weighs 5 gms which is 73.5% protein and 26.5% salts and water of hydration.
(b) Most oils weigh 14 gms per tablespoon.
(c) Most sugars weigh 12 gms per tablespoon in dry form.

range between 5 and 7 gm per 100 ml (Table VII). The types of carbohydrates used most frequently include glucose (dextrose), sucrose (table sugar), and honey, which contains 40.5% fructose, 34.2% glucose, 1.9% sucrose and 23.4% water.

The formula is brought to a liter volume with sterile tap water, which is preferred as a source of trace elements that are not present in the core. Since this formula does not contain vitamins, multivitamins with E are given as a supplement.

A concentration of 1 gm per 100 ml of the core formula is offered at first to test the patient's tolerance to casein. If this concentration is tolerated, the core formula is increased to 3.0 gm per 100 ml. Fat is added next, first at 1.4 gm per 100 ml and then in increments as described in Table VII until a final concentration of 4.2 gm per 100 ml is achieved. Finally, sugar is added in the same manner (Table VII) starting at 1 gm per 100 ml with increases to a final concentration of 5 to 7 gm per 100 ml. If a particular concentration causes diarrhea, that concentration is either maintained or reduced slightly until the intestine develops tolerance, and then is again advanced until the desired concentration is achieved. As a patient is weaned to Modular Formula, decisions about formula changes are based on the frequency and quality of the stools. Nursing personnel note all stool volumes and check the pH, glucose and reducing substance. The pH is tested easily by touching nitrazine paper to fresh stool. Fecal glucose is checked with glucose oxidase test tape. Reducing substance is determined by taking a small amount of stool and diluting it with twice its volume of water. Fifteen drops of this suspension are added to a Clinitest tablet (Ames Company), and the reducing substance concentration is determined by comparing the solution to the color chart provided. When the stool pH drops below 6.0, or glucose or reducing substance begins to appear in the stool, the formula is reduced to the previously tolerated mixture. If the infant cannot tolerate the protein core alone, we resort to total parenteral nutrition for two to three weeks and then attempt again to wean him to Modular Formula.

The changes in the formula are generally made every 12 hours, so that a formula of relatively high caloric value is achieved very rapidly. Initially, most infants can tolerate a formula that is complete in protein and fat (i.e., 2.2 gm of protein and 4.2 gm of fat per 100 ml) with glucose in quantities of 2 to 3 gm per 100 ml. This formula has approximately 55 calories per 100 ml. Until a full caloric density formula is tolerated, it is imperative that a solution with 10% dextrose is infused intravenously in order to prevent the occurrence of hypoglycemia. With the incomplete formula as described above in conjunction with intravenous glucose, most infants are able to gain weight.

All infants on total parenteral nutrition are weaned to oral feedings according to the schedule described above. The transition from intravenous feeding to oral feeding is much easier with this technique. When the infants have tolerated the complete formula for several weeks, they are then given a conventional formula that most closely matches in composition the tolerated concentrations of the Modular Formula.

Indications for the use of this formula:

Acquired glucose intolerance, or chronic protracted diarrhea of infancy;
Surgical short gut syndrome with secondary multiple nutrient intolerançes;
Weaning from total parenteral nutrition;
Sequential challenge of the intestine for diagnostic purposes;
Modification of renal solute load in children with renal or cardiac disease.

Table VIII summarizes the potential complications resulting from the use of this formula.

Infants with complex malabsorptive problems have responded very well to treatment with the Modular Formula. We have been able to achieve good energy intake and have found that the ability to challenge the intestine sequentially with various food stuffs has supplied us with helpful diagnostic information. Modular Formula is obviously more difficult to use than the average conventional formula but is certainly no more complex than many other medical treatments. We have found that the modular concept of formula preparation has been valuable in the teaching of basic nutritional principles.

Potential complications with the use of this formula fall almost entirely into the realm of human error. Improper mixing can result in an increased renal solute load and hypernatremia if the formula core is used in high concentrations. This is a real danger since most medical personnel are

Table VIII

Potential Complications Associated With the Use of Modular Formula

Complications	Causes	Prevention
Hypoglycemia	Low carbohydrate intake	Intravenous glucose during weaning
	Malnutrition	
	Sepsis	
	High Protein load	
	Antecedent TPN*	
Hypernatremia	Improper mixing of formula	Training of personnel
Essential fatty acid deficiency	Use of medium-chain triglycerides	Addition of safflower oil to formula
	Antecedent TPN*	
Hypophosphatemic rickets	Low phosphate formula Antecedent TPN*	Surveillance
Hypovitaminosis	Failure to provide vitamin supplement	Oral or intravenous vitamins (or both)
Trace element deficiency	Inadequate trace elements in formula	Use of sterile tap water

*Total Parenteral Nutrition

familiar with formulas that require one scoop of formula to 2 oz. of water to achieve appropriate concentrations. Using this ratio with the Modular Formula would be disastrous since the proper dilution for this formula is one scoop of formula to 5½ oz. of water. Improper addition of fat and carbohydrate to the formula can also result in a hypocaloric mixture and therefore an inadequate nutrient intake. As in all formulas, poor mixing techniques can result in bacterial contamination and associated enteric infections.

Hypoglycemia can result from feeding a carbohydrate-free formula to malnourished infants who have marginal glycogen reserves. This problem can be prevented by supplying an alternate source of glucose intravenously while a formula containing less than 3% carbohydrate is being fed orally. Above this concentration more than 20% of the calories ingested are carbohydrate, which seems adequate to inhibit gluconeogenesis and protect glycogen stores.

Since this formula does not contain vitamins, supplementation with a multi-vitamin preparation is imperative. The best multivitamin preparations to use are those that do not contain carbohydrate in the carrier medium. On occasion, we have caused an increase in acid diarrhea by the addition of this small amount of carbohydrate in children with severe monosaccharide intolerance.

All of the major trace elements have been added to the formula; it is anticipated that the others will be supplied by mixing the formula with tap water. Since little is known presently about the requirements for many trace nutrients and this formula represents a chemically defined diet, possible deficiencies are always a danger and should be looked for. In our experience, we have not had definable problems with trace nutrient deficiency syndromes.

Since the protein in Modular Formula is casein, infants with casein hypersensitivity will not tolerate this formula. This diagnosis has been rare in our experience because Modular Formula allows us to do a specific challenge of the intestinal tract with protein. We have noted, though, that allergic reactions to casein are more frequent in children with severe monosaccharide intolerance, but this problem is usually resolved after total parenteral nutrition has allowed for healing of the damaged intestinal mucosa.

The nutritive value of any protein is determined by the ratio of essential amino acid present in that protein. The amino acid present in the smallest amount limits the utilization of the rest for protein synthesis. In casein, this limiting amino acid is methionine. We have allowed for this by adding methionine to the formula at a level of 0.2% of the casein. When the formula is prepared in its normal concentration, the protein accounts for 13% of the calories, which is adequate to supply the protein requirements of the infant.

The type of fat added to the formula must be individualized according to the patient's ability to absorb fat. If the patient has a defect in the amount of lipolytic enzymes available as in cystic fibrosis, an impairment in bile salt metabolism such as in biliary atresia, or a depleted bile acid pool as a result of protracted diarrhea, medium-chain triglycerides in the form of fractionated coconut oil are used. It is important to remember that medium-chain triglycerides do not contain sufficient amounts of essential fatty acid (linoleic acid), which can be added to the formula in the form of safflower oil, which is extremely rich in linoleic acid. Only 3 ml of safflower oil per liter of formula are sufficient to prevent fatty acid deficiency; it will provide 3% of the calories as linoleic acid. Fat can be added to the formula in greater amounts than recommended to increase the caloric content, but ketosis may result if more than 65% of the ingested maintenance calories are fat.

The choice of carbohydrates has been discussed above. When glucose is used, problems may develop with osmotic diarrhea. Since glucose is a relatively small molecular weight compound, its contribution to the osmotic density of the formula is large, and it is the nutrient used in the highest concentration. When a hypertonic solution enters the lumen of the gut rapidly, an osmotic gradient develops causing water to shift into the lumen. This process distends the gut, stimulating peristalsis, and results in diarrhea. Depending upon its composition, Modular Formula can have an osmotic density as high as 600 mOsm per liter so that diarrhea of this nature is possible. We have found that by increasing the concentration gradually, as recommended, this problem is minimized. When diarrhea does occur, uncertainty with respect to the actual cause may result since the diarrheal stool caused by a high osmolar load in the intestine could contain reducing sugar just as that of carbohydrate intolerance. If a patient can only tolerate 2 to 3% glucose in the formula, substitution of honey may allow an increase in the carbohydrate concentration, because two independent pathways are used for the absorption of the glucose and fructose present in honey.

Chapter 3

Normal Diets

Basic Principles

The starting point in the management of the dietary or nutritional needs of any age group is a basic fundamental understanding of what constitutes an optimal diet in terms of available knowledge that will allow maintenance of good physical and mental health. This entails a knowledge of nutrient requirements for most individuals and, in turn, allowances which will cover the great majority and, hopefully, all individuals, regardless of varying physical, environmental, social, ethnic and other differences.

In dealing with children, not only must we consider the total daily nutritional needs in terms of basal metabolism, specific dynamic action (S.D.A.), activity, losses via skin, lungs, feces and urine, any organic disease causing an excess or deficiency of one or multiple nutrients (any interruption of normal pathways for digestion, absorption, metabolism, excretion, etc.), but we must constantly be aware of the factor of growth and growth-rate. This growth factor varies inversely with the age of the growing organism. There is also the adolescent growth spurt when most needs are increased. The nutritional needs are likewise correlated with the specific type of growth occurring, as multiplication of cell number or increase in cell size. The various tissues of the body have different growth and maintenance requirements as well as means of adaptation to periods of stress, insufficient intake, food imbalances, etc. In contrast, the mature individual's needs are based on the fundamental requirements to maintain a state of equilibrium involving the aforementioned basic needs and losses without the factor of growth.

Each individual food contributes varying amounts of one to numerous different nutrients and in varying proportions to each other. Obviously, to calculate the total amount of each fundamental nutrient obtained from a mixed diet is time-consuming and laborious for the dietitian but this is how diet calculation had its beginning. Since the nutritive value of foods can be quite variable depending upon geographical location, soil composition, climatic conditions and many other factors too numerous and obvious to enumerate, and each individual likewise has varying discrepancies in needs, the overall picture is fairly well balanced out by using standard figures for food composition which have taken all of these influencing factors into consideration.

To achieve simplicity in planning and calculating diets, foods have been divided into four major groups—the milk group, the meat group, the vegetable and fruit group and the cereal and bread group, with an additional, optional, fifth group, fats and sweets. The last group contributes very little nutritional value in terms of protein, minerals or vitamins but may represent a major source of calories. In planning a normal dietary pattern, foods from each of these basic four food groups are selected in proper amounts to furnish the pre-determined nutritional needs of the particular individual (or group) in terms of protein, carbohydrate, fat, minerals, vitamins and calories. The fifth group assumes relatively small importance in the pediatric age group except during adolescence (Table IX).

The term "daily requirement" is used to indicate the minimum amount of a particular nutrient necessary to prevent clinical signs of deficiency. This may vary from one individual to another, as well as from time to time for any given individual, and be influenced by environmental conditions, disease and other factors. Nutritional requirements may vary with age, sex, genetic make-up, activity, temperature, physiological state, etc. While data concerning requirements are invaluable in controlled studies and research, they are of minimum value in planning practical diet patterns for every day use. These requirements are not to be confused with the N.R.C. allowances which are approximately fifty per cent over the minimum daily requirements.

The Food and Nutrition Board of the National Research Council, in 1943, prepared their first "Recommended Daily Dietary Allowances" to be used as a guide in planning the needs of healthy individuals from infancy to old age. These were termed allowances since they were "designed to afford a margin of sufficiency above average physiological requirements to cover variations among essentially all individuals in the general population." These allowances subsequently have been revised, the latest being the eighth edition, 1974 (Table X). This publication provides invaluable information regarding each nutrient and the interrelationship and interdependence of the various nutrients as well as the basis for the establishment of allowance values.

In planning a dietary pattern for any age group, one first determines the total daily caloric need for that particular individual (or intelligently-approximated average value for a group) in terms of aforementioned maintenance and activity needs. The main purpose of eating food is that it supplies the body with necessary energy. Food energy units derived from proteins, carbohydrates and fats are termed kilocalories (one kilocalorie is the amount of heat necessary to raise 1 kg of water from 15 to 16 degrees C.). The accepted international unit of energy is the joule (one joule equals 10^7 ergs, or the energy expended when 1 kg is moved 1 m by 1 newton). The factor 4.2 is used to convert energy allowances from kilocalories to kilojoules (1 kcal equals 4184 J exactly). The classical Atwater energy conversion factors of 4 kcal/gram of food protein and carbohydrate and 9 kcal/gram of food fat have been verified and are adequate for energy content computation of customary U.S. diets. Energy values, in kilojoules per gram of substance, are protein and carbohydrate, 17; fat, 38; and alcohol, 30 (N.R.C.-1974).

Since protein, in many ways, may be considered the "key" nutrient in planning a diet, one next determines the protein needs. Foods equivalent to this amount of protein are then chosen from the meat group and the milk group. These are distributed among the number of meals or feedings desired per day. The caloric value derived from protein is subtracted from the total caloric allowance. The carbohydrate contribution is then selected from the vegetable and fruit group and the cereal-bread group and dis-

Table IX

A Guide to Good Eating—Daily Recommendations

Milk Group	Meat Group	Vegetables Fruits	Breads Cereals
3 or more glasses milk—Children smaller glasses for some children under 8 4 or more glasses—Teenagers 2 or more glasses—Adults Cheese, ice cream and other milk-made foods can supply part of the milk	2 or more servings Meats, fish, poultry, eggs, or cheese—with dry beans, peas, nuts as alternates	4 or more servings Include dark green or yellow vegetables; citrus fruit or tomatoes	4 or more servings Enriched or whole grain Added milk improves nutritional values

A guide to good eating helps you plan or choose pleasing and satisfying meals that provide good nutrition. It suggests minimum amounts of food from each of 4 food groups which should be included in each day's meals. This menu plan shows one way to include the 4 important food groups in a day's meals:

Breakfast	Dinner	Lunch or Supper
Fruit	Main Protein Dish	Vegetable
Cereal or Egg or Both	Vegetable Potato	Bread and Butter
Toast or Roll and Butter	Bread or Roll and Butter	Main Protein Dish
Milk	Milk Dessert	Milk Fruit

Vary your menus to suit your taste. In using the dairy foods for their important calcium . . .

1 glass milk = 8 ounces or ¼ quart
1 slice American cheese (1 oz.) = ¾ glass milk
½ cup creamed cottage cheese = ⅓ glass milk
½ cup (¼ pint) ice cream = ¼ glass milk

In the meat group, 2 servings should give at least as much protein as 4 ounces cooked lean meat (⅓ pound raw). About equal amounts of protein come from . . .

1 ounce cooked lean meat, poultry, or fish
1 egg
1 slice cheese, American or Swiss (1 ounce)
2 rounded tablespoons cottage cheese (2 ounces)
2 tablespoons peanut butter (1 ounce)
½ cup cooked dried beans or peas

An average serving of vegetables or fruits is ½ cup; of bread, 1 slice; of cereal, ½ to ¾ cup.

National Dairy Council, 1964, Chicago.

Table X

Recommended Daily Dietary Allowances, N.R.C., 1974

								Fat-Soluble Vitamins				Water-Soluble Vitamins							Minerals					
	Age (years)	Weight		Height		Energy	Protein	Vitamin A Activity		Vitamin D	Vitamin E Activity[e]	Ascorbic Acid	Folacin[f]	Niacin[g]	Riboflavin (B_2)	Thiamin (B_1)	Vitamin B_6	Vitamin B_{12}	Calcium	Phosphorus	Iodine	Iron	Magnesium	Zinc
		(kg)	(lbs)	(cm)	(in)	(kcal)[b]	(g)	(RE)[c]	(IU)	(IU)	(IU)	(mg)	(μg)	(mg)	(mg)	(mg)	(mg)	(μg)	(mg)	(mg)	(μg)	(mg)	(mg)	(mg)
Infants	0.0-0.5	6	14	60	24	kg × 117	kg × 2.2	420[d]	1,400	400	4	35	50	5	0.4	0.3	0.3	0.3	360	240	35	10	60	3
	0.5-1.0	9	20	71	28	kg × 108	kg × 2.0	400	2,000	400	5	35	50	8	0.6	0.5	0.4	0.3	540	400	45	15	70	5
Children	1-3	13	28	86	34	1300	23	400	2,000	400	7	40	100	9	0.8	0.7	0.6	1.0	800	800	60	15	150	10
	4-6	20	44	110	44	1800	30	500	2,500	400	9	40	200	12	1.1	0.9	0.9	1.5	800	800	80	10	200	10
	7-10	30	66	135	54	2400	36	700	3,300	400	10	40	300	16	1.2	1.2	1.2	2.0	800	800	110	10	250	10
Males	11-14	44	97	158	63	2800	44	1,000	5,000	400	12	45	400	18	1.5	1.4	1.6	3.0	1200	1200	130	18	350	15
	15-18	61	134	172	69	3000	54	1,000	5,000	400	15	45	400	20	1.8	1.5	2.0	3.0	1200	1200	150	18	400	15
	19-22	67	147	172	69	3000	54	1,000	5,000	400	15	45	400	20	1.8	1.5	2.0	3.0	800	800	140	10	350	15
	23-50	70	154	172	69	2700	56	1,000	5,000		15	45	400	18	1.6	1.4	2.0	3.0	800	800	130	10	350	15
	51+	70	154	172	69	2400	56	1,000	5,000		15	45	400	16	1.5	1.2	2.0	3.0	800	800	110	10	350	15
Females	11-14	44	97	155	62	2400	44	800	4,000	400	12	45	400	16	1.3	1.2	1.6	3.0	1200	1200	115	18	300	15
	15-18	54	119	162	65	2100	48	800	4,000	400	12	45	400	14	1.4	1.1	2.0	3.0	1200	1200	115	18	300	15
	19-22	58	128	162	65	2100	46	800	4,000	400	12	45	400	14	1.4	1.1	2.0	3.0	800	800	100	18	300	15
	23-50	58	128	162	65	2000	46	800	4,000		12	45	400	13	1.2	1.0	2.0	3.0	800	800	100	18	300	15
	51+	58	128	162	65	1800	46	800	4,000		12	45	400	12	1.1	1.0	2.0	3.0	800	800	80	10	300	15
Pregnant						+300	+30	1,000	5,000	400	15	60	800	+2	+0.3	+0.3	2.5	4.0	1200	1200	125	18+[h]	450	20
Lactating						+500	+20	1,200	6,000	400	15	80	600	+4	+0.5	+0.3	2.5	4.0	1200	1200	150	18	450	25

[a]The allowances are intended to provide for individual variations among most normal persons as they live in the United States under usual environmental stresses. Diets should be based on a variety of common foods in order to provide other nutrients for which human requirements have been less well defined. See text for more detailed discussion of allowances and of nutrients not tabulated. See Table I (p. 6) for weights and heights by individual year of age (1).

[b]Kilojoules (kJ) = 4.2 × kcal

[c]Retinol equivalents

[d]Assumed to be all as retinol in milk during the first six months of life. All subsequent intakes are assumed to be half as retinol and half as β-carotene when calculated from international units. As retinol equivalents, three fourths are as retinol and one fourth as β-carotene.

[e]Total vitamin E activity, estimated to be 80 percent as α-tocopherol and 20 percent other tocopherols. See text for variation in allowances (1).

[f]The folacin allowances refer to dietary sources as determined by *Lactobacillus casei* assay. Pure forms of folacin may be effective in doses less than one fourth of the recommended dietary allowance.

[g]Although allowances are expressed as niacin, it is recognized that on the average 1 mg of niacin is derived from each 60 mg of dietary tryptophan.

[h]This increased requirement cannot be met by ordinary diets; therefore, the use of supplemental iron is recommended.

From The Food Nutrition Board of the National Research Council.

tributed among the meals or feedings. The difference, if any, that remains, after subtracting the carbohydrate calories, can be selected from an appropriate group, or, if allowed on the diet being planned, from the fifth group (fats and sweets). At the present time, carbohydrate and fat make nearly equal contributions to the energy content of the national diet: carbohydrate 46 per cent, fat 42 per cent. The total protein content of the food has remained nearly constant at 11-12 per cent of total energy intake (N.R.C.-1974).

In infant feeding, it is assumed that a baby being breast-fed by a well-nourished, healthy mother receives adequate amounts of high quality dietary protein. The efficiency of utilization of human milk protein is 100 per cent. All of the proprietary formulas designed for infant feeding are formulated to simulate human milk. The recommended dietary protein allowance for infants during the first year of life is 1.8 gm/100 kcal, based on the composition of human milk. Proteins of lower quality should be fed in proportionately higher amounts. These proteins are introduced in progressively larger amounts after about six months and thus the allowance per kilogram of body weight should be corrected for the lower utilization, approximately 70 per cent. The Food and Nutrition Board has emphasized that if the dietary protein is significantly less than 8 per cent of total kilocalories as provided by human milk, it is not possible to feed the infant enough food to meet the protein requirement. Appropriate increments of protein to allow for proper growth for children beyond one year were added to the maintenance protein allowance on the basis that gain in body weight is eighteen per cent protein.

There is no basis for assessing a minimal daily requirement or allowance for carbohydrate. Munro (1951) has stated that there are specific needs by the body for carbohydrate as a source of energy for the brain and certain other specialized purposes. Beyond these needs, carbohydrate and fat seem to be interchangeable as dietary sources of energy and have comparable nitrogen-sparing effects. Carbohydrate is easily converted to fat in vivo but fatty acids containing an even number of carbon atoms cannot be utilized in carbohydrate synthesis. Gamble[1] explains that while human beings are capable of adapting to very low intakes of carbohydrate, those adults having grown accustomed to normal diets require a minimum of 100 grams of carbohydrate per day to prevent excessive tissue protein breakdown, ketosis and possibly other metabolic derangement. Tissue storage of carbohydrate in man as glycogen is normally less than 1800 kcal; consequently, inadequate dietary sources result in the utilization of dietary or body tissue protein, ketosis, loss of cations, especially sodium and involuntary dehydration.

There is no basis for an exact daily allowance for fat but it is our most concentrated source of energy, serves as carrier for fat-soluble vitamins (A, D, E and K) and other substances essential for the human body. It likewise adds much satiety value through flavor, texture and appearance.

1. Gamble, J. L. *Companionship of Water and Electrolytes in the Organization of Body Fluids, in Lane Medical Lectures,* Vol. 5 No. 1; Stanford University Press; Stanford, California; 71, 1951.

All cells of the body utilize fatty acids as a source of energy except the central nervous system and erythrocytes. Excess kilocalories from carbohydrate and/or fat are stored primarily in adipose cells which form a dynamic tissue. Contrary to popular opinion, most dietary fats are readily digested by normal healthy people. Factors influencing the digestion and metabolism of food fats include carbon chain length, melting point and degree of saturation of individual fatty acids.

It should be remembered that as the per cent of total kilocalories furnished by polyunsaturated fatty acids increases, so does the requirement for vitamin E. Present evidence indicates that the suggested ratio of dietary alpha-tocopherol: PUFA of 0.6 (mg/g) is higher than necessary and that satisfactory diets in the United States have average ratios of about 0.4.

Fat contributes approximately fifty per cent of total kilocalories in both human and cow's milk. In order to meet the caloric requirements in infants, because of their limited capacity for intake, it is essential to provide at least 15 per cent of the total kilocalories as fat (N.R.C.—1974).

Linoleic acid and arachidonic acid are the only polyunsaturated fatty acids known to be essential for growth, nutritional well-being and dermal integrity in the human infant (N.R.C., 1974). Arachidonic acid can be formed from linoleic acid by the human being but linoleic acid cannot be synthesized and must therefore be supplied in the diet. The requirement is low—one percent of the total kilocalories as linoleate. Hansen (1962)[2] has recommended the allowance in infant formulas as three per cent of the total kilocalories.

High concentrations of linoleic acid are found in various edible vegetable oils (corn, cottonseed, peanut, safflower, soybean) but *not* in coconut oil or olive oil.

Deficiency of essential fatty acids in man include dermatitis and derangements in lipid transport. While deficiencies have not been seen in adults on an ordinary diet, they have been reported in hospitalized patients maintained exclusively on intravenous feeding for prolonged periods (N.R.C.-1974) and on early hyperalimentation regimes.

Physiological role of the essential fatty acids includes tissue metabolism, in phospholipids, in maintaining the function and integrity of cellular and subcellular membranes; aid in the regulation of cholesterol metabolism, especially transport, transformation into metabolites and ultimate excretion; and as precursors of prostaglandins, important in the regulation of widely diverse physiological processes (N.R.C.-1974).

Table XI gives the "Recommended Daily Food Intake for Children" or the "House Diet" for Texas Children's Hospital based on the N.R.C.-R.D.A., 1974.

Table XII provides an analysis of a suggested meal pattern for the "regular" house diet compared with the calculated values while Table XIII furnishes the same comparison of the "Chopped Diet".

2. Hansen, A. E., R. A. Stewart, G. Hughes and L. Söderhjelm, "The Relation of Linoleic Acid to Infant Feeding," *Acta Paediatr 51*:Suppl, 137:1 1962.

Table XI

Recommended Daily Food Intake Patterns for Children
(House Diet)
(Assuming No Food Intolerances)

Age Group/ Years	Average Height/ Inches	Average Weight/ Pounds	Median KCAL/ Age Group	CHO/ grams (50% of Calories)	PRO/ grams (15%of Calories)	FAT/ grams (35% of Calories)	Milk Group/ Ounces	Meat Group	Bread-Cereal Group	Vegetable—Fruit Group			Miscellaneous	
										Po-tatoes*	Other Veg**	Fruit†	FAT/ teasp. butter††	Desserts and Sweets
1-3	34	28	1300	163	49	51	16	1 egg 2-1 oz. servings	2 sl. bread ½ c. cereal	2¼ cup servings	2¼ cup servings	3⅓ cup servings	2	Plain desserts: cake, cookies, puddings, ice cream, gelatin desserts, fruit whips
4-6	44	44	1800	225	68	70	16	1 egg 2-2 oz. servings	3 sl. bread ½ c. cereal	2¼ cup servings	2¼ cup servings	2½ cup servings	3	
7-10	54	66	2400	300	90	93	24	1 egg 2-2½ oz. servings	3 sl. bread ½ c. cereal	2½ cup servings	2½ cup servings	3½ cup servings	4	
11-14 Male	63	97	2800	350	105	109	32	1 egg 2-3 oz. servings	4 sl. bread ¾ c. cereal	2½ cup servings	2½ cup servings	3½ cup servings	5	Desserts and Sweets in moderation to give satiety to the diet and increase grams of carbohydrate and total calories
11-14 Female	62	97	2400	300	90	93	24	1 egg 2-3 oz. servings	3 sl. bread ¾ c. cereal	2½ cup servings	2½ cup servings	3½ cup servings	4	
15-18 Male	69	134	3000	375	113	117	32	1 egg 2-4 oz. servings	5 sl. bread ¾ c. cereal	2¾ cup servings	2½ cup servings	3½ cup servings	6	
15-18 Female	65	119	2100	263	79	82	24	1 egg 2-3 oz. servings	3 sl. bread ¾ c. cereal	2½ cup servings	2½ cup servings	3½ cup servings	5	

*May be replaced by equal amount of macaroni, noodles, spaghetti or rice
**One serving should include a dark leafy green or deep yellow vegetable for Vitamin A
†One serving should be rich in Ascorbic Acid (Vitamin C)
††One slice of bacon may be substituted for one teaspoon butter or margarine

Table XII

Analysis of a Suggested Meal Pattern for "Regular" House Diet Compared with Calculated Values

FOOD	AMOUNT	CALORIES	PROTEIN (gm)	FAT (gm)	CARBOHYDRATE (gm)	CALCIUM (mg)	PHOSPHORUS (mg)	IRON (mg)	SODIUM (mg)	POTASSIUM (mg)	VITAMIN A (I.U.)	THIAMINE (mcg)	RIBOFLAVIN (mcg)	NIACIN (mg)	VITAMIN C (mg)	VITAMIN D (I.U.)	VITAMIN E (I.U.)	FOLACIN (mcg)	VITAMIN B_6 (mg)	VITAMIN B_{12} (mcg)	IODINE (mcg)	MAGNESIUM (mg)
BREAKFAST																						
Orange Juice	1/2 c.	58.1	0.9	0.1	13.4	11	20	0.1	1	233	250	113	13	0.4	56							
Scrambled Egg	One	111.2	7.3	8.4	1.6	52	123	1.1	167	95	702	52	182	0.1	0							
Cream of Wheat	1/2 c.	80.8	2.5	0.4	16.8	11	75	0.5	91	-	0	64	13	-	0							
Sugar	1 tsp.	11.6	0.0	0.0	2.9	0	0	-	-	-	0	0	0	0.0	0							
Toast	1 slice	61.5	2.0	0.7	11.8	20	23	0.6	118	24	-	46	48	0.6	-							
Margarine	1 tsp.	36.9	-	4.1	-	1	1	0.0	49	1	165	-	-	-	0							
Grape Jelly	1 Tbsp.	39.6	-	-	9.9	3	1	0.2	2	11	1	1	4	-	1							
Milk	1 c.	156.4	8.4	8.4	11.8	283	223	-	120	346	336	72	408	0.2	2							
LUNCH																						
Broiled Chicken	2oz.	105.5	17.6	3.9	0.0	8	141	1.1	53	198	96	72	114	3.2	-							
Rice	1/2 c.	79.7	1.5	0.1	18.2	8	21	0.7	281	21	0	83		0.8	0							
Green Beans	1/2 c.	18.1	0.9	0.1	3.4	29	16	1.0	153	62	306	20	33	0.2	3							
Carrot Sticks	50 gm.	22.9	0.6	0.1	4.9	19	18	0.4	24	171	5500	30	25	0.3	4							
Bread	1 slice	60.7	2.0	0.7	11.6	19	22	0.6	117	24	-	58	48	0.6	-							
Margarine	2 tsp.	72.9	-	8.1	-	2	2	0.0	99	2	330	-	-	-	0							
Cherry Jelly	1 Tbsp.	39.6	-	-	9.9	3	1	0.2	2	11	1	1	4	-	2							
Canned Pear Halves	2 halves	81.0	0.2	0.2	19.6	5	7	0.2	1	84	-	10	20	0.1	1							
Milk	1 c.	156.4	8.4	8.4	11.8	283	223	-	120	346	336	72	408	0.2	2							
DINNER																						
Broiled Beef Patty	2 oz.	167.8	14.5	12.2	0.0	7	116	1.9	28	270	24	54	126	3.2	-							
Baked Potato	100 gm.	95.7	2.6	0.1	21.1	9	65	0.7	4	503	-	100	40	1.7	20							
Spinach	1/4 c.	15.4	1.5	0.2	1.9	57	22	1.1	26	167	3950	35	75	0.2	10							
Bread	1 slice	60.7	2.0	0.7	11.6	19	22	0.6	117	24	-	58	48	0.6	-							
Margarine	2 tsp.	72.9	-	8.1	-	2	2	0.0	99	2	330	-	-	-	0							
Apple Jelly	1 Tbsp.	39.6	-	-	9.9	3	1	0.2	2	11	1	1	4	-	1							
Peach Half	1 half	42.1	0.2	0.1	10.1	2	6	0.2	1	65	215	5	10	0.3	2							
Yellow Cake	50 gm.	183.2	2.3	6.4	29.1	36	56	0.2	129	39	75	10	40	0.1	-							
White Icing	10 gm.	39.5	0.1	0.7	8.2	2	1	-	5	2	27	-	2	-	-							
Milk	1 c.	156.4	8.4	8.4	11.8	283	223	-	120	346	336	72	408	0.2	2							
TOTAL CALCULATIONS OF DIET		2066.2	83.9	80.6	251.3	1177	1431	11.6	1929	3058	12981	1029	2073	13.0	106							
ANALYSIS OF DIET		2333.0	86.2	91.9	274.3	826	1342	18.9	2473	2983	7309	643	2298	13.6	80	78	30	38481	1.2	1.0	1402	26
RDA FOR 8-YEAR OLD CHILD						800	800	10.0			3300	1200	1200	16.0	40	400	10	300	1.2	2.0	110	250

Table XIII

Analysis of a Suggested Meal Pattern for "Chopped" Diet Compared with Calculated Values

FOOD	AMOUNT	CALORIES	PROTEIN (gm)	FAT (gm)	CARBOHYDRATE (gm)	CALCIUM (mg)	PHOSPHORUS (mg)	IRON (mg)	SODIUM (mg)	POTASSIUM (mg)	VITAMIN A (I.U.)	THIAMINE (mcg)	RIBOFLAVIN (mcg)	NIACIN (mg)	VITAMIN C (mg)	VITAMIN D (I.U.)	VITAMIN E (I.U.)	FOLACIN (mcg)	VITAMIN B_6 (mg)	VITAMIN B_{12} (mcg)	IODINE (mcg)	MAGNESIUM (mg)
BREAKFAST																						
Orange Juice	1/2 c.	58.1	0.9	0.1	13.4	11	20	0.1	1	233	250	113	13	0.4	56							
Hard Cooked Egg	One	75.9	6.2	5.5	0.4	26	98	1.1	59	62	566	43	134	-	0							
Cream of Wheat	1/4 c.	39.4	1.2	0.2	8.2	6	37	0.3	45	-	0	31	6	-	0							
Margarine	1 tsp.	36.9	-	4.1	-	1	1	0.0	49	1	165	-	-	-	0							
Sugar	1 tsp.	11.6	0.0	0.0	2.9	0	0	-	-	-	0	0	0	0.0	0							
Milk	1 c.	156.4	8.4	8.4	11.8	283	223	-	120	346	336	72	408	0.2	2							
LUNCH																						
Broiled Chicken	1 oz.	53.2	8.8	2.0	0.0	4	71	0.5	26	99	48	36	57	1.6	-							
Rice	1/4 c.	39.6	0.8	-	9.1	4	11	0.3	140	11	0	41		0.4	0							
Spinach	1/4 c.	15.4	1.5	0.2	1.9	57	22	1.1	26	167	3950	35	75	0.2	10							
Bread	1 slice	60.7	2.0	0.7	11.6	19	22	0.6	117	24	-	58	48	0.6	-							
Margarine	1 tsp.	36.9	-	4.1	-	1	1	0.0	49	1	165	-	-	-	0							
Grape Jelly	1 Tbsp.	39.6	-	-	9.9	3	1	0.2	2	11	1	1	4	-	1							
Canned Pear Halves	2 halves	81.0	0.2	0.2	19.6	5	7	0.2	1	84	-	10	20	0.1	1							
Milk	1/2 c.	78.2	4.2	4.2	5.9	142	112	-	60	173	168	36	204	0.1	1							
DINNER																						
Broiled Beef Patty	1 oz.	84.1	7.3	6.1	0.0	3	58	1.0	14	135	12	27	63	1.6	-							
Mashed Potatoes	1/4 c.	49.0	1.1	2.2	6.2	12	24	0.2	166	125	85	40	25	0.5	5							
Green Beans	1/4 c.	9.7	0.5	0.1	1.7	15	8	0.5	77	31	153	10	16	0.1	1							
Bread	1 slice	60.7	2.0	0.7	11.6	19	22	0.6	117	24	-	58	48	0.6	-							
Margarine	1 tsp.	36.9	-	4.1	-	1	1	0.0	49	1	165	-	-	-	0							
Apple Jelly	1 Tbsp.	39.6	-	-	9.9	3	1	0.2	2	11	1	1	4	-	1							
Canned Peach Half	1 half	42.1	0.2	0.1	10.1	2	6	0.2	1	65	215	5	10	0.3	2							
Milk	1/2 c.	78.2	4.2	4.2	5.9	142	112	-	60	173	168	36	204	0.1	1							
TOTAL CALCULATIONS OF DIET		1183.2	49.5	47.2	140.1	759	858	7.1	1181	1777	6448	653	1339	6.8	81							
ANALYSIS OF DIET		1395.6	50.6	50.3	175.6	693	827	11.5	1938	1874	1788	466	1348	7.7	58	31	14	21031	0.7	0.7	1749	17
RDA FOR 2-YEAR OLD CHILD						800	800	15.0			1100	700	800	9.0	40	400	7	100	0.6	1.0	60	150

Table XIV

Recommended Dietary Allowances for Infants Expressed In Relation to Energy Needs (amounts per 100 kcal)

	Unit	0.0-0.5 yr	0.5-1.0 yr
Protein	gm	1.9	1.85
Vitamin A	IU	200	206
Vitamin D	IU	57	41
Vitamin E	IU	.569	.5
Ascorbic Acid	mg	4.98	3.6
Folacin	mcg	7.12	5.14
Niacin	mg-equiv.	.7	0.82
Riboflavin	mg	0.056	0.062
Thiamine	mg	0.043	0.051
Vitamin B_6	mg	0.043	0.041
Vitamin B_{12}	mcg	0.043	0.031
Calcium	mg	51.28	55.56
Phosphorus	mg	34.19	41.15
Iodine	mcg	4.98	4.63
Iron	mg	1.42	1.54
Magnesium	mg	8.55	7.20
Zinc	mg	0.427	0.51

The calorie allowances for children of both sexes are about 80 kcal/kg up to ten years. After ten years of age, the kcal/kg values gradually decline to 50 for adolescent males and 35 for adolescent females.

The N.R.C. recommended allowances for infants, expressed in relation to energy needs are listed in Table XIV.

The essential nutrients of a well-balanced nutritious diet are identical for all age groups but the amounts vary with individual needs. Thus the child has a relatively large requirement for growth and activity, requiring the nutrient composition of the food consumed to be high in protein, minerals and vitamins with adequate caloric value. At various age levels adaptation of diet to meet particular handicaps or lack of functional maturity must be made—the fluid consistency of formula prior to the cutting of teeth, gradual introduction of complex foods with enzyme readiness, finger-food for the toddler, etc. Starting in the second year, most children experience new and rapidly changing attitudes and emotional reactions to foods and food habits. Understanding and wise guidance during this period can establish wholesome food selection and attitudes for the future. Consequently, a wide variety of foods are offered and repeated at periodic intervals. As the infant with his very rapid growth rate has a large appetite, the toddler slows down in his intake corresponding to the slower growth rate during the second year. Mother cannot help but feel that he just is not eating enough and fears for his well-being.

It is at this time that many faulty food habits are introduced—like offering a bottle at any time, some fruit juice, a cookie, just anything as the "poor, little dear just didn't have a thing for breakfast."

Self-feeding should be encouraged and "tolerated" when the individual child shows readiness for it. Very small portions should be offered in order that the child may feel the capability and sense of pride in finishing one serving and wanting or asking for more—thus imitating adults. Each child is an individual! Each child will vary in preferences for foods and amounts.

Chapter 4

Standard Hospital Diets

Regular House Diet

Principle: The Regular House Diet is designed to meet the nutritional requirements of children who are not acutely ill and who have no food intolerance.

Adequacy: The diet provides the Recommended Daily Dietary Allowances for all nutrients, if consumed in suggested amounts. (See Recommended Daily Food Intake Patterns for Children, Table XI and the full analysis of Suggested Meal Pattern for Regular House Diet, Table XII).

Foods	**Foods Allowed**	**Foods To Avoid**
Beverages	Milk, milk drinks; tea; carbonated beverages (in moderation)	*Coffee
Breads	All; emphasize whole grain breads; crackers	None
Cereals	All; emphasize whole grain cereals	None
Desserts	All	Coconut or nuts when indicated
Fats	All	None
Fruits and Fruit Juices	All; include one serving citrus fruit or juice daily	Peel or remove seeds as indicated
Meat, Fish, Poultry, Cheese, and Eggs	All	Fish with small bones
Potatoes or Substitutes	Potatoes, white or sweet; corn; macaroni; noodles; rice; spaghetti	None

Foods	Foods Allowed	Foods to Avoid
Soups	All	None
Sweets	All (in moderation)	Coconut or nuts when indicated
Vegetables and Vegetable Juices	All; include one serving dark green or yellow vegetable daily	None unless some cause individual distress
Miscellaneous	Salt; spices; peanut butter; cream sauces; sour cream; yogurt; mustard; catsup; pickles; chocolate	*Black pepper; foods that are highly seasoned for young children

*Coffee and Black Pepper are usually not served unless specifically requested.

Chopped Diet

Principle: The Chopped Diet is used as a transition from pureed foods to the Regular House Diet. It is a soft diet moderately low in cellulose and connective tissue, as well as containing no fried or highly seasoned foods. The diet is designed to teach the child to chew and enjoy chopped foods. Finger foods help promote motor development and encourage the chewing process. It may be used between the ages of one and three years.

Adequacy: The diet provides the Recommended Daily Dietary Allowances for all nutrients, if consumed in suggested amounts. (See recommended Daily Food Intake Patterns for Children, Table XI and the full analysis of Suggested Meal Pattern for Chopped Diet, Table XIII.)

Foods	Foods Allowed	Foods To Avoid
Beverages	Milk, milk drinks; tea; carbonated beverages (in moderation)	*Coffee
Breads	Emphasize refined wheat bread; crackers, saltine and graham	Whole or cracked grain; seeds (sesame, poppy, caraway)
Cereals	Refined cooked and prepared cereals	Whole grain cereals
Desserts	Plain desserts; cookies, cakes, custards, puddings, ice cream, gelatin, fruit whips, sherbet, popsicles, fudgesicles	Coconut; nuts; rich pastries
Fats	Butter; margarine; cream; mayonnaise	Bacon; lard

*Coffee and Black Pepper usually are not served unless specifically requested.

Foods	Foods Allowed	Foods to Avoid
Fruits and Fruit Juices	All fruit juices; ripe banana; raw peeled apple; orange or grapefruit sections; canned fruit without seeds; include one serving citrus fruit or juice daily	Any fruit with seeds or tough skins
Meat, Fish, Poultry, Cheese, and Eggs	Lean, tender, chopped: beef, lamb, liver, pork, chicken, turkey; boneless fish, eggs, cheese	Fish with small bones; fried, smoked or highly seasoned meat or meat products
Potatoes or Substitutes	White potatoes, mashed or dehydrated sweet potatoes; macaroni; noodles; refined rice; spaghetti	Skins of potatoes; fried potatoes; potato chips; corn and corn chips; wild rice
Soups	Clear or cream soups with allowed foods	Highly seasoned soups
Sweets	Honey; jelly; sugar; syrup; plain candy (all in moderation)	Candy with nuts or coconut; small hard candy; jams; marmalade
Vegetables and Vegetable Juices	All vegetables as tolerated and accepted; include one serving dark green or yellow vegetable daily	Raw vegetables that are difficult for the young child to chew
Miscellaneous	Salt; mild spices; smooth peanut butter; cream sauces; yogurt; sour cream; catsup; mustard	*Black pepper; highly seasoned foods; herbs; nuts; olives; popcorn; pickles

Soft Diet

Principle: The Soft Diet is moderately low in cellulose and connective tissue and contains no fried or highly seasoned foods. It is used most commonly as a post-operative diet, as a progressive step from a liquid diet to the Regular House Diet.

Adequacy: The diet provides the Recommended Daily Dietary Allowances for all nutrients, if consumed in suggested amounts. (See Recommended Daily Food Intake Patterns for Children, Table XI).

Foods	Foods Allowed	Foods To Avoid
Beverages	Milk, milk drinks; tea; carbonated beverages (in moderation)	*Coffee
Breads	Emphasize refined wheat bread; crackers, saltine and graham	Whole or cracked grain; breads or crackers with fruits or seeds; hot rolls, biscuits or cornbread; waffles or pancakes

*Coffee and black pepper usually are not served unless specifically requested.

Foods	Foods Allowed	Foods to Avoid
Cereals	Refined cooked and prepared cereals	Whole grain cereals
Desserts	Plain desserts: cookies, cake, custards, ice cream, puddings, sherbet, popsicles, fruit whips, gelatin	Coconut; nuts; rich pastries
Fats	Butter; margarine; cream; mayonnaise	Bacon; lard
Fruits and Fruit Juices	Any fruit juice; canned pears, peaches, peeled apricots, applesauce, pineapple, fruit cocktail; orange and grapefruit sections without connective membranes; fresh soft cooked apples, pears, peaches; ripe banana When tolerated (older children), canned cherries and plums	Fresh fruits except those permitted; dried fruits; berries
Meat, Fish, Poultry, Cheese, and Eggs	Lean, tender broiled, boiled or baked: beef, veal, lamb, pork, liver, turkey, chicken; boneless fish; eggs; cottage and mild cheese	Smoked, spiced, salted fried: meats, fish, ham, poultry, eggs; sharp cheese
Potatoes or Substitutes	White potatoes, mashed or dehydrated sweet potatoes; macaroni; noodles; rice; spaghetti; hominy	Skins of potatoes; fried potatoes; potato chips; corn and corn chips
Soups	Clear or cream soups with allowed foods	Highly seasoned soups
Sweets	Honey; jelly; syrup; sugar; plain candy (all in moderation)	Candy with nuts or coconut; jams; marmalades
Vegetables and Vegetable Juices	Tender cooked: asparagus, beets, carrots, green or wax beans, green peas, mushrooms, pumpkin, turnips, chopped greens, squash, okra, eggplant, stewed tomatoes, all mild vegetable juices	All others; fried vegetables
Miscellaneous	Salt; mild spices; vanilla extract; natural gravies; smooth peanut butter; cream sauces; catsup; prepared mustard	*Black Pepper; highly seasoned foods; herbs; nuts; olives; popcorn; pickles

Suggested Meal Pattern

Breakfast	Lunch	Dinner
Orange Juice	Roast Beef	Broiled Chicken
Scrambled Egg	Whipped Potatoes	Buttered Noodles
Cream of Wheat	Buttered Chopped Spinach	Buttered Carrots
Toast	Refined Wheat Bread	Refined Wheat Bread
Butter	Butter	Butter
Milk	Sliced Peaches	Sugar Cookies
	Milk	Milk

Dental Soft Diet

Principle: The Dental Soft Diet is individualized to meet the needs of children who have difficulty in chewing or swallowing. This diet is a modification of the Soft Diet and includes pureed or soft-textured foods.

Adequacy: The diet provides the Recommended Daily Dietary Allowances for all nutrients, if consumed in suggested amounts. (See Recommend Daily Food Intake Patterns for Children, Table XI).

Foods	Foods Allowed	Foods To Avoid
Beverages	Milk, milk drinks; tea; carbonated beverages (in moderation)	*Coffee
Breads	Emphasize refined wheat bread; graham and saltine crackers if softened in milk or soup; hot breads if tolerated	Whole or cracked grain; breads or crackers with fruits or seeds
Cereals	Refined cooked and prepared cereals	Whole grain cereals
Desserts	Plain soft desserts: cake, cookies, custards, puddings, ice cream, sherbet, popsicles, fruit whips, fudgesicles, gelatin	Coconut; nuts; crisp pastries
Fats	Butter; margarine; cream; mayonnaise	Bacon
Fruits and Fruit Juices	Any fruit juice; canned pears, peaches, peeled apricots, applesauce, pineapple, fruit cocktail; orange and grapefruit sections without connective membranes if tolerated; soft cooked apples, pears, peaches; ripe banana When tolerated (older children), canned cherries and peeled plums	Fresh fruits except those permitted; raisins; dates; berries

Foods	Foods Allowed	Foods to Avoid
Meat, Fish, Poultry, Cheese & Eggs	Tender, lean, broiled, boiled, ground or pureed: beef, veal, lamb, pork, liver, turkey, chicken, boneless fish; eggs; soft cheese	Smoked, spiced, salted, fried: meats, fish, ham, poultry, eggs
Potatoes or Substitutes	White potatoes, mashed or dehydrated sweet potatoes; macaroni; noodles; rice; spaghetti; hominy	Skins of potatoes; fried potatoes; potato chips; corn and corn chips
Soups	Clear or cream soups with allowed foods	Highly seasoned soups
Sweets	Honey; jelly; syrup; sugar; chocolate sauce (all in moderation)	Candy; nuts; coconut; gum; jams; marmalades
Vegetables and Vegetable Juices	Tender cooked or pureed: asparagus, beets, carrots, green or wax beans, green peas, mushrooms, pumpkin, turnips, chopped greens, squash, okra, eggplant; all mild vegetable juices	All others; fried vegetables
Miscellaneous	Salt; mild spices; vanilla extract; natural gravies; smooth peanut butter; cream sauces; catsup; prepared mustard	*Black pepper; highly seasoned foods; herbs; nuts; olives; popcorn; pickles

Suggested Meal Pattern

Breakfast	Lunch	Dinner
Orange Juice	Ground Roast Beef	Ground Chicken
Scrambled Egg	Whipped Potatoes	Buttered Noodles
Cream of Wheat	Buttered Chopped Spinach	Buttered Green Peas
Toast	Refined Wheat Bread	Refined Wheat Bread
Butter	Butter	Butter
Milk	Applesauce	Vanilla Pudding
	Milk	Milk

Liquid Diets

Clear Liquid Diet

This modification provides a source of fluids in the form of clear liquids only. It furnishes little, if any, caloric contribution but may provide electrolyte support, especially in infants and young children, with the use of Pedialyte[3] or Lytren[4]. These are particularly useful for vomiting and/or

*Coffee and black pepper usually are not served unless specifically requested

3. Ross Laboratories
4. Mead-Johnson Company

diarrhea or other gastrointestinal pathology. Because of its gross nutrient inadequacy, its use is restricted to very limited periods of time and is most often used in the pre-operative and immediate post-operative periods as a step in progression to a regular or other diet.

For gastrointestinal surgery, most surgeons prefer a restricted clear liquid diet in the immediate post-operative period. This is confined to warm tea, broth or bouillon and jello. Carbonated beverages are not allowed.

As the patient progresses satisfactorily, a soft-surgical diet, which is actually a combination of full liquid and low residue diet, is used before going on to a soft-bland or soft diet, etc.

Clear Liquid Diet

Principle: The Clear Liquid Diet is designed to provide fluids without stimulating extensive digestive processes, to relieve thirst and to provide oral feedings which will promote a gradual return to normal food intake. Due to the absence of residue, this diet is used most frequently pre-and post-operatively.

Adequacy: This diet is inadequate in all nutrients.

Foods	Foods Allowed	Foods To Avoid
Beverages	Tea; carbonated beverages	*Coffee; all others
Desserts	Clear flavored gelatin; popsicles	All others
Soups	Clear broth; bouillon; consomme	All others
Sweets	Sugar; plain hard candy (in moderation)	All others

*Coffee usually is not served unless specifically requested.

Suggested Meal Pattern

Breakfast	Lunch	Dinner
Broth	Consomme	Broth
Cherry Flavored Gelatin	7-Up	Coke
Tea	Orange Flavored Gelatin	Strawberry Flavored Gelatin

Polycose (Glucose Polymer)

Polycose is predominantly medium chain length glucose polymers although other lengths are present.

Chain Length	Approx. Percentage
Free glucose	< 2%
1-4 glucose units	29%
5-9 glucose units	48%
10 or more glucose units	23%

Salivary, pancreatic and intestinal maltases and amylase rapidly hydrolyze polycose to free glucose with rapid absorption into portal blood; pancreatic amylase speeds hydrolysis but is not essential.

Polycose is a carbohydrate source of calories that can be used to help overcome caloric deficits in persons unable to meet their total caloric needs from regular diets. It can be used as the sole energy source for short periods, or as a supplement indefinitely.

Approximate analysis:

	Powder (100 gm)	Liquid 100 kcal/100 ml	
Calories	400	100	200
Carbohydrate	94 gm	25	50 gm
Moisture	6 gm	35	70 gm
Ash	0.5 gm	0.13	0.25 gm

Minerals do not exceed the following values:

	mg/mEq	mg/mEq	
Sodium	122/5.3	30/1.3	70/3
Potassium	8/0.2	1.6/0.04	4/0.1
Chloride	234/6.6	50/1.4	110/3.1
Calcium	14/0.7	6.0/0.3	16/0.8
Phosphorus*	9/0.9	1.2/0.12	3/0.3

(contains no protein, fat or vitamins)

Approximate Calorie Equivalents:

Powder		Liquid	
1 level Tbsp	= 30 kcal	1 ml	= 2 kilocal
1 oz (8.25 gm)	= 110 kcal	1 fl oz	= 60 kilocal
100 gms	= 400 kcal	100 ml	= 200 kilocal

Advantages:
1. Low osmolarity
2. Low sweetness
3. Rapidly absorbed as glucose with negligible gut residue
4. Low electrolyte levels
5. May be mixed with most solid foods and beverages. Water soluble. Unflavored.

Polycose is available as powder, in 14 oz cans, 6 per case; liquid, (43% w/w aqueous solution) in 4 fl oz bottles, 12 bottles per tray, 4 trays per case.

Liquid: Clear with a faint yellowish color that slightly darkens with age and has a moderately sweet taste.

Caloric value of 43% (w/w) aqueous solution = 2 kcal/ml
Osmolarity = 570 mOsm/l
Density = 1.2 gm/ml
Viscosity = 32 centipoise at 24°C

*Valence of 3 used

Administration Guide for Maintenance and Replacement of Losses in Mild to Moderate Diarrhea

Pedialyte†

Infants and Young Children														
Weight (lbs)	7	10	13	17	20	22	24	28	30	32	34	36	38	40
Weight (kg)	3.18	4.54	5.90	7.71	9.07	9.98	10.89	12.70	13.61	14.51	15.42	16.33	17.24	18.14
Approx. Surface Area (Sq. meters)	.21	.26	.30	.35	.40	.44	.47	.53	.58	.61	.64	.67	.71	.74
Pedialyte— Oz/Day Maintenance	10 to 14	13 to 17	15 to 20	17 to 23	20 to 26	22 to 29	23 to 31	26 to 35	29 to 38	30 to 40	32 to 42	33 to 44	35 to 47	37 to 49
Pedialyte— Oz/Day Maintenance and Replacement	15 to 19	19 to 24	24 to 29	29 to 35	33 to 40	37 to 44	40 to 47	45 to 54	49 to 59	52 to 62	55 to 66	58 to 69	61 to 73	65 to 77

For children 5 years or older: 2 or more quarts daily
†Ross Laboratories

Lytren† Dosage Guide for Infants and Young Children

Body Weight Kg.	Body Weight Lb.	Average Surface Area Sq. Meter*	Lytren Solution Daily Dosage: Maintenance Approx. Fl. Oz.**	Lytren Solution Daily Dosage: Maintenance plus Replacement of Moderate Losses Approx. Fl. Oz.***
3	6-7	0.2	10	16
5	11	0.29	15	23
7	15	0.38	19	30
10	22	0.49	25	40
12	26	0.55	28	44
15	33	0.64	32	51
18	40	0.76	38	61

*Surface area based on average height for each weight shown.
**Based on water requirement of 1500 ml. (50 fl. oz.) per sq. meter.
***Based on water requirement of 2400 ml. (80 fl. oz.) per sq. meter.
†Mead-Johnson Co.

Full Liquid Diet

This modification is defined as a diet consisting of a variety of foods that are liquid or liquefy at body temperature.[5] This diet usually meets the Recommended Daily Allowances for calcium, phosphorus, riboflavin and ascorbic acid but it is inadequate in all other nutrients. The physical consistency must be such that it pours. Again, it is most often used for relatively short periods as a progression toward a more normal diet.

Some indications in addition to post-operative care include situations requiring low mechanical irritation of bowel surgery involving mouth, throat or neck, fractured jaw, inability to chew and difficulty in swallowing.

If physical consistency is the only requirement for the full liquid diet, like wired, fractured jaw, for example, then wider selection of strained foods can be thinned to pour with milk or other fluid. This could then be made nutritionally adequate and used for longer periods either orally or as a tube feeding. Selective vitamin or mineral supplementation may be necessary.

Full Liquid Diet

Principle: The Full Liquid Diet is used to provide nourishment which is easy to consume with very little stimulation to the gastrointestinal tract. As postoperative diet, it is used as a progressive step from the Clear Liquid Diet to the Soft Diet. The Full Liquid Diet expands the Clear Liquid Diet by allowing milk products, fruit juices and cereal gruel. The diet allows foods that are liquid or that liquefy at body temperature.

Adequacy: The Full Liquid Diet meets the Recommended Daily Allowances for calcium, phosphorus, riboflavin and ascorbic acid. It is inadequate in all other nutrients.

Foods	Foods Allowed	Foods To Avoid
Beverages	Milk, milk drinks; tea; carbonated beverages (in moderation)	*Coffee
Breads	None	All
Cereals	Cereal gruel made from refined cereals	All others
Desserts	Ice cream, sherbet, flavored gelatin, pudding, custard, fruit ice, fruit whips, popsicles (all without nuts, coconut or whole fruits)	All others
Fats	Butter; margarine; cream	All others
Fruits and Fruit Juices	Juices; include one serving citrus juice daily	All others

5. Turner, Dorothea, *Handbook of Diet Therapy*, 5th Ed., University of Chicago Press: 35, 1970.

Foods	Foods Allowed	Foods to Avoid
Meat, Fish, Poultry, Cheese, and Eggs	Mild cheese sauce; cream soups; egg cooked in custards or puddings	All others
Potatoes or Substitutes	Mashed potato in strained creamed soup	All others
Soups	Broth; strained cream soup	All others
Sweets	Sugar; strained honey; plain hard candy (all in moderation)	All others
Vegetables and Vegetable Juices	Mild-flavored pureed vegetables in soups	All others
Miscellaneous	Salt; mild spices; artificial flavorings	All others

*Coffee usually is not served unless specifically requested

Suggested Meal Pattern

Breakfast	Lunch	Dinner
Orange Juice	Cream of Potato Soup	Cream of Chicken Soup
Cream of Wheat Gruel	Grape Juice	Lemonade
Milk	Milk	Milk
Butter	Custard Sauce	Vanilla Ice Cream
Sugar		

T & A Diets

Liquid: Following a T and A or throat surgery, a modified liquid diet is usually allowed with iced or cold liquids being preferred to aid in hemostasis. Warm and hot foods are avoided.

Soft: Approximately twenty-four (24) hours later, a T & A #1 soft diet is introduced consisting of full liquid, excluding citrus fruit juices, plus scrambled or poached eggs. If the patients remain in the hospital more than two (2) days, they progress to the T & A #2 Soft.

T & A Liquid Diet

Principle: The T & A Liquid Diet is used after tonsillectomy and adenoidectomy surgery for a very short period of time (one or two meals). It eliminates foods that are thermally, mechanically and chemically irritating to the throat. Ice cold foods are preferred to minimize hemorrhaging, nausea and pain.

Adequacy: This diet is inadequate in all nutrients.

Foods	Foods Allowed	Foods To Avoid
Beverages	Cold beverages only; milk, milk drinks, tea and carbonated beverages (if tolerated)	Hot beverages; all others

Foods	Foods Allowed	Foods to Avoid
Desserts	Popsicles; ice cream; sherbet; flavored gelatin; puddings; custards (all without fruit; nuts or coconut)	All others
Fruits and Fruit Juices	Grape juice; apple juice; fruit nectars	All others
Miscellaneous	Sugar; artificial flavorings	All others

Suggested Meal Pattern

Cherry Flavored Gelatin
Vanilla Ice Cream
Apple Juice
Milk

T & A #1 Soft Diet

Full Liquid Diet excluding citrus fruit juices, plus scrambled or poached eggs.

T & A #2 Soft Diet

Principle: The T & A Soft Diet is a progressive step from the T & A Liquid Diet to the Regular House Diet. It is generally ordered as the third meal following a tonsillectomy. Cold and soft foods are more soothing and tend to maintain hemostasis. Meat is omitted until the patient progresses to the Regular House Diet.

Adequacy: The diet meets the Recommended Daily Allowances for calcium, phosphorus and riboflavin. It is inadequate in all other nutrients; however, the diet is recommended for only one or two days.

Foods	Foods Allowed	Foods To Avoid
Beverages	Milk, milk drinks; tea and carbonated beverages (if tolerated)	All others
Cereal	Refined cooked cereal	All others
Desserts	Flavored gelatin, ice cream, sherbet, puddings, custards (all without nuts, coconut or fruit)	All others
Fruit and Fruit Juices	Grape juice; apple juice; fruit nectars	All others
Fat	Butter; margarine; cream	All others
Meat, Fish, Poultry, Cheese and Eggs	Soft-cooked eggs; cottage and mild cheese	Fried eggs; sharp cheese; all others

Foods	Foods Allowed	Foods to Avoid
Potatoes or Substitutes	White potatoes (cooked without skin); rice; noodles; macaroni; spaghetti; macaroni & cheese	All others
Soups	Strained cream soups	All others
Sweets	Sugar	All others
Vegetables and Vegetable Juices	Pureed vegetables in cream soups	All others
Miscellaneous	Artificial flavorings; cream sauce	All Others

Suggested Meal Pattern

Breakfast	Lunch	Dinner
Grape Juice Soft Scrambled Egg Cream of Wheat Sugar Butter Milk	Strained Cream of Chicken Soup Buttered Mashed Potatoes Apple Juice Vanilla Ice Cream Milk	Strained Cream of Potato Soup Buttered Noodles Apricot Nectar Raspberry Flavored Gelatin Milk

Chapter 5

Tube Feedings

Basic Principles

This modification of diet is a source of fluid and nourishment which requires that the material be sufficiently fluid to flow through a naso-gastric tube. In cases of esophageal obstruction, a gastrostomy is used. The tube feeding should be nutritionally adequate and can be used for short periods of time or indefinitely. It should meet the patient's individual needs, be easily digested and be well tolerated by the patient without untoward reactions such as vomiting, diarrhea, distention or constipation. It should be easily prepared and reasonable in cost.

Blenderized Feedings

Any food that can be blenderized can be used unless contraindicated in the particular situation one is treating. A combination of food with specified restrictions, if any, is selected. The use of regular foods is usually much more favorably received by the patient. The food is thinned with sufficient liquid (milk, water) to facilitate blenderizing or liquefaction. The homogenate is strained before using. Fluid requirements are met as usual and the protein and caloric intake adjusted as required. Usually, dilute feedings are introduced followed by more concentrated ones—a very important practical point. Raw eggs should never be used.

Protein (approximately 15%)

That there is an adequate amount of high quality protein in the tube feeding is vitally important since it is essential for building and repairing body cells and tissues. However, an excess can cause dehydration or hypernatremia as well as result in the production of additional urea needing to be excreted by the kidneys.

Carbohydrate (approximately 50%)

Carbohydrates are included for their caloric content, to cover the protein utilization and satiety value. The sources used most frequently are glucose, sucrose, corn syrup solids and the lactose in the milk. Honey is sometimes better tolerated by infants. Some patients may have specific intolerances or enzyme deficiencies.

Fats (approximately 35%)

Fats are included for their caloric concentration, source of essential fatty acid carrier for fat soluble vitamins and satiety value.

Excessive amounts of fat can cause slow passage of food from the stomach with regurgitation and subsequent aspiration. With malabsorption, there can be steatorrhea. In this situation, MCT oil can be tried. One must provide the essential fatty acid, linoleic acid, and the fat soluble vitamins.

Tube feedings for infants and children are planned similarly by first determining the total caloric needs, the protein, carbohydrate and fat distribution, fluid requirements and then selecting calculated amounts of appropriate foods to meet the nutritional needs. Where there is a milk intolerance, tube feedings with Meat Base Formula or other cow's milk substitutes (Soybean formulas, Nutramigen, Portagen, etc.) may be used alone or with proper additions. In cases of specific carbohydrate intolerances or disaccharidase deficiencies, proper substitutions can be made. Likewise, specific oils or combinations, including MCT oil, may be selected in cases of fat malabsorption. In combination with the strained baby foods, a regular or modified diet may easily be converted to a tube feeding.

Commercially Prepared Tube Feedings

With the current trend toward prepackaged, individualized and disposable products, most doctors and hospitals have adopted the use of the many commercially prepared tube feedings available. One of the most attractive aspects of this system is the possibility of eliminating contamination; another key feature is the conservation of time spent in the preparation and the cost of the "contamination-free" area for preparation. The individual units allow the use of a fresh package or can with each feeding which eliminates much waste when the order is changed or the patient cannot continue on a product for any reason. It also allows immediate introduction of the specific feeding without waiting for the preparation.

Some products on the market have natural foods as a base and virtually replace the freshly-made tube feeding—Formula 2 (prepared by Gerber and marketed by Cutter) and Compleat-B (Doyle). Others are combinations of protein (egg albumin, caseinate, skimmed milk, soy-protein isolate, crystalline or hydrolyzed amino acids), carbohydrate (maltodextrin, sucrose, corn syrup solids) and fat (soy oil, vegetable oil, MCT oil, coconut oil, safflower oil, corn oil) plus vitamins and minerals. Some contain lactose, some are lactose-free. Some have very low residue, some moderate and others rather high residue. For an analysis of the composition of these various tube feedings, see Table XV. Sources of protein, carbohydrate and fat in the various tube feedings and supplementary feedings

Table XV

Nutrient Composition of Tube Feedings, Elemental Feedings and Supplementary Feedings

PER 100 mls.	COMPANY	DILUTION	KILOCALORIES PER 100 ml./PER oz.	PROTEIN (gms.)	FAT (gms.)	CARBOHYDRATE (gms.)	VITAMIN A (I.U.)	VITAMIN D (I.U.)	VITAMIN E (I.U.)	ASCORBIC ACID (mg.)	VITAMIN B1 (mcg.)	VITAMIN B2 (mcg.)	NIACIN (mcg.)	VITAMIN B6 (mcg.)	SODIUM (mEq./mg.)	POTASSIUM (mEq./mg.)	CHLORIDE (mEq./mg.)	CALCIUM (mEq./mg.)	PHOSPHORUS (mEq./mg.)	IRON (mg.)	RENAL SOLUTE LOAD (mOsm/liter)	INTESTINAL SOLUTE (mOsm/liter water)
COMPLEAT B	Doyle	R/F	97.9 / 29.4	3.9	3.9	11.8	307	25	1.8	3.7	86	104	613	123	4.8 / 110	3.6 / 141	2.5 / 88	3.7 / 74	5.2 / 135	1.10	331	468
ENSURE	Ross	R/F	106.1 / 31.8	3.7	3.7	14.5	265	21	3.2	16.0	170	180	2120	210	3.2 / 74	3.2 / 127	3.0 / 106	2.1 / 42	1.6 / 42	0.95	305	448
FLEXICAL	Mead Johnson	5:7[a]	101.4 / 30.4	2.2	3.4	15.5	250	20	1.5	5.0	72	80	900	100	1.6 / 36	3.9 / 152	3.4 / 120	2.6 / 52	1.7 / 44	0.50	214	805
FORMULA 2	Cutter	R/F	99.6 / 29.9	3.8	4.0	12.1	50	23	2.1	5.0	70	120	1000	150	2.0 / 45	5.4 / 210	5.4 / 190	6.5 / 130	4.3 / 110	1.50	345	435-500
ISOCAL	Mead Johnson	R/F	105.2 / 31.6	3.4	4.4	13.0	260	21	3.9	15.6	200	225	2604	258	2.3 / 52	3.3 / 130	2.9 / 104	3.1 / 63	2.0 / 52	0.94	279	350
MERITENE (LIQUID)	Doyle	R/F	99.7 / 29.9	6.0	3.3	11.5	417	33	2.5	8.3	167	167	833	167	4.0 / 92	4.3 / 167	4.5 / 160	[b] 7.1 / 142	4.8 / 125	1.67	470	539
MERITENE (POWDER)	Doyle	1:2[c]	114.9 / 34.5	7.6	3.7	12.8	625	42	5.0	9.4	292	417	3125	250	4.5 / 104	8.2 / 321	6.3 / 225	12.5 / 250	8.0 / 208	1.88	623	608
NUTRI-1000	Syntex	R/F	105.5 / 31.7	3.4	5.5	10.6	264	21	1.6	5.3	106	106	793	106	2.3 / 53	3.8 / 148	2.9 / 103	6.4 / 127	3.7 / 95	0.63	284	500
PRECISION HIGH NITROGEN	Doyle	1:8[d]	125.3 / 37.6	5.2	0.1	25.9	208	17	1.3	2.9	83	83	417	83	5.1 / 117	2.8 / 108	2.6 / 91	1.7 / 33	1.3 / 33	0.75	401	580
PRECISION LR	Doyle	1:8[d]	132.1 / 39.6	2.9	0.1	29.9	347	28	2.1	4.9	139	139	694	139	3.6 / 83	2.7 / 104	2.4 / 85	2.8 / 56	2.2 / 56	1.25	252	600
SUSTACAL (LIQUID)	Mead Johnson	R/F	99.9 / 30.0	6.0	2.3	13.8	464	37	2.8	5.6	139	167	1945	194	4.0 / 93	5.3 / 206	4.4 / 156	5.0 / 100	3.6 / 92	1.67	479	756
SUSTACAL (POWDER)	Mead Johnson	1:8[e]	133.3 / 40.0	8.0	3.3	17.9	619	49	3.7	13.0	185	222	2593	259	5.3 / 122	8.6 / 337	5.0 / 178	14.0 / 281	9.8 / 252	2.22	645	1000
SUSTAGEN	Mead Johnson	1:1[f]	185.6 / 55.7	11.1	1.6	31.7	529	42	4.8	31.7	402	455	5285	529	5.5 / 127	8.6 / 338	6.7 / 237	16.9 / 338	9.8 / 254	1.90	841	1200
TCH TUBE FEEDING MILK BASED		[g]	100.9 / 30.3	3.9	4.5	11.2	293	20	-	7.1	91	156	680	44	2.6 / 60	3.5 / 135		3.8 / 77	3.3 / 84	2.81 [j]	283	
TCH TUBE FEEDING SOY BASED		[h]	100.5 / 30.2	3.7	4.5	11.3	355	25	0.7	5.0	109	140	1270	99	2.6 / 60	3.0 / 118		3.6 / 72	3.0 / 78	3.14 [j]	267	
VIVONEX HN	Eaton	1:8.5[i]	101.7 / 30.5	4.2	0.1	21.0	167	13	1.7	2.3	40	40	443	67	3.3 / 77	1.8 / 70	5.2 / 186	1.3 / 27	1.0 / 27	0.33	342	844
VIVONEX STANDARD	Eaton	1:8.5[i]	99.3 / 29.8	2.0	0.1	22.6	278	22	1.7	3.9	67	67	739	111	3.7 / 86	3.0 / 117	5.1 / 180	2.2 / 44	1.7 / 44	0.56	232	1170

a 5:7 indicates 5 packed level scoops (2 oz.) of Flexical powder to 7 oz. water.
b 125 mg./6.2 mEq. of calcium in chocolate Meritene liquid.
c 1:2 indicates 1 tablespoon of Meritene powder to 8 oz. (1 cup) of cold, whole milk.
d 1:8 indicates one packet (3 oz.) of Precision powder to 8 oz. (1 cup) of cold water.
e 1:8 indicates one packet (1.9 oz.) of Sustacal powder to 8 oz. (1 cup) of cold, whole milk.
f 1:1 indicates 1 cup (150 gms.) of Sustagen powder to 1 cup (8 oz.) of water.
g See Table XVII for proportion of ingredients. Prepared formulas are recommended due to availability of complete nutritional analysis, sanitation and accurate dilution.
h See Table XVIII for proportion of ingredients. Prepared formulas are recommended due to availability of complete nutritional analysis, sanitation and accurate dilution.
i 1:8.5 indicates one packet (2.82 oz.) of Vivonex powder to 8.5 oz. of cold water.
j Values for chloride not available.

are listed in Table XVI. A comparison of 1500 mls. of the various tube and supplementary feedings with the R.D.A. for children 7-10 years old may be found in Table 5-A in the appendix.

Indications for Tube Feeding

- Oral surgery
  - Congenital defects, trauma
  - Orthopedic problems (wired jaw)
  - Extensive dental surgery
    - Peridontal conditions
- Radical neck or upper respiratory system surgery
- Gastrointestinal surgery, resection
- Inability to chew or swallow adequately
- Esophageal obstruction
- Comatose patient
- Neurogenic palsies or paralysis
- Traumatic nerve damage
- Anorexia nervosa
- Depression or other mental illness
- Burns
- Malignancy
- Weakness

This mode of feeding, when indicated and tolerated, is much safer than the I.V. route, can be nutritionally adequate and can be used more easily and economically for much longer periods of time. It can likewise be adapted to any age group, including small infants. Any modification can be adjusted to tube feeding—like substitution of polyunsaturated for saturated fatty acids, eliminating specific sugars, selecting a specific protein, carbohydrate or fat, etc.

Judicious planning of the composition of the tube feeding is imperative because it has been shown that high-protein tube feedings may cause severe, potentially fatal dehydration and hypernatremia in spite of the sodium intake, fluid intake and urinary output being within reasonable, normal limits—apparently resulting from a relative sodium retention by the kidney. This work was done on adults by Gault et al (1968)[1]. Hypernatremia (elevation of serum sodium concentration above 145 or 150 mEq per liter), in the majority of cases occurs with dehydration of infants and elderly people when water losses exceed sodium losses. This usually occurs with reduced fluid intake or severe fecal or renal loss of water. This situation is particularly important where the patient is unable to respond to thirst and ask for water (infant, stuporous condition, laryngectomy or cerebrovascular accident).

Treatment is simply the provision of water without protein or sodium for 24-48 hours but it is important to proceed with caution so as to

1. Gault, M. H., M. E. Dixon, M. Doyle and W. M. Cohen, Ann. Int. Med. *68*:778-791, 1968.

Table XVI
Sources of Protein, Carbohydrate and Fat in Commercially Prepared Tube Feedings, Elemental Diets and Supplementary Feedings

Blended Foods	Protein	Carbohydrate	Fat
Compleat B	Beef Puree, Non-fat dry milk	Maltodextrin, Sucrose, Fructose (Peas, green beans, peaches, orange juice)	Corn Oil
Formula 2	Non-fat dry milk, Beef, Egg Yolks	Sucrose (carrots, green beans orange juice, farina), Microcrystalline cellulose	Corn Oil
Elemental			
Vivonex Standard and HN	Crystalline 1-amino acids	Glucose, Glucoseoligosaccharides	Safflower Oil
Low Residue			
Flexical	Casein Hydrolysate + Amino acids added	Sucrose, Corn Syrup Solids, Tapioca Starch	Soy Oil 80% MCT Oil 20%
Precision LR & HN	Egg Albumin Solids	Sugar, Maltodextrins	Vegetable Oil, Mono & Diglycerides
Medium Residue			
Ensure	Sodium and Calcium Caseinates, Soy Protein Isolates	Sucrose, Corn Syrup Solids	Corn Oil
Nutri-1000	Skimmed Milk	Sucrose, Dextrin-Maltose, Dextrose (corn)	Soy Oil, Hydrogenated Coconut Oil, Soy lecithin, Mono-and Diglycerides
Isocal	Sodium Caseinate, Soy Protein Isolates 13%	Corn Syrup Solids	50% MCT Oil 7% Soy Oil 30%
High Residue			
Meritene Liquid	Sodium Caseinate, Conc'd Sweet Skim Milk	Sucrose, Corn Syrup Solids	Vegetable Oil
Meritene Powder	Specially processed non-fat dry milk	Sugar, Maltodextrin	....
Sustacal Liquid	24% Conc'd sweet skim milk, Na caseinate, Ca caseinate, Soy Protein Isolate	55% Sugar, Corn Syrup Solids (lactose)	Partially hydrogenated Soy Oil 21%
Sustacal Powder*	Non fat dry milk	Sugar, Corn Syrup Solids	....
Sustagen	Non-fat dry milk, Powdered whole milk, Ca caseinate	Corn Syrup Soilds, Dextrose, Sugar	Butter fat in whole milk

* Must be mixed with milk to be nutritionally complete.

avoid symptoms of water intoxication. This may occur when the brain, which retains hypertonic levels of sodium longer than the plasma, becomes edematous.

All tube feedings should be sterilized and used while fresh because of possible contamination, especially with salmonella. Feedings should be refrigerated, then warmed to room temperature when used, as cold feedings can cause distress. Diarrhea, a common problem in the past, is usually due to a too-concentrated feeding, too rapid rate of infusion, excessive fat content, hyperosmolality, improper residue, improper positioning of the tube or bacterial contamination. Dehydration can be caused by excessive intake of protein, sugars or electrolytes, chronic vomiting and/or diarrhea, insufficient fluid intake and fever. When introducing a feeding, a dilute feeding should be used to evaluate patient tolerance and to insure adequate fluid intake.

More concentrated feedings are gradually given leading up to full strength—about 1 kcal per 1 ml. Food intolerances, allergies and enzyme deficiencies should be recognized and proper substitutions made. The tube feeding should always be checked for nutrient excesses or deficiencies.

The calculated analysis of the T.C.H.'s milk-based tube feeding compared with the R.D.A. for the 1-2 year old child is found in Table XVII; a similar comparison for the soy-based tube feeding is found in Table XVIII.

Elemental Diets

Elemental diets are chemically defined diets that provide complete nutritional requirements in a predigested, easily absorbable form. The term chemically defined means that each nutrient is known and quantitated. Studies in both adults and children have shown that these diets can promote normal growth over extended time periods in selected patients.

These diets come in a powdered form which when reconstituted with water in a full strength solution provide 1 calorie/ml. The distinguishing characteristic of an elemental diet is that it provides protein in a predigested or hydrolyzed form, or, in a synthetic form of amino acids. Carbohydrate is added to provide approximately 150 calories per each gram of nitrogen, insuring maximum protein sparing effect on body tissues. This means that 90% of the calories in these products is in the form of sugar, and usually as simple glucose or dextrins. Fat is added in small amounts to provide the essential fatty acid, linoleic acid (safflower oil). Vitamins and minerals are added to provide the normal daily requirements. Vitamin K may be deficient in some products.

Unfortunately, some of the elemental diets are not truly chemically defined and do not contain simple, predigested ingredients. Sugars may be in the form of sucrose or oligosaccharides in place of glucose, fats may include large amounts of soy and coconut oil (medium chain triglyceride), and even protein in one product is in the form of egg albumin rather than amino acids. This variation in composition makes it essential to read labels carefully to choose the right product for each individual

Table XVII

Analysis of TCH Milk-Based Tube Feeding Compared with the R.D.A. for the 1-2 Year Old Child

FOOD	AMOUNT	CALORIES	PROTEIN (gm.)	FAT (gm.)	CARBOHYDRATE (gm.)	CALCIUM (mg.)	PHOSPHORUS (mg.)	IRON (mg.)	SODIUM (mg.)	POTASSIUM (mg.)	VITAMIN A (I.U.)	THIAMINE (mcg.)	RIBOFLAVIN (mcg.)	NIACIN (mg.)	VITAMIN C (mg.)	VITAMIN D (I.U.)	VITAMIN E (I.U.)	FOLACIN (mcg.)	VITAMIN B_6 (mg.)	VITAMIN B_{12} (mcg.)	IODINE (mcg.)	MAGNESIUM (mg.)
Soft Cooked Egg	One	75.9	6.2	5.5	0.4	26	98	1.1	59	62	570	40	130	-	-	23						
Strained Beef	3.5 oz.	90.5	13.4	4.1	-	7	106	1.8	180	193	-	12	147	2.6	3.8				0.20			
Strained Squash	4.5 oz.	34.6	1.1	0.2	7.1	31	24	0.5	129	194	1692	32	34	0.5	10.7				0.08			
Homogenized Milk	14 oz.	284.1	15.8	14.9	21.7	522	410	0.2	222	623	628	172	768	0.4	3.5	175						
Strained Rice	9 Tbsp.	78.9	1.5	0.9	16.2	141	177	21.3	3	66	-	600	450	3.0	-				0.12			
Strained Orange Juice	4.2 oz.	64.9	0.7	0.5	14.4	8	12	0.4	3	213	39	55	20	0.3	52.4				0.04			
Safflower Oil	1 1/3 Tbsp.	167.4	-	18.6	-	-	-	-	-	-	-	-	-	-	-	-	-	-	-	-	-	-
Corn Syrup	3 1/2 Tbsp.	207.2	-	-	51.8	32	11	2.8	-	-	-	-	7	-	0.4	-	-	-	-	-	-	-
Water	90 ccs																					
TOTAL CALCULATIONS		1003.5	38.7	44.7	111.6	767	838	28.1	596*	1351	2929	911	1556	12.7*	70.8	198			0.44			
RDA FOR 1-3 YEAR OLD			23.0			800	800	15.0			2000	700	800	9.0	40.0	400	10	100	0.60	1.0	60	150

Table XVIII

Analysis of TCH Soy-Based Tube Feeding Compared with the R.D.A. for the 1-2 Year Old Child

FOOD	AMOUNT	CALORIES	PROTEIN (gm.)	FAT (gm.)	CARBOHYDRATE (gm.)	CALCIUM (mg.)	PHOSPHORUS (mg.)	IRON (mg.)	SODIUM (mg.)	POTASSIUM (mg.)	VITAMIN A (I.U.)	THIAMINE (mcg.)	RIBOFLAVIN (mcg.)	NIACIN (mg.)	VITAMIN C (mg.)	VITAMIN D (I.U.)	VITAMIN E (I.U.)	FOLACIN (mcg.)	VITAMIN B_6 (mg.)	VITAMIN B_{12} (mcg.)	IODINE (mcg.)	MAGNESIUM (mg.)
Strained Lamb	5.2 oz.	144.8	22.7	6.0	-	9	174	2.1	246	287	-	131	269	4.7	4.2				0.53			
Strained Squash	4.5 oz.	34.6	1.1	0.2	7.1	31	24	0.5	129	194	1692	32	34	0.5	10.7				0.08			
Neo-Mull-Soy	20 oz.	387.4	11.2	21.0	38.4	510	384	5.1	222	540	1266	318	636	4.4	38.0	252	6.6		0.26			
Strained Rice	9 Tbsp.	78.9	1.5	0.9	16.2	141	177	21.3	3	66	-	600	450	3.0	-				0.12			
Apricot Nectar	2 oz.	37.7	0.2	0.1	9.0	6	7	0.1	-	93	587	7	7	0.1	2.0							
Safflower Oil	3 1/2 tsp.	146.7	-	16.3	-	-	-	-	-	-	-											
Corn Syrup	2 Tbsp. & 2 1/2 tsp.	167.6	-	-	41.9	26	9	2.3	-	-	-	0	6	-	0.3							
Water	10 ccs																					
TOTAL CALCULATIONS		997.7	36.7	44.5	112.6	723	775	31.4	600	1180	3545	1088	1402	12.7	50.2	252	6.6		0.99			
RDA FOR 1-3 YEAR OLD			23			800	800	15.0			2000	700	700	9.0	40.0	400	10	100	0.60	1.0	60	150

* 6.8 mg. preformed niacin; 5.9 mg. niacin provided by tryptophan. (Tryptophan calculated as 1% of the protein content of the complete protein foods. 6.0 mg. tryptophan are equivalent to 1 mg. niacin)

case. Table XV gives the nutrient composition of the most commonly used elemental diets.

Uses and Advantages

Because elemental diets contain a minimum amount of bulk and are predigested, they are of value in a wide range of digestive and absorptive problems. In preoperative patients these diets decrease intestinal contents and the low residue leads to decreased colonic bacteria while providing adequate nutrition. Post-operatively these diets are non-irritating and are used to replace the traditional clear liquids.

In the short bowel syndrome rapid absorption of pre-digested nutrients is essential because of the reduction in intestinal capacity. The elemental diets circumvent the need for complex digestive processes and allow rapid absorption of a complete nutritional source.

Either internal or external fistulae of the intestinal tract create unique problems where predigested diets are helpful. Rapid absorption high in the intestine decreases flow through the fistula, decreasing fluid losses and, in some cases, allowing healing and closure of the fistula. Bacterial overgrowth of the upper intestine is frequently associated with fistulae and significant maldigestion results. The predigested elemental diet can be utilized to overcome this complication.

Other disorders where these diets are beneficial include inflammatory bowel disease and radiation-induced enteropathy where there is frequently malabsorption, fistulous tracts, and partial obstruction. Chronic pancreatitis may also benefit from the elemental diet because of the very low stimulus to pancreatic secretion by the predigested contents. Any diet is contraindicated in acute pancreatitis.

Disadvantages

The most troublesome characteristic of elemental diets is their poor taste, and in spite of the many flavors available, patient acceptance is poor. If kept very cold they are more palatable, but many children refuse to drink even small amounts and tube feedings are often necessary to insure adequate intake for normal nutrition.

A second major problem is the high osmotic load these liquid diets present to the gastrointestinal tract. This frequently leads to rapid secretion of water into the intestine with diarrhea and dehydration. To avoid this complication, it is necessary to start with dilute amounts of the diets with gradual increasing concentration as intestinal adaptation occurs. Using a continuous drip by NG tube, rather than intermittent large amounts, also helps reduce the effects of the hyperosmolar fluid. Because of the hyperosmolality of the elemental diets, children under 10 months of age may have difficulty tolerating more than 0.4 kcal/ml. Older children can usually develop tolerance to the standard 1 kcal/ml.

Careful monitoring of weight, electrolytes, hemoglobin, and urine sugar is essential, and supplementation with vitamin K is necessary with some products.

Ingredient List of Tube Feedings and Supplemental Feedings

Compleat-B

Deionized water, beef puree, maltodextrin, green bean puree, pea puree, nonfat dry milk, corn oil, sucrose, peach puree, reconstituted orange juice, sodium tripolyphosphate, hydroxylated lecithin, potassium chloride, carrageenan, magnesium oxide, calcium carbonate, ferric ammonium citrate, ascorbic acid, alpha tocopheryl acetate, calcuim pantothenate, manganese sulfate, copper gluconate, niacin, zinc sulfate, thiamine hydrochloride, pyridoxine hydrochloride, riboflavin, biotin, folic acid, vitamin A palmitate, vitamin D_2, vitamin B_{12}.

Ensure

Water, corn syrup solids, sucrose, corn oil, sodium and calcium caseinates, soy protein isolate, potassium citrate, magnesium chloride, soy lecithin, potassium chloride, calcium carbonate, sodium hexametaphosphate, choline chloride, ascorbic acid, carrageenan, zinc sulfate, ferrous sulfate, alpha-tocopheryl acetate, niacin, vitamin A palmitate, copper sulfate, vitamin D, phytonadione, calcium pantothenate, pyridoxine hydrochloride, riboflavin, thiamine hydrochloride, manganese chloride, biotin, potassium iodide, folic acid, and cyanocobalamin. Artificial flavoring added.

Flexical

Sugar (sucrose), dextrin, enzymatically hydrolyzed casein, soy oil, medium chain triglycerides (fractionated coconut oil), citric acid, artificial flavor, mono and diglycerides, lecithin, artificial coloring, amino acids (L-methionine, L-tyrosine, L-tryptophan), vitamins (vitamin A palmitate, ergocalciferol, d-alpha-tocopheryl acetate, sodium ascorbate, folic acid, thiamine hydrochloride, riboflavin, niacinamide, pyridoxine hydrochloride, cyanocobalamin, biotin, calcium pantothenate, phytonadione, choline chloride), and minerals (calcium citrate, potassium chloride, dibasic magnesium phosphate, potassium citrate dibasic calcium phosphate, ferrous sulfate, cupric sulfate, zinc sulfate, manganese sulfate, and potassium iodide).

Formula 2

Water, nonfat dry milk, beef, sucrose, carrots, corn oil, orange juice concentrate, egg yolks, green beans, wheat flour, cellulose gum, artificial flavor, magnesium oxide, sodium ascorbate, ferrous sulfate, tocopheryl acetate, niacinamide, zinc sulfate, cupric sulfate, pyridoxine hydrochloride, thiamine hydrochloride, cyanocobalamin, folic acid, calciferol (vitamin D) and potassium iodide.

Isocal

Water, corn syrup solids, soy oil, calcium caseinate, sodium caseinate, MCT oil, soy protein isolate, potassium citrate, calcium citrate, lecithin, magnesium chloride, dibasic magnesium phosphate, sodium citrate, calcium chloride, dibasic calcium phosphate, potassium chloride, carrageenan, ferrous sulfate, vitiams (vitamin A palmitate, calciferol, d-alpha-tocopheryl acetate, phytonadione, sodium ascorbate, folic acid, thiamine hydrochloride, riboflavin, niacinamide, pyridoxine hydrochloride, cyanocobalamin, biotin, calcium pantothenate and choline chloride) and minerals (zinc sulfate, manganese sulfate, cupric sulfate, and potassium iodide).

Meritene Liquid Concentrated sweet skim milk, corn syrup solids, vegetable oil, sodium caseinate, sucrose, artificial flavoring, salt, carrageenan, vitamins and minerals. Chocolate flavor also includes cocoa, cellulose flour, artificial color and cellulose gum.

Meritene Powder Specially-processed nonfat dry milk, sugar, malto-dextrin, magnesium sulfate, iron pyrophosphate, ascorbic acid, natural and imitation vanilla, lecithin, vitamin E (alpha tocopheryl), niacin, ribofiavin, copper gluconate, calcium pantothenate, vitamin A palmitate, thiamin hydrochloride, pyridoxine hydrochloride, folic acid, vitamin D_2.

Nutri-1000 Skim milk, corn oil, sucrose, corn syrup solids, mono and diglycerides, lecithin, vanilla extract, sodium hexametaphosphate, calcium carrageenan, sodium ascorbate, magnesium oxide, choline chloride, ferrous sulfate, dl-a-tocopheryl acetate, niacinamide, zinc, cupric and manganese sulfates, vitamin A palmitate, thiamine hydrochloride, d-calcium pantothenate, pyridoxine hydrochloride, vitamin D_3, riboflavin, folic acid, d-biotin, potassium iodide, vitamin B_{12}.

Precision Lr Diet Maltodextrin, pasteurized egg white solids, sugar, calcium glycerophosphate, vegetable oil, citric acid, natural and imitation flavors, magnesium sulfate, dipotassium phosphate, mono and diglycerides, choline bitartrate, iron pyrophosphate, ascorbic acid, alpha tocopheryl acetate, copper gluconate, artificial color, d-calcium pantothenate, manganese sulfate, niacin, zinc sulfate, vitamin A palmitate, thiamin hydrochloride, pyridoxine hydrochloride, riboflavin, d-biotin, potassium iodide, folic acid, vitamin D_2, cyanocobalamin.

Precision High Nitrogen Diet Maltodextrin, pasteurized egg white solids, sugar, natural and imitation flavors, citric acid, calcium glycerophosphate, magnesium sulfate, dipotassium phosphate, vegetable oil, choline bitartrate, mono and diglycerides, iron pyrophosphate, ascorbic acid, artificial color, alpha tocopheryl acetate, zince sulfate, vitamin A palmitate, copper gluconate, d-calcium pantothenate, niacin, manganese sulfate, pyridoxine hydrochloride, thiamin hydrochloride, riboflavin, vitamin D_2, d-biotin, potassium iodide, folic acid, cyanocobalamin.

Sustacal Liquid Water, sugar (sucrose), concentrated sweet skim milk, corn syrup solids, partially hydrogenated soy oil, sodium caseinate, calcium caseinate, soy protein isolate, potassium citrate, magnesium chloride, artificial flavor, dibasic magnesium phosphate, sodium citrate, calcium chloride, carrageenan, ferrous citrate, vitamin A palmitate, calciferol, d-alpha-tocopheryl acetate, sodium ascorbate, thiamine hydrochloride, riboflavin, pyridoxine hydrochloride, cyanocobalamin, niacinamide, folic acid, calcium pantothenate, choline bitartrate, biotin, zinc sulfate, manganese sulfate, cupric sulfate and sodium iodide.

In addition to the above, Chocolate liquid contains Dutch process cocoa (alkalized), potassium chloride and artificial color. It does not contain sodium caseinate or vegetable stabilizer.

Sustacal Vanilla Powder

Nonfat dry milk, sugar, corn syrup solids, artificial flavor, dibasic magnesium phosphate, vitamin A palmitate, calciferol, d-alpha-tocopheryl acetate, sodium ascorbate, thiamine hydrochloride, niacinamide, ferric pyrophosphate, pyridoxine hydrochloride, cyanocobalamin, calcium pantothenate, folic acid, zinc sulfate, cupric carbonate, and manganese sulfate.

Sustacal Chocolate Powder

Nonfat dry milk, sugar, corn syrup solids, Dutch process cocoa (alkalized), artificial flavor, lecithin, artificial color, dibasic magnesium phosphate, vitamin A palmitate, calciferol, d-alpha-tocopheryl acetate, sodium ascorbate, thiamine hydrochloride, niacinamide, ferric pyrophosphate, pyridoxine hydrochloride, cyanocobalamin, calcium pantothenate, folic acid, zinc sulfate, cupric carbonate, and manganese sulfate.

Sustagen

Whole milk and non-fat milk solids, calcium caseinate, maltose and dextrins, dextrose, ferrous sulfate, vitamins and imitation vanilla flavor. (Chocolate-flavored Sustagen also contains cocoa and sucrose.)

Vivonex

Glucose oligosaccharides, L-glutamine, magnesium gluconate dihydrate, calcium glycerophosphate, sodium citrate dihydrate, l-arginine hydrochloride, L-aspartic acid, potassium citrate monohydrate, glycine, l-tyrosine ethyl ester hydrochloride, l-leucine, safflower oil, sodium glycerophosphate, l-lysine hydrochloride, l-proline, l-phenylalanine, l-valine, l-alanine, l-methionine, l-threonine, l-isoleucine, l-serine, potassium sorbate, potassium chloride, l-histidine hydrochloride monohydrate, l-tryptophan, polysorbate 80, choline bitartrate, inositol, ferrous ammonium sulfate hexahydrate, ascorbic acid, zinc acetate dihydrate, alpha-tocopheryl acetate, niacinamide, manganous acetate tetrahydrate, d-calcium pantothenate, cupric acetate monohydrate, pyridoxine hydrochloride, Vitamin A acetate, riboflavin phosphate sodium salt, thiamine hydrochloride, d-biotin, potassium iodide, folic acid, Vitamin K_1, Vitamin D_2, Vitamin B_{12}.

Vivonex High Nitrogen

Glucose oligosaccharides, l-glutamine, l-aspartic acid, glycine, l-phenylalanine, l-proline, l-leucine, l-lysine hydrochloride, l-alanine, l-arginine hydrochloride, magnesium gluconate dihydrate, sodium citrate dihydrate, l-valine, l-methionine, l-threonine, l-isoleucine, l-serine, potassium citrate monohydrate, l-tyrosine ethyl ester hydrochloride, l-histidine hydrochloride monohydrate, calcium glycerophosphate, sodium glycerophosphate, safflower oil, l-tryptophan, potassium sorbate, polysorbate 80, choline bitartrate, inositol, ferrous ammonium sulfate hexahydrate, ascorbic acid, zinc acetate dihydrate, alpha-acetate tetrahydrate, d-calcium pantothenate, cupric acetate monohydrate, pyridoxine hydrochloride, vitamin A acetate, riboflavin phosphate sodium salt, thiamine hydrochloride, d-biotin, potassium iodide, folic acid, vitamin K_1, vitamin D_2, vitamin B_{12}.

Chapter 6

Total Parenteral Nutrition (TPN)

William J. Klish, M.D. and Joseph Rogers, M.D.

I. Indications

A. Clinically established indications

1. Lesions of the gastrointestinal tract precluding adequate oral intake or absorption of nutrients. Examples: Necrotizing enterocolitis, ruptured omphalocele, massive resection of the small bowel, small bowel atresias, meconium peritonitis, etc.

2. Chronic diarrhea and/or malabsorption with malnutrition.

B. Indications more or less investigational in different centers

1. Very low birth weight infants in whom adequate oral intake can not be promptly established.

2. Severe burns.

3. Inflammatory bowel disease unresponsive to surgery, corticosteroids and/or azulfidine.

4. Acute renal failure.

II. Currently stocked TPN solutions

Table XIX lists formulas for mixing different TPN solutions with glucose, minerals and vitamins for central or peripheral venous infusion. The peripheral solution is also used initially in central infusions to stimulate insulin production so that the patient can tolerate the high glucose loads.

III. Technique

A. Catheter placement

A thin-walled, radiopaque silastic catheter with external diameter of approximately an 18 gauge needle is inserted by cutdown into the mid-superior vena cava under direct visualization with fluoroscopy, using strict aseptic surgical technique. The external end is then tunneled 3-4 inches subcutaneously cephalad to emerge through the parietal scalp behind the ear. The catheter is sutured to the scalp. A needle-hub adapter is attached, to which a 0.22 millipore filter is affixed with extension tubing. The I.V. tubing from the TPN solution is then put directly into the filter. Betadine ointment is applied to the catheter-skin exit site and dressed.

B. Catheter care

The dressing is changed at least every two days. The skin around the catheter is treated with tincture of iodine followed by fresh Betadine ointment. The catheter site can be protected from the searching hands of the patient by creating a cap from stockenette with the tubing existing from the center.

C. Principles of TPN infusion

A constant infusion pump (IVAC) is essential to the procedure. Initial infusion begins with "starter" solution at a rate that satisfies water requirements. The infusion rate is advanced to approximately 140 ml/kg/day as the patient tolerates higher glu-

Table XIX
Composition of Available Protein Hydrolysate TPN Solutions

	Using Amisol 5% Solution		Using Aminosol 5% D_5W Solution		Using Amigen 5% D_5W Solution	
	Full Strength ml	Peripheral ("starter") ml	Full Strength ml	Peripheral ("starter") ml	Full Strength ml	Peripheral ("starter") ml
Amigen 5% D_5W	......	......	......	......	290.0	160.0
Aminosol 5%	265.0	160.0	......	......	......	......
Aminosol 5% D_5W	......	......	290.0	160.0	......	......
$D_{50}W$	210.0	100.0	182.0	80.0	190.0	80.0
D_5W	......	215.0	......	235.0	......	240.0
NaCL, 14.6% (2.5 mEq NA/cc)	4.4	4.4	4.4	4.4	......	2.0
Ca gluconate, 10% (9.7 mg Ca^{++}/cc)	13.0	9.0	13.0	9.0	10.0	7.4
$MgSO_4 \cdot 7H_2O$ (0.81 mEq Mg^{++}/cc)	5.8	5.8	5.8	5.8	5.0	5.4
K phosphate (4.4 mEq K^+/cc) (93 mg Pi/cc)	1.5	1.0	1.5	1.0	......	......
KCl (2 mEq K^+/cc)	1.0	2.0	1.0	2.0	4.0	4.0
MVI concentrate	1.0	1.0	1.0	1.0	1.0	1.0
TOTAL	500.0	500.0	500.0	500.0	500.0	500.0
Calories/ml	0.94	0.55	0.96	0.54	1.0	0.54
Glucose concentration	21.0%	12.0%	21.0%	12.0%	22.0%	12.0%
Protein concentration	2.9%	1.6%	2.9%	1.6%	2.9%	1.6%

cose loads (based on absence of glucosuria). Full strength solution is then infused at approximately 110-120 ml/kg/day and titrated upward to a final rate of 140 ml/kg/day. This "weaning" period should last approximately 5 days. Table XX summarizes the amount of each constituent delivered per kg. each day at this rate.

The following supplements are given weekly by I.M. injection:

	Infants	**Older Children**
Vitamin K (Aquamephyton)	1 mg	5 mg
Vitamin B_{12}	10 micrograms	100 micrograms
Folate	1 mg	5 mg

D. Metabolic variables to be monitored:

<table>
<tr><th></th><th colspan="2">Frequency</th></tr>
<tr><th></th><th>1st Week</th><th>Later</th></tr>
<tr><td>Urine glucose</td><td colspan="2">every urine</td></tr>
<tr><td>Urinalysis</td><td colspan="2">prn</td></tr>
<tr><td>WBC & differential</td><td colspan="2">prn</td></tr>
<tr><td>HCT</td><td>q.o.d.</td><td>weekly</td></tr>
<tr><td>blood glucose</td><td>daily</td><td>3 times weekly</td></tr>
<tr><td>BUN</td><td colspan="2">twice weekly</td></tr>
<tr><td>Electrolytes</td><td>q.o.d.</td><td>twice weekly</td></tr>
</table>

<table>
<tr><th></th><th colspan="2">Frequency</th></tr>
<tr><th></th><th>1st Week</th><th>Later</th></tr>
<tr><td>Calcium</td><td colspan="2">weekly</td></tr>
<tr><td>Phosphate</td><td colspan="2">weekly</td></tr>
<tr><td>SGOT</td><td colspan="2">weekly</td></tr>
<tr><td>SGPT</td><td colspan="2">weekly</td></tr>
<tr><td>Alk. phos.</td><td colspan="2">weekly</td></tr>
<tr><td>Serum proteins</td><td colspan="2">weekly</td></tr>
<tr><td>Serum ammonia</td><td colspan="2">prn</td></tr>
<tr><td>Chest x-ray</td><td colspan="2">weekly</td></tr>
<tr><td>Weight</td><td colspan="2">daily</td></tr>
<tr><td>Length and FOC</td><td colspan="2">weekly</td></tr>
<tr><td>I & O</td><td colspan="2">hourly</td></tr>
</table>

IV. Major complications

A. Mechanical (catheter related)	Remarks
1. Plugging	Prevention: Insure constant infusion rate, especially during patient transport.
2. Dislodgement	Dislodgement can lead to rebound hypoglycemia if not detected early.
3. Thrombosis of major vessels	Prevention: Weekly chest x-rays to verify correct position in superior vena cava.
4. Extravasation of fluid	Severe rock-hard edema will be noted and requires catheter removal.
5. Contact dermatitis	Prevention: Tincture of benzoin to taping sites.
B. Infectious	
1. Local skin infection	Prevention: Strict aseptic technique during dressing changes.
	Treatment: Topical and/or systemic antibiotics after appropriate cultures.
2. Septicemia	Monilial sepsis requires immediate catheter removal. Bacterial sepsis can be treated with antibiotics; if there is not prompt clinical improvement, catheter removal is essential.

Table XX
Nutrients per kg per Day Furnished by Various TPN Solutions at 140 cc/kg/24 Hours

	Aminosol 5% D_5W		Aminosol 5%		Amigen 5% D_5W	
	Full Strength	Peripheral ("starter") ml	Full Strength	Peripheral ("starter") ml	Full Strength	Peripheral ("starter") ml
Protein	4.0 gm	2.3 gm	3.7 gm	2.3 gm	4.0 gm	2.4 gm
Glucose	29.5 gm	16.8 gm	29.3 gm	17.1 gm	29.5 gm	16.7 gm
Sodium	3.1 mEq	3.1 mEq	3.1 mEq	3.1 mEq	2.8 mEq	3.0 mEq
Magnesium	1.3 mEq	1.3 mEq	1.3 mEq	1.3 mEq	1.3 mEq	1.3 mEq
Calcium	35.3 mg	24.5 mg	35.2 mg	24.5 mg	35.3 mg	24.6 mg
Potassium	3.7 mEq	3.1 mEq	3.7 mEq	3.1 mEq	3.8 mEq	3.1 mEq
Phosphorus	39.1 mg	26.1 mg	38.9 mg	26.1 mg	37.7 mg	20.8 mg
Calories	134.0 cal	67.2 cal	131.6 cal	77.0 cal	138.8 cal	76.2 cal

C. Metabolic

1. Glucose disorders

a. Hyperglycemia	Prevention: Each urine checked for glucose. Gradual increase in glucose concentration while advancing infusion to final rate.
b. Hypoglycemia	Occurs if TPN is suddenly stopped, e.g. dislodgement of catheter.
2. Electrolyte, mineral, and acid-base disorders	Prevention: Adherence to a strict schedule of chemical monitoring. See Table XXI.
3. Azotemia	Prevention: Limiting total protein intake to no more than 4 gm/kg/day.
4. Hyperammonemia	More common with crystalline amino acid mixtures. This has not been a significant problem with protein hydrolysate mixtures at suggested infusion rates.
5. Essential fatty acid deficiency	Prevention: Intravenous fat emulsion (Intralipid)

V. Assessment of efficacy
Success of this procedure is dictated by the following parameters:
1. Progressive weight gain.
2. Absence of complications.

Table XXI
Composition of Crystalline Amino Acid Solution (FreAmine II 8.5%)

	Full Strength ml	Peripheral ("starter") ml
Fre Amine II 8.5%	150.0	100.0
$D_{50}W$	200.0	90.0
D_5W	120.0	285.0
NaCl, 14.6% (2.5 mEq NA^+/cc)	3.8	4.0
Ca gluconate, 10% (9.7 mg/ml)	13.0	9.0
$MgSO_4 \cdot 7H_2O$ (0.81 mEq/ml)	5.8	5.8
K Phosphate (4.4 mEq K^+/ml) (93 mg P/ml)	1.0	0.5
KCl (2 mEq/ml)	4.5	4.5
MVI	1.0	1.0
TOTAL	500.0	500.0

Guidelines for the Use of Intralipid In Total or Partial Parenteral Nutrition For Infants and Children

I. Indications

A. Same as those for total parenteral nutrition using hypertonic infusions of protein hydrolysate and glucose via central venous catheter.

B. Treatment or prevention of essential fatty acid deficiency.

II. Solutions

A. Intralipid	10% soybean oil 1.2% egg yolk phosphatides (emulsifier)
Caloric concentration 1.1 cal/ml.	2.25% glycerin (bringing solution to 280 m°sm/liter

		Amigen 5% D5W	Aminosol or 5%
B. Protein hydrolysate, glucose		180 ml	180 ml
		+	+
	D5W	240 ml	215 ml
Protein Concentration 1.8%	D50W	60 ml	78 ml
Glucose Concentration 10.0%	Potassium phosphate 3mM/ml	0.5 ml	1.5 ml
Caloric Concentration 0.48 cal/ml	Calcium gluconate 10%	10.0 ml	13 ml
	Magnesium Sulfate 10%	5.4 ml	5.8 ml
	KCL, 2 mEq/ml	6.0 ml	1.0 ml
	NaCl, 2.5 mEq/ml	2.0 ml	4.4 ml
	MVI concentrate	1.0 ml	1.0 ml
		500 ml	500 ml

III. Methods of Administration

A 21, 23, or 25 gauge butterfly needle is inserted into a scalp vein. To this is attached an I.V. catheter plug with a rubber nipple (McGaw Labs, catalog No. N 2046). Intravenous tubing (Abbott Soluset with micro-drip chamber) from the separate Intralipid and Amigen-glucose bottles are inserted by needles through the plug. The Intralipid tubing should be above the Amigen-glucose tubing; this prevents the less dense fat emulsion from floating up into the Amigen-glucose solution.

No micropore filters can be used with the Intralipid administration set.

Constant flow rates are maintained by 2 IVAC infusion pumps.

IV. Suggested Flow Rates of Intralipid and Protein-Glucose Infusions

A. Total Parenteral Nutrition

Day	Protein-glucose (ml /Kg)	Intralipid (ml /Kg)	Total volume (ml /Kg)	Total calories (cal /Kg)
1	110	10	120	64
2	120	20	140	80
3	130	30	160	95
4 +	140	40	180	110

Note: When the initial Intralipid volumes are too small to accurately infuse over a 24 hour period, at least an 8 hour infusion is suggested to prevent hyperlipidemia.

Weekly I.M. supplements during TPN

	Infants	Older Children
Vitamin K (Aquamephyton)	1 mg	5 mg
Vitamin B_{12}	10 micrograms	100 micrograms
Folate	1 mg	5 mg

B. Treatment or prevention of essential fatty acid deficiency.

During TPN by central venous protein-glucose infusions, essential fatty acid deficiency can be prevented or corrected by administering 8% of total daily caloric intake as Intralipid. This can be done as an intermittent infusion of 30 ml/Kg, every 4th day for those receiving 100-120 cal/Kg/day and every 3rd day for patients getting 130+cal/Kg/day.

V. Metabolic Parameters to be Monitored

As of this writing (2/4/76) neither plasma Intralipid levels nor lipoprotein electrophoreses are available for objective determination of fat emulsion clearance during Intralipid infusion. These should be available in the near future. In the interim, visible serum turbidity (as judged by examining plasma in a microhematocrit tube) should be checked twice daily. The Intralipid infusion rate is adjusted so that there is no gross lipidemia.

Chapter 7

Therapeutic Hospital Diets

Generalized Gastrointestinal Disorders

Knowledge and data are both very meager regarding the actual effects of foods (both individually and in a mixed diet) on the gastrointestinal tract (secretions, motility, vascularity, mucosal integrity). Most opinions are based on unsubstantiated ideas regarding food as it appears on the plate with little or no proven evidence of its effect on the digestive system or the effect of metabolism on the food. Many opinions are based on tradition—using terms such as "bland" with many differences of opinion as to its definition. Foods have been categorically labeled according to taste (mild), consistency (soft, low-fiber, low-residue), color (white, etc.) again, with little agreement.

Since there is no well-documented evidence that the actual diet alters the course or produces healing in many of the more common gastrointestinal disorders (peptic ulcer, regional enteritis, biliary tract disease, ulcerative colitis, diverticulitis, functional bowel disease), there seems to be no justifiable reason to have *all* patients with a common disorder adhere to a rigid dietary regimen. These dietary patterns are often unattractive, unpalatable, monotonous and costly. Many foods produce varying effects in different people. *It seems wiser to seek the reaction of each individual patient to each specific food using a well-balanced regular diet as a basis.* The elimination of milk has been beneficial to some, but certainly not to all, patients with ulcerative colitis. Some patients with peptic ulcer can eat almost any food including orange juice or fresh pineapple; others will have gastrointestinal distress. Patients with active peptic ulcer disease would naturally benefit from avoiding known gastric acid stimulants (caffeine, alcohol).

Currently, there is much in the literature regarding the amount of bulk or roughage in the diet. Some feel that the "Western" diet, with all of the refined and processed foods and low-fiber content, is responsible for the prevalence of gastrointestinal disorders and the apparent scarcity of these illnesses in the undeveloped countries where the unrefined foods are consumed. Bran causes increased intestinal motility in some patients, however, and constipation in others.

Specific Gastrointestinal Disorders

The above discussion does not necessarily apply to infants and young children. Many of them have congenital or hereditary conditions (lactase deficiency, celiac disease), whereas adults are more likely to have acquired abnormalities (lactose intolerance, diverticulitis). Any age group can have malabsorption following bowel resection.

Rigid dietotherapy is mandatory in specific gastrointestinal conditions: 1) The elimination of gluten (wheat, barley, rye, oats) in celiac disease (gluten-induced enteropathy), 2) The elimination of all sources of galactose in galactosemia, 3) The elimination of lactose in lactase deficiency; other specific sugars for corresponding enzyme deficiencies, 4) The substitution of fructose for glucose and galactose in defective transport mechanism of monosaccharides, 5) The use of a low-phenylalanine diet in phenylketonuria, 6) The selection of a "substitute formula" in cow's milk intolerance.

Because of the increasing awareness and intensified interest in the metabolic role of specific carbohydrates, information regarding the individual percentage composition of various foods has become necessary. Hardinge, Swarner and Crooks[1] have compiled such information from currently available data (Appendix, Table A-1) bringing much scattered material together for ready reference. With specific carbohydrates being incriminated in the cause and/or control of certain metabolic disorders, this information is often desired and so it has been included.

Information concerning carbohydrates with only limited data available, compiled by the same authors, is presented in Appendix, Table A-2. Since sorbitol, a sugar alcohol, can be metabolized apparently without the action of insulin, it is of interest in the management of diabetes. Omission of dietary galactose is of prime importance in the control of galactosemia. Lactose, raffinose, stachyose, other sugars and the polysaccharide, galactan, yield galactose on hydrolysis.

Minimum Residue Diet
(Surgical Soft)

Principle: The Minimum Residue Diet provides the least amount of residue of any of the restricted residue diets. It is recommended when a minimum amount of gastrointestinal residue is desired, especially for pre- and post-operative gastrointes-

1. Hardinge, M. G., J. B. Swarner and H. Crooks; "More Common Carbohydrates in Foods per 100 gm. Edible Portion., *46*:197, 1965.

tinal surgery. The diet allows no milk, fruit or vegetables. This diet supplants the diet previously referred to as "surgical soft."

Adequacy: While this diet can be adequate in protein, carbohydrate and fat, IT IS GROSSLY INADEQUATE IN ALL MINERALS AND VITAMINS. It should be used for a limited time only (one or two days).

Foods	Foods Allowed	Foods to Avoid
Beverages	Carbonated beverages; tea	* Coffee, milk; all others
Breads	Emphasize refined wheat bread; melba toast; saltine crackers	All others
Cereals	Refined cooked cereal: cream of wheat, cream of rice, grits, farina	All others
Desserts	Plain desserts: gelatin, arrowroot and sugar cookies, vanilla wafers, angel food cake, sponge cake, popsicles, fruit ices	All others
Fat	Butter; margarine	All others
Fruits and Fruit Juices	None	All
Meat, Fish, Poultry, Cheese and Eggs	Lean, tender broiled, boiled or baked: beef, veal, lamb, pork, liver, turkey, chicken, boneless fish; eggs	Spiced or fried: meats, fish, ham, poultry, eggs; cheese and cheese products
Potatoes or Substitutes	Macaroni; spaghetti; noodles; refined rice	Potatoes; hominy; all others
Soups	Specially prepared clear soups; soups prepared with allowed foods	Commercial soups
Sweets	Sugar; syrup; strained honey; jelly; plain candy (all in moderation)	Candy with nuts or coconut; jams; marmalades; all others
Vegetables and Vegetable Juices	Tomato Juice	All others
Miscellaneous	Iodized Salt	All others

* Coffee usually is not served unless specifically requested.

Suggested Meal Pattern

Breakfast	Lunch	Dinner
Tomato Juice	Roast Beef	Broiled Chicken
Scrambled Egg	Buttered Rice	Buttered Noodles
Refined Wheat Toast	Melba Toast	Melba Toast
Cream of Rice	Butter	Butter
Butter	Jello Cubes	Sugar Cookies
Sugar	Iced Tea	Iced Tea
	Sugar	Sugar

Low Residue Diet

Principle: The Low Residue Diet is low in cellulose and gastrointestinal residue. It contains more residue than the minimum residue diet and is usually the second step in restricted residue diets. This diet provides milk, fruit and vegetables in limited quantities only.

Adequacy: The diet provides the Recommended Dietary Allowances for Vitamin A, Riboflavin, Niacin and Vitamin C.

Foods	Foods Allowed	Foods to Avoid
Beverages	Milk and milk drinks limited to two cups per day (for children under 12 years of age, only one cup per day) ; tea; carbonated beverages	* Coffee, all others
Breads	Emphasize refined wheat bread; hot rolls; saltine crackers	Whole grain or cracked grains; quick breads; breads or crackers with fruits or seeds
Cereals	Cooked refined, enriched cereals: grits, cream of wheat, cream of rice, malt-o-meal, oatmeal; refined prepared cereals	Whole grain cereals
Desserts	Plain desserts: sherbet, cake, cookies, custards, ice cream, puddings (using recommended milk allowance), gelatin desserts, fruit whips (with gelatin base and using allowed fruits), popsicles, fruit ices	Pies; pastries; doughnuts; coconut; nuts

*Coffee and Black Pepper usually are not served unless specifically requested

Foods	Foods Allowed	Foods to Avoid
Fat	Butter; margarine	Fried foods; highly seasoned gravy; bacon
Fruits and Fruit Juices	Two servings daily, including one citrus juice: strained fruit juices, cooked or canned peaches, pears, apples, applesauce, apricots, ripe banana	Raw fruit; cooked or canned fruit with seeds; pineapple; dried fruits; avocado
Meat, Fish, Poultry, Cheese, and Eggs	Lean, tender broiled, boiled or baked: beef, veal, lamb, pork, liver, turkey, chicken, boneless fish; eggs; cottage and mild cheese (not more than two ounces daily)	Spiced or fried: meats, fish, ham, poultry, eggs; sharp cheese
Potatoes or Substitutes	White potatoes, mashed or dehydrated sweet potatoes; macaroni; noodles; refined rice; spaghetti; hominy	Skins of potatoes; fibrous sweet potatoes; fried potatoes; potato chips; corn and corn chips; wild rice
Soups	Clear or cream soups with allowed foods (within milk allowance)	Highly seasoned soups
Sweets	Strained honey; jelly; syrup; sugar; plain candy (all in moderation)	Candy with nuts or coconut; jams; marmalades
Vegetables and Vegetable Juices	Two servings daily; tender, cooked asparagus, beets, carrots, green or wax beans, green peas, summer or mashed winter squash, chopped spinach, mushrooms, eggplant, mild vegetable juices	Fried or raw vegetables; tomatoes; okra; gas forming vegetables: broccoli, cauliflower, cabbage, brussel sprouts, dried beans or peas, turnips, green pepper, onion, greens of kale, mustard, dandelion and turnips
Miscellaneous	Salt; mild spices; vanilla extract; natural gravies; smooth peanut butter; cream sauces; catsup; prepared mustard	* Black pepper; highly seasoned foods; herbs; nuts; olives; popcorn; pickles

* Coffee and black pepper usually are not served unless specifically requested.

Suggested Meal Pattern

Breakfast	**Lunch**	**Dinner**
Strained Orange Juice	Roast Beef	Broiled Chicken
Scrambled Egg	Mashed Potatoes	Buttered Rice
Refined Wheat Toast	Buttered Carrots	Buttered Green Beans
Cream of Rice	Refined Wheat Bread	Refined Wheat Bread
Butter	Butter	Butter
Sugar	Angel Food Cake	Sliced Peaches
1 cup Milk	Iced Tea	1 cup Milk
	Sugar	

Carbohydrate Intolerance and Enzyme Deficiencies

Inability to digest and absorb carbohydrates is a frequent cause of chronic watery diarrhea, often leading to dehydration and failure to thrive. Both simple and complex sugars may provoke diarrhea when given in sufficient quantity, and elimination of the offending sugar from the diet readily reverses this diarrhea. Most carbohydrates in the diet occur as the disaccharides, maltose, isomaltose, sucrose and lactose: the quantity varying with age. In early infancy, lactose (milk sugar) comprises 100% of the dietary carbohydrate, while an adult ingests little lactose, but far more starch and sucrose. In some special formulas and elemental diets, the monosaccharides glucose and fructose may be the only carbohydrates.

Each disaccharide must be split into its component monosaccharide, glucose, galactose or fructose, before absorption can occur. This process of digestion takes place at the surface of cells lining each intestinal villus, and is brought about by disaccharidase enzymes specific for each sugar. Once the disaccharides are split, there is active transport of glucose and galactose, but only passive transport of fructose. The sequence in digestion and absorption is shown below.

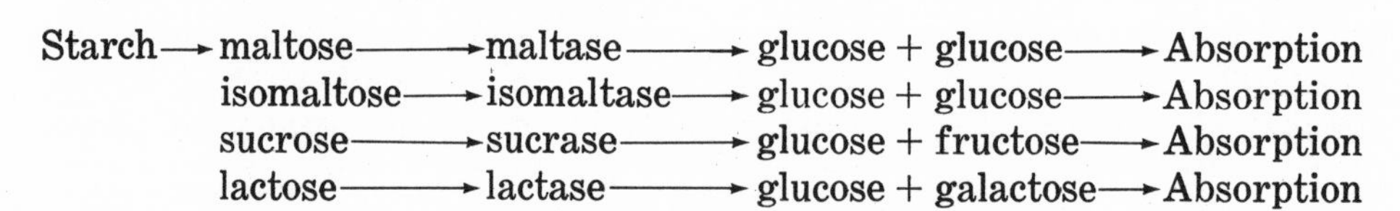

Accumulation of undigested disaccharides in the bowel lumen results from lack of disaccharidase enzymes, with or without damage to the intestinal villus cells. Accumulation of monosaccharides results from congenital absence of transport mechanisms or damage to villus cells with loss of surface area.

The effect of unabsorbed disaccharides or monosaccharides in the small intestine is secretion of water and electrolytes. This increased volume of fluid causes distention and an increase in motility, with dumping of carbohydrate rich fluids into the colon. It is here that bacterial action brings about fermentation, with the production of gas and acidic components, and a diarrheal stool, high in carbohydrate and of low pH. It is the increase fluid and gas production in the bowel that leads to distention, cramping and diarrhea. The loss of water and electrolytes usually leads to dehydration. Diagnosis of carbohydrate intolerance includes: 1) Improvement with withdrawal of a specific sugar; 2) Finding acid stools less than pH 6.0, with positive reducing sugar (2+ or more); 3) Specific oral tolerance tests with 2 gm/kg of sugar up to maximum of 50 gm.; 4) Measurement of disaccharidase enzymes, by small bowel biopsy; 5) Perfusion studies of the upper small intestine, measuring specifically the amount of a given sugar that can be absorbed over a short segment of jejunum.

There are several common clinical disorders where carbohydrate intolerance leads to acute and/or chronic diarrhea. Lactose intolerance is frequently seen following acute infection, or in conditions where there is more serious damage to the upper intestinal mucosa, such as in celiac disease, infestation with Giardia Lamblia, and in chronic malnutrition, where there is atrophy of the intestinal villi. Elimination of lactose containing formulas from the diet, with substitution of either a sucrose or a glucose containing formula is curative. Most of these conditions are transient and readily reversible with recovery from the initial illness. Lactose intolerance is also seen in older aged children and adults as an acquired defect, probably environmental and genetic in origin. The severity of the intolerance is variable, and it is often possible to provide some milk, as long as it is small in amount and used at the time of other food intake. Sucrose intolerance is seen with congenital absence of the specific disaccharidase, leading to diarrhea with the introduction of fruit and vegetables. This is a life long problem, but may improve with age. Severe mucosal damage from a variety of insults, may result in transient intolerance to sucrose, with full recovery following recovery of the basic disease. Intolerance to maltose and isomaltose occurs with severe mucosal damage, and a generalized malabsorption. The most severe form of sugar intolerance is in the severely malnourished infant with chronic diarrhea, who has generalized disaccharidase deficiency and acquired glucose-galactose malabsorption. As the upper bowel is damaged from a variety of insults, villi are lost and the absorptive surface decreases leading to a total malabsorption of all sugars, fats and proteins. At this point, we often see diarrhea resulting from only a 3-5% glucose solution. During the treatment phase of this type of illness, intravenous glucose is mandatory to prevent hypoglycemia. These infants often have to be hyperalimented, with gradual introduction of oral feedings over several weeks.

The use of various formulas to treat diarrhea requires knowledge of the components of the formulas, as well as the side effects that occur. For example, elimination of lactose from the diet and substitution of any of the soy formulas, provides sucrose as the main sugar, which is generally well tolerated. In sucrose intolerance, the infants would do well on human or cows milk, or on a glucose containing formula, but would not tolerate the usual soy formulas. In those infants with glucose malabsorption, formulas such as CHofree can be used, but until an oral carbohydrate can be started, IV-glucose must be provided. Pregestimil, a glucose containing formula, with hydrolyzed casein and medium chained triglycerides, would also be useful in an infant with generalized carbohydrate malabsorption;

however, Pregestimil has a very high osmotic load, which may produce secretion of water and electrolytes into the small bowel in an infant with a severely damaged mucosa.

In summary, the most important aspects of carbohydrate intolerance include identifying and eliminating the offending sugar, and providing intravenous glucose in those cases where all carbohydrate must be removed transiently from the diet.

Milk Free Diet

Foods	Foods Allowed	Foods to Avoid
Beverages	Carbonated beverages; tea; soy-based formulas; Meat Base (MBF) Formula; cocoa made with water or milk substitute; milk-free cocoa	Milk—fresh, evaporated, dry, malted, buttermilk; cream; cocomalt; ovaltine; cocoa; coffee*
Breads	Homemade milk-free breads; plain crackers	All commercial breads containing milk, milk solids or whey; zwieback; commercial bread crumbs and breading mixes (check labels carefully)
Cereals	Any dried or cooked cereal not containing milk or milk solids	Special K; Cocoa Krispies; Concentrate; Cocoa Puffs; Cocoa Pebbles
Desserts	Fruit Ices; popsicles; flavored gelatin; homemade cookies, cakes and pies prepared without milk or milk products; angel food cake; puddings prepared with fruit juice or milk substitutes	Ice cream; sherbet; custard; puddings; cakes, cookies, pies and pie crusts prepared with milk and milk products; whipped toppings; junket
Fat	Milk-free margarine (such as Marparv); vegetable oils and shortenings; salad dressings and mayonnaise prepared without milk or milk products; crisp bacon	Butter; margarine; cream cheese; sour cream
Fruits and Fruit Juices	All	None
Meat, fish, poultry, cheese and eggs	Beef, veal, lamb, pork, liver, turkey, fish; eggs-prepared in any way without milk or milk products; Kosher meat products are milk free	Yogurt; cheese and cheese products; all creamed and breaded foods; luncheon meats; frankfurters (check labels carefully)

*** Coffee and black pepper usually are not served unless specifically requested.**

Foods	Foods Allowed	Foods to Avoid
Potatoes or substitutes	Potatoes, rice, noodles, spaghetti, macaroni, hominy—all prepared without milk or milk products	Instant potatoes; frozen french fries (if lactose is used as a browning agent)
Soups	Broth-based soups	Cream soups
Sweets	Sugar; syrup; honey; plain candy; jelly; jam; marmalade; marshmallows and marshmallow cream	Caramels; chocolate candy; butterscotch
Vegetables	All frozen, fresh or canned vegetables prepared without milk or milk products; all vegetable juices	None
Miscellaneous	Catsup; mustard; pickles; unbuttered popcorn; iodized salt; vinegar; spices; herbs; peanut butter	All others

Celiac Disease

Celiac disease is now considered a specific disease entity, gluten-induced enteropathy (celiac sprue, adult celiac disease) and is considered to be the same as adult idiopathic steatorrhea (Rubin, et al., 1960, 1970).[1,2] The exact pathogenesis of the deleterious effect of gluten (gliadin) remains obscure (Anderson, et al., 1972).[3] Diagnosis depends upon the demonstration of impaired intestinal absorption, characteristic histological changes in the duodenal and jejunal mucosa and definite clinical response to elimination of dietary gluten with relapse following reintroduction (Anderson et al., 1960,[4] Meeuwisse, 1970[5]). It is uncommon in the United States but the exact incidence is unknown. It is familial but the genetic pattern of inheritance is unclear. The onset is insidious and correlates with the introduction of cereals (gluten) into the diet. There is a higher

1. Rubin, Cyrus E., Lloyd L. Brandborg, Patricia C. Phelps and Hawley C. Taylor, Jr.; "Studies of Celiac Disease, I. The Apparent Identical and Specific Nature of the Duodenal and Proximal Jejunal Lesion in Celiac Disease and Idiopathic Sprue," *Gastroenterology 38*:28-49, 1960.
2. Rubin, Cyrus E, Samuel Eidelman and Wilfred M. Weinstein; "Sprue by any Other Name," *Gastroenterology 58*:409-413, 1970.
3. Anderson, Charlotte M., Michael Gracey and Valerie Burke; "Coeliac Disease, Some Still Controversial Aspects," *Arch. of Disease in Childhood 47*:292-298, 1972.
4. Anderson, Charlotte M.; "Histological Changes in the Duodenal Mucosa in Coeliac Disease, Reversibility During Treatment with a Wheat Gluten Free Diet," *Arch Disease in Childhood 35*:419-427, 1960.
5. Meeuwissem, G. W.; "Diagnostic Criteria in Coeliac Disease," (Discussion, European Society for Paediatric Gastroenterology), *Acta. Paediatrica Scandinavica 59*:461-463, 1970.

incidence in females than males. Other causes of malabsorption must be excluded (cystic fibrosis, post-bacterial and viral gastroenteritis, a-beta-lipoproteinemia, protein-calorie malnutrition, starch intolerance, secondary disaccharidase intolerance following enteric infections—more common in young infants).

Symptoms may include pallor, poor weight gain or weight loss, growth retardation (weight and height), muscle wasting, abdominal distention, diarrhea (but may have normal or constipated stools), steatorrhea (may be absent—McNicholl and Egan-Mitchell, 1971),[6] occasional vomiting, anorexia and irritability. Asymptomatic patients do exist (MacDonald et al., 1965)[7] and may reveal no malabsorption of carbohydrate or fat (Anderson, 1966).[8] Deficiencies in iron, folate, calcium, as well as fat-soluble vitamins A, D and K are not uncommon. Intestinal biopsy is the most positive and reliable index of malabsorption. The characteristic mucosal findings are not specific (Anderson, 1966) and great care must be taken in obtaining, handling and interpreting the specimens. The proximal small intestine shows the most severe lesion—the villi are usually absent and the mucosa flat. The distal mucosal changes are less marked (Rubin et al, 1960).

Therapy consists of the elimination of gluten (gliaden) from the diet with the exclusion of wheat, rye, barley and oats. Wheat and rye are apparently the worst offenders with barley being less so and oats tolerated by some. Buckwheat is eliminated by some and included by others. Such products should be tested on an individual basis.

In the acutely ill child with large fluid losses from the intestine, milk is withheld because of the probability of secondary disaccharidase deficiency. In this case, as in that of milk intolerance, a milk-substitute formula is used.

Total caloric intake is high initially to cover past and present fecal losses and malabsorption (120-200 kcal/kg/day). The protein is that maximally utilizable by the body in the earlier stage (3-4 gms/kg per day) to allow for maintenance and excessive losses and lowered with improvement. Carbohydrate is recommended in the form of simple sugars in the early stage and later disaccharides. The fat content of the diet is best held at not more than six per cent of the total kilocalories. Improved fat absorption is usually achieved with the use of medium-chain triglycerides (Isselbacher, 1966).[9] There must be an adequate supply of linoleic acid and the fat-soluble vitamins; at times this is most safely accomplished with a supplement.

6. McNicholl, Brian and Bridget Egan-Mitchell; "Infancy Celiac Diease Without Diarrhea," *Peds. 49*:85-91, 1972.
7. MacDonald, W. C., W. O. Dobbins, III., and C. E. Rubin; "Studies of the Familial Nature of Celiac Sprue Using Biopsy of the Small Intestine," *New England, J. Med. 272*:448-456, 1965.
8. Anderson, Charlotte M.; Intestinal Malabsorption in Childhood" *Arch. Disease in Childhood 41*:571-569, 1966.
9. Isselbacher, Kurt J.; "Biochemical Aspects of Fat Absorption," *Gastroenterology 50*:78-82, 1966.

Frequent and small feedings are essential at first. Later, caloric intake is adjusted to a regular diet with the elimination of gluten. The consensus is that it best be maintained for life.

Gluten Restricted Diet

Principle: The gluten-free diet is designed to meet the nutritional needs of children with gluten-induced enteropathy (celiac disease). Each diet must be individualized to encourage sufficient caloric intake. Wheat, rye, oats and barley products or their derivatives are excluded from the diet.

Adequacy: The diet provides the Recommended Daily Dietary Allowances for all nutrients. In the acute stage anorexia may prohibit adequate intake, and when indicated a vitamin and mineral supplement may be necessary.

Foods	Foods Allowed	Foods to Avoid
Beverages	Milk, milk substitutes; tea; carbonated beverages (in moderation)	*Coffee; prepared drinks with malt, wheat, rye, barley or oats
Breads	Any made from rice, corn, soybean, potato starch, buckwheat (if tolerated) or wheat starch flours	All containing wheat, rye, barley, or oats; all commercial yeast and quick bread mixes; all crackers; bread crumbs; rusk; zwieback; melba toast; muffins; pancakes; rolls; pretzels; Ry-Krisp
Cereals	Any made from rice or corn	All containing wheat, rye, barley or oats. The labels of any new products should be read carefully for ingredients.
Desserts	Homemade fruit-flavored ices, popsicles, sherbet, ice cream, fruit whips, puddings, cakes, cookies made with gluten-free flours	Any prepared with wheat, rye, oats or barley; commercially prepared desserts or mixes not on special list
Fats	Vegetable oils; margarine; butter; pure mayonnaise; salad dressings included on special list; cream; crisp bacon	Salad dressings thickened or emulsified with wheat, rye, oats, or barley products
Fruits and Fruit Juices	All; include one serving of citrus fruit or juice daily	Peel or remove seeds as indicated

Foods	Foods Allowed	Foods to Avoid
Meat, Fish, Poultry, Cheese and Eggs	Lean, tender broiled, boiled or baked: beef, veal, lamb, pork, liver, turkey, chicken, boneless fish, all-meat frankfurters; eggs; cottage, cheddar, swiss, parmesan, processed cheese (if tolerated); if fat is tolerated, meats may be fried in allowed fats	All breaded meats; luncheon meats or frankfurters with cereal; canned chili.
Potatoes or Substitutes	White or sweet potatoes; rice; hominy; potato chips; corn chips; cheetos; low protein pastas	Macaroni; noodles; spaghetti; stuffings made with commercial bread
Soups	Bouillon; broth; consomme; homemade vegetable or cream soups with allowed foods	Commercial soups containing wheat, rye, oats, or barley
Sweets	Honey; jam; jelly; syrup; sugar; hard candy without soft centers (check all labels carefully)	Candies made with wheat, rye, barley, or oats
Vegetables and Vegetable Juices	All frozen, fresh or canned vegetables or vegetable juices	Any vegetables cooked with cream sauce thickened with flour
Miscellaneous	Salt; pure spices; peanut butter; pickles; vinegar; gravy or sauce thickened with allowed flours or starches	Bottle meat sauce; condiments with wheat, rye, barley, or oats; flavoring syrups; cocoa mixes; gravies or sauces with wheat, rye, barley or oats

* Coffee is usually not served unless specifically requested.

Gluten-Free Commercial Products

Gluten-Free Cereals

Minute Rice (General Foods)
Post Cocoa Pebbles Cereal (General Foods)
Post Fruity Pebbles Cereal (General Foods)
Post Frosted Rice Krinkles Cereal (General Foods)
Kellogg's Puffa Puffa Rice Cereal (Kellogg's)
Kellogg's Sugar Pops Cereal (Kellogg's)

Gluten-Free Desserts

Dream Whip Whipped Topping Mix (General Foods)
D-Zerta Low Calorie Gelatin Desserts (General Foods)
D-Zerta Low Calorie Pudding and Pie Fillings (General Foods)
D-Zerta Low Calorie Whipped Topping Mix (General Foods)
Jello 1-2-3 Dessert Mixes (General Foods)
Jello Gelatin Desserts (General Foods)
Jello Golden Egg Custard Mix (General Foods)
Jello Lemon Chiffon Pie Filling (General Foods)
Jello Pudding and Pie Filling (General Foods)
Jello Tapioca Puddings (General Foods)
Jello Whip'n Chill Dessert Mixes (*except chocolate flavor*—contains malt extract) (General Foods)
Minute Tapioca (General Foods)
Birds Eye Cool Whip Non-Dairy Whipped Topping (General Foods)
Birds Eye Cool'n Creamy Puddings (General Foods)
Birds Eye Thick'n Frosty Frozen Thick Shake Concentrate (General Foods)
Merimix Real Egg Custard (Delmark)
Delmark Quick Egg Custard (Delmark)
Delmark Quick Tapioca Pudding Mix (Delmark)
Delmark Quick Creamy Pudding Mix (Delmark)
Snack-Pack Puddings (Hunt-Wesson Foods)
Kroger Ice Cream
Kroger Ice Milk
Kroger Sherbet

Gluten-Free Sweets

Baker's Chocolate Products (General Foods)
Log Cabin Syrup (all varieties) (General Foods)
Nestle's Semi-Sweet Chocolate Bars (Nestle's)
Nestle's Semi-Sweet Chocolate Morsels (Nestle's)
Milk Chocolate Kisses (Hershey's)
Milk Chocolate Bar (Plain and with Almonds) (Hershey's)
Block Milk Chocolate (Hershey's)
Mr. Goodbar (Hershey's)
Krackel Bar (Hershey's)
Special Dark Bar (Hershey's)
Semi-Sweet Chocolate Chips (Hershey's)
Milk Chocolate Chips (Hershey's)
Sweet Chocolate Sprigs (Hershey's)
Baking Chocolate (Hershey's)
Chocolate Flavored Syrup (Hershey's)
Milk Chocolate Fudge Topping (Hershey's)
Candy Coated Hershey-ets (Hershey's)
Milk Chocolate Covered Candy Coated Peanuts (Hershey's)

Coconut Cream Egg (Hershey's)
Reese's Peanut Butter Egg (Hershey's)
Reese's Peanut Butter Cup (Hershey's)

Gluten-Free Miscellaneous Items

Baker's Coconut (all varieties) (General Foods)
Calumet Baking Powder (General Foods)
Certo Fruit Pectin (General Foods)
Sure-Jell Fruit Pectin (General Foods)
Sugar Sweetened Kool-Aid Instant Soft Drink Mixes (General Foods)
"Regular" Kool-Aid Instant Soft Drink Mixes (General Foods)
Kool-Pops Pop Bars (General Foods)
Good Seasons Salad Dressing Mixes (except Riviera, French and Low Calorie Italian) (General Foods)
Good Seasons Thick'n Creamy Salad Dressing Mixes (Italian, French, and Bleu Cheese *only*) (General Foods)
Cheetos (Frito-Lay)
Doritos (Frito-Lay)
Funyuns (Frito-Lay)
Lay's and Ruffles Potato Chips (Frito-Lay)
Carnation Instant Breakfast (except Chocolate Malt flavor) (Carnation)
Delmark Egg Nog (Delmark)
Delmark Milk Shake Mix (Delmark)
Bennett's Mayonnaise (Doxsee)
Bennett's Salad Dressing (Doxsee)
Bennett's French Dressing (Doxsee)
Bennett's Italian Dressing (Doxsee)
Bennett's Bleu Cheese Dressing (Doxsee)
Bennett's Chili Sauce (Doxsee)
Doxsee Cocktail Sauce (Doxsee)
French's Prepared Mustard (R. T. French Company)
Pillsbury Instant Breakfast (Pillsbury)
Pillsbury Food Sticks (Pillsbury)
Cocoa (Hershey's)
Instant Cocoa Mix (Hershey's)
Hot Cocoa Mix (Hershey's)
Lipton California Onion Dressing
Lipton Deluxe French Dressing
Lipton Garlic French Dressing
Lipton Green Goddess Dressing
Lipton Italian Dressing
Lipton Italian Rose Dressing
Lipton Russian Dressing
Lipton Thousand Island Dressing
Ketchup (Hunt-Wesson)
Chili Sauce (Hunt-Wesson)

Low Sucrose Diet

Foods	Foods Allowed	Foods to Avoid
Beverages	Whole, low fat, or skim milk, buttermilk; tea and koolaid made with artificial sweeteners; dietetic carbonated beverages	Sweetened condensed milk; chocolate milk; malted milks; carbonated beverages with sugar; punch; coffee*
Breads	Wheat flour; corn meal; soda crackers, saltine crackers; homemade biscuits or muffins without sugar; homemade breads made with honey	Yeast breads; commercial biscuits or muffins; bread mixes; bread crumbs
Cereals	Shredded wheat, puffed wheat, puffed rice, cream of wheat, cream of rice, oatmeal, grits, farina	Cereals containing sugar; sugar coated cereals
Desserts	Dietetic gelatin (D'zerta) Dietetic pudding (D'zerta)	All containing sugar, such as cakes, pies, ice cream, cookies, sherbet, donuts, sweet rolls, puddings, custard, candy, ice milk, mellorine
Fats	Margarine; oil; homemade salad dressings prepared without sugar	Commercial salad dressings; sweet cream butter
Fruits and Fruit Juices	Any fresh, dried, fresh frozen, or canned without sugar; unsweetened fruit juices	Syrup-packed fruits; sweetened fruit juices
Meats, Fish, Poultry, Cheese and Eggs	Beef, veal, lamb, fresh pork, chicken, turkey; fish; cheese, prepared without sugar; eggs prepared in any way	Ham, bacon, luncheon meats, frankfurters and any others containing sugar; peanut butter
Potatoes or Substitutes	White potato; macaroni; noodles; spaghetti; rice	Sweet potato
Soup	Homemade soups prepared without sugar	Commercial soups and broths
Sweets	Honey; glucose; artificially sweetened candy, jams and jellies	Sugar of all types; jam, jelly, syrups, marmalade, preserves, corn syrup

* Coffee and black pepper are usually not served unless specifically requested.

Foods	Foods Allowed	Foods to Avoid
Vegetables	Asparagus, green beans, wax beans, broccoli, Brussels sprouts, cabbage, cauliflower, celery, chard, collards, cucumbers, eggplant, kale, lettuce, mushrooms, okra, peppers, parsley, spinach, tomato, watercress, pumpkin, fresh corn, radishes, squash	All others
Miscellaneous	Salt; herbs; spices; vanilla; lemon; popcorn; unsweetened pickles (dill and sour); mustard; cornstarch	Black Pepper* catsup; chili sauce; steak sauce; chewing gum

Sodium Restricted Diet

Basic Principles

This is a modification of the normal diet in which the sodium content is restricted to varying degrees below the average intake.

The average adult on a customary mixed diet consumes approximately two to four mEq/kg or 8 to 16 g/day (137-274 mEq/day) of NaCl. Thus, a 2800 kcal diet supplying 12 grams of NaCl would be equivalent to twelve mEq/100 k cal. Human milk contains on the average about 7 mEq Na per liter. An infant consuming human milk as the sole source of nourishment will receive about 5-10 mEq Na/day. Breast-fed babies do not develop sodium deficiency. The sodium requirement for growth of infants can be readily met by 1.3-1.8 mEq of Na/day. Estimated average loss of Na in sweat in infants is about 2.2 mEq/day (less with lower temperature) and 1-2 mEq/day in the stool. Requirements during the first year for both growth plus losses are easily met by 4-8 mEq Na/day.

Surveys on American infants show average intakes of NaCl to range from 0.3-2.2 mEq/100 kcal (9 mEq/day) for younger infants and 5.7-6.4 mEq per 100 kcal (60 mEq/day) for those around one year of age.

Since sodium is the ion of importance, one should refer to a specific amount (or range) in terms of mg or mEq of sodium (500 mg or 22 mEq sodium) rather than "salt-free", "low-salt", "moderate-salt", or even "low-sodium".

The restriction of sodium has been found beneficial in a variety of conditions such as congestive heart failure, hypertension, edema, ascites, cirrhosis and various diseases involving kidney function. Dietary restriction of sodium may be used as the only form of therapy or in conjunction with drug therapy or dialysis. Such a diet will almost always involve an alteration in protein, potassium and other essential nutrients.

Hemodialysis is being used more widely at the present time for the prolongation of life in patients with chronic renal disease to prevent earlier death from uremia. Since a normal diet between dialyses could prove fatal

* Coffee and black pepper usually are not served unless specifically requested.

from cardiac arrest due to hyperkalemia, the interim diet has assumed prominent significance. The food ingested significantly influences the products of catabolism, sodium, potassium and fluid and, consequently, necessitates restrictions of these nutrients, but one must simultaneously provide adequate amounts of other essential nutrients and calories. In this situation, potassium is the limiting factor. Jordan et al, (1967)[11] have outlined a basic diet plan for use in such patients with lists arranged in food groups giving protein, sodium, potassium and water content with a list of foods to be avoided.[11]

The sources of sodium include its wide natural occurrence, especially in animal foods (milk, cheese, eggs, meat, fish, poultry). Organ meats and all shellfish are very rich sources. Some vegetables, particularly certain greens, contain significant quantities. Most other vegetables, cereals and fruits are relatively low.

In addition to the natural sources of sodium, other significant contributions that must be considered include that added in processing, preservation and preparation of food, that occurring in water, that used in water softeners, that added at the table in the form of NaCl, etc. Salt is used in the quality-separation of vegetables, to prevent discoloration of fruit, in the brining process for such foods as pickles, sauerkraut, corned beef, in the koshering of meat, as a preservative for frozen or dried fish, ham and other manufacturing processes.

Many sodium-containing compounds are used in the manufacture of foods for various purposes—monosodium glutamate, sodium acetate, sodium alginate, sodium benzoate, sodium citrate, sodium propionate and sodium sulfite. Baking soda and baking powder are widely used in the preparation of food. Potassium bicarbonate can be substituted for sodium bicarbonate but is not very palatable. Sodium-free baking powder can be purchased or prepared by the pharmacist. The acknowledgement of the addition of salt is now required on all labels by the F.D.A.

Many drugs contain sodium—antihistamines, sodium salicylate, sodium ascorbate, antiacids and alkalizers, antibiotics, cough medicines, laxatives, pain relievers and sedatives. Some dentifrices contain sodium, in which case it would be well to rinse thoroughly and not swallow. Products labeled as dietetic foods are required to list the sodium content in an average serving and in 100 grams of the food.

A joint committee of the American Dietetic Association, the American Heart Association and the U.S. Public Health Service has planned a list of food groups for planning sodium-restricted diets in terms of units of sodium. These groups are similar to those used for the calculation of diabetic diets. Foods to be avoided because of their high sodium content are listed, as well as a "free list" of foods that may be used freely because of low sodium content. The "free list" simplifies the addition of calories where possible (75 kilo-calories per unit).

11. Jordan, Wanda L., James E. Cimino, M.D., Alice C. Grist, Grace E. McMahon and Maureen M. Doyle; "Basic Pattern for a Controlled Protein, Sodium and Potassium Diet", *Journal American Dietetic Association*, *50*:137-141, 1967.

Milk is just as important for its nutrient contribution to the basic diet of the sodium-restricted modification as the normal diet. It is very difficult to plan a diet adequate in calcium, as well as protein and riboflavin, without milk unless a supplement is given. Other high quality protein foods (meat, eggs) are restricted because of their natural sodium content. Because of the high sodium content of most protein foods, it is impossible to plan a "high protein-low sodium" diet from natural foods.

There are numerous references in recent literature concerning the excessive content of salt in processed baby foods. Dahl[12] has investigated this subject extensively and states "there can be no question about the high concentrations of NaCl in processed baby foods; except for fruits, they contain concentrations of NaCl, added by the processors, that range from about 5 to more than 100 times that of the original natural products".

The daily requirement of NaCl for the normal infant appears to be relatively small as is evidenced by the proven adequacy of breast milk for normal growth and development with its low sodium content of about 7 mEq/liter. Thus the normal infant consumes approximately 5 to 10 mEq Na daily from human milk.

McCance and Widdowson[13] have estimated a requirement of 75 mEq Na for each kilogram of new tissue formed in the process of growth. Thus, growth during the first year would be satisfied by approximately 1.3-1.8 mEq daily and following cessation of growth, the daily requirement would be approximately 1 mEq or less.

Requirements for sodium (infants) other than growth:

Obligatory losses

a. Stool (Gamble et al)[14]
  0.2-1.7 mEq/day
  Daily allowance of 1-2 mEq appears adequate and is comparable with adult losses.

b. Sweat (Cooke, Pratt and Darrow)[15]
  1.8-7.6 mEq /liter (average 4.9)
  Environmental temperature of 91° F.
  Calculated daily volume of sweat 45-65 mg/kg
 Daily average loss (5 month old, 7 kg) = 2.2 mEq Na
 More temperate conditions: approximately 1 mEq/day

c. Urine
  Data concerning urinary losses in infants are not available. Ac-

12. Dahl, L. K.; "Salt in Processed Baby Foods," *American Journal Clinical Nutrition 21*:787-792, 1968.
13. McCance, R. A. and E. M. Widdowson, "Mineral Metabolism of the Foetus and Newborn," *British Medical Bulletin, 17*:132-136, 1961.
14. Gamble, J. L., W. M. Wallace, L. Eliel, M. A. Holliday, M. Cushman, J. Appleton, A Shenberg and J. Piotti; "Effects of Large Loads of Electrolytes," *Pediatrics 7*:305-320, 1951.
15. Cooke, R. E., E. L. Pratt and D. C. Darrow; "The Metabolic Response of Infants to Heat Stress," *Yale Journal Biological Medicine 22*:227-249, 1950.

cording to Dole et al (1950)[16], adults with good renal function excreted only 0.21 to 1.52 mEq/day in the urine on prolonged daily sodium intakes averaging 2.17 mEq. In Dahl's (1968)[17] opinion, equal effectiveness of infant kidney function is indicated by the fact that breast-fed infants do not develop sodium deficiency. He therefore feels that the requirement for sodium during the first year of life, including growth plus losses, would generously be met by daily intakes of 4-8 mEq.

The largest problem presented with the sodium-restricted diet is patient acceptance due to lack of palatability. This becomes even a larger obstacle since it is most frequently required in cases of long-term usage. Great ingenuity is required in the preparation of such food to keep it varied, attractive and flavorful enough to help the patient to adhere to it for any length of time. Counseling is very important so that the patient fully understands the reasons for the restrictions and the healthful benefits to be derived.

Certain herbs and spices are very helpful in achieving flavor for taste appeal. Salt substitutes sound good but are not widely accepted; they contain potassium which would be contraindicated with renal damage. Therefore, these should be used only as ordered by the physician.

Various low-sodium products and recipes have been developed that aid greatly in planning a diet. Various bread products can be made using low-sodium baking powder or soda, part of the milk and egg allowance, or by substituting low-sodium milk (Lonalac)*.

When prescribing a sodium-restricted diet, one must be aware of the fact that it can cause sodium depletion, and watch for symptoms. Greater than expected sodium depletion may result from a combination of low-salt diet and vomiting, diarrhea, heat stress, excessive sweating, adrenal insufficiency, renal damage, surgery and/or diuretics. Symptoms of sodium depletion include mottled peripheral circulation, lethargy, weakness, abdominal cramping, oliguria, azotemia, etc. The etiology of these symptoms is usually documented by blood electrolyte disturbances but must be differentiated from excess water retention.

Salt Consumption of Infants

Food	Amount/Day	mEq Na/Kg/Day
Breast Milk	150-200 ml/kg	1 -1.4
Undiluted Cow's Milk	150-200 ml/kg	3.7-5.0

* Special formula by Mead-Johnson

16. Dole, V. P., L. K. Dahl, G. C. Cotzias, H. A. Eder and M. E. Krebs; "Dietary Treatment of Hypertension. Clinical and Metabolic Studies of Patients on the Rice-Fruit Diet," *Journal of Clinical Investigation 29*:1189-1206, 1950.
17. Dahl, L. K.; "Salt in Processed Baby Foods," *American Journal Clinical Nutrition 21*:787-792, 1968.

Strained Foods (no salt added)	mEq Na/100 gm food	
Fresh Fruits	0.1	grapefruit, oranges, peaches, pears, plums, apples, apricots, bananas, cherries
Fresh Vegetables	0.1-0.6	white potatoes, squash, tomatoes, green beans, lima beans, peas
Carrots	1.3	
Dry Cereals	0.1	cream of wheat, oatmeal, wheatena
Meats (cooked)	2-4	veal, beef, chicken, lamb, liver, pork
Eggs	5-6	

In usual amounts consumed (even several hundred grams/day), these foods would contribute only small amounts of NaCl—1 mEq. Na/Kg body wt. per day or less.

Nearly all strained infant and "junior" foods except fruits and fruit juices contain added salt. Canned soups are likewise high in salt content.

Puyau and Hampton (1966)[18] have shown that the average daily intake of sodium by infants 11-13 months of age to be approximately 60 mEq. or 0.35 Gm of NaCl/kg/day. This represents 13.4 Gm of NaCl per M^2/day.

Dahl et al (1963)[19] analyzed some strained foods on the market and found the following values:

		Na/100 Gms.	
Meats	16 samples	293-510 mg	(12.7-22.2 mEq)
		Avg 359	Avg 15.6
Vegetables & Mixtures	14 samples	144-357	(6.2-15.5)
		Avg 244	Avg 16.6

Cereals similarly analyzed by the Department of Agriculture (Handbook No. 8) showed the following values: 421-653 mg. (Avg 537); 18.3-28.5 (Avg 23.4). Therefore, processed foods contained sodium content that exceeded natural foods by the following approximate factors:*

Meats	5-6
Vegetables	6-60
Cereals (dry)	Excess of 100

* Fortunately baby food manufacturers have recently begun to lower the sodium content of infant products.

18. Puyau, F. A. and Hampton, L. P.; "Infant Feeding Practices," *Am. J. Dis. Children, 111*:370-373, 1966.

19. Dahl, L. K., M. Heine and L. Tassinari; "High Salt Content of Western Infant's Diet: Possible Relationship to Hypertension in the Adult," *Nature 198*:1204, 1963.

Gerber's "No Salt Added" Pureed Meats

These products have been prepared by Gerber's Company for use where restricted salt intake is beneficial.

Product	Sodium Content
Beef	(2.0 mEq) 46.9 mg /100 Gms
Chicken	(1.3 mEq) 30.0 mg /100 Gms
Veal	(2.5 mEq) 56.6 mg /100 Gms

The sodium content of each pack will vary slightly as a result of variations in the animals' diets. A higher maximum is declared on labels in order to cover all packs. For all three products (beef, chicken and veal), the declared sodium content is 75 mg (3.3 mEq) per 100 gms.

Summary of Na Intake by Infants

5 Kilo Infant	Sodium (mEq/kg/day)
Breast Milk 200 ml milk/kg Unsalted foods ½ jar vegetables (50 gm) ½ jar meat (50 gm)	1.8
Cow's Milk Unsalted foods ½ jar vegetables ½ jar meat	4.4-6.0
Cow's Milk Processed foods ½ jar vegetables ½ jar meat	7-8
If infants also consume Heavily Salted Cereals	10+*

* 500-1000% above probable requirements.

While this has not proven harmful for short-term periods, there is the obvious possibility of eventual damage or harm after prolonged high intakes in either the cardiovascular or renal system functions, or both.

Sodium and Potassium Values Special Solutions and Products

Product	Amount	mg/mEq Na	mg/mEq K
Hospital Coffee (premix)	100 cc	10.3/.45	67/1.7
Hospital Tea (premix)	100 cc	10.3/.45	5.9/.15
Hospital Water	100 cc	10.3/.45	———
*Coca Cola, Hospital	100 cc	11.5/.5	3.9/.1
*Tab, Hospital	100 cc	17.3/.7	3.9/.1
*Sprite, Hospital	100 cc	18.4/.8	3.9/.1
*Fresca, Hospital	100 cc	27.6/1.2	3.9/.1
**Gingerale	100 cc	8.3/.36	0.8/0.2
*Carbonated water, hospital dispenser	100 cc	14.9/.6	3.9/.1
Kool-Aid	100 cc	*negligible	*negligible
Root Beer	100 cc	negligible	negligible
Skim Milk	100 cc	53/2.3	168/4.3
**Pedialyte	100 cc	69/3	78/2
† Lytren	100 cc	57/2.5	98/2.5
**Polycose, Liquid	100 cc	70/3	4/0.1
**Polycose, Powder	100 gm	122/5.3	8/0.2
Jello Water	100 cc	48.3/2.1	Negligible
Consomme, Broth, Bouillon	100 cc	375/16.3	53.5/1.4

* Sodium and potassium values will vary depending upon the local water supply where the finished product is produced.
** Ross Laboratories
†Mead Johnson Co.

Table XXII

Milligrams of Sodium Allowed for Each Food Category of Sodium-Restricted Diets
Texas Children's Hospital

Food Category	250 mgs	500 mgs Infant	500 mgs	800 mgs	1000 mgs	1500 mgs	2000 mgs
Beverages	14	157	247	328	388	388	388
Breads	3	....	3	36	36	393	240
Cereals	2	19	2	2	2	100	100
Desserts	12	....	12	64	197	197	197
Fats	7	....	9	9	9	9	9
Fruits and Fruit Juices	10	17	10	15	15	15	15
Meat, Fish, Poultry, Cheese, and Eggs	166	206	166	166	166	166	166
Potatoes or Substitutes	10	....	10	15	15	15	200
Soups	....	....	....	....	....	....	....
Sweets	10	....	10	10	10	10	10
Vegetables and Vegetable Juices	15	82	15	70	70	70	550
Miscellaneous	5	....	5	5	5	5	5
Tap Water	....	....	....	75	75	75	75
						50*	50*
Total	254	481	489	795	988	1493	2005

* 1 teaspoon regular baking powder in quick breads and desserts increases the sodium value 35-50 milligrams per serving

250 Milligram Sodium Diet (11 mEq)

Food Category		Milligrams of Sodium
Beverages	2 cups Low Sodium Milk	14
Breads	3 slices Low Sodium Bread	3
Cereals	1 serving Low Sodium Cereal	2
Desserts	Low Sodium Bakery Items	12
Fats	2 Tablespons Unsalted Butter Unsalted Salad Dressing	7
Fruits and Fruit Juices		10
Meat, Fish, Poultry, Cheese, and Eggs	4 ounces Unsalted Meat 1 unsalted Egg	100 66
Potatoes or Substitutes		10
Soups	Low Sodium Homemade with Allowed Ingredients	—
Sweets		10
Vegetables and Vegetable Juices	Low Sodium Vegetables	15
Miscellaneous		5
Distilled Water must be used for drinking and food preparation		—
	Total	**254**

250 Milligram Sodium Diet (11 mEq)

Foods	Foods Allowed	Foods to Avoid
Beverages	Low sodium milk** (not to exceed 2 cups per day); tea; distilled water to be used for drinking and food preparation	*Coffee; whole, skim or chocolate milk; buttermilk; prepared or instant milk-based beverages; tap water; all carbonated beverages
Breads	Low sodium bread; low sodium crackers; low sodium melba toast; unsalted biscuits, cornbread, muffins, all made with	All enriched, whole grain breads; quick breads or yeast rolls prepared with salt;

* Coffee and black pepper usually are not served unless specifically requested.

** Lonolac powder prepared by Mead Johnson is a low sodium milk containing 7 milligrams of sodium per cup when reconstituted with distilled water.

Foods	Foods Allowed	Foods to Avoid
	allowed ingredients (low sodium baking powder, low sodium milk, egg) ; unsalted yeast rolls	all other crackers; commercial bread mixes; self-rising flour
Cereals	cookes, all made with allowed wheat, puffed rice, shredded wheat, low sodium cornflakes	Instant cereals; all other ready-to-eat cereals
Desserts	Low sodium gelatins; homemade unsalted puddings, pies, cakes, cookies, all made with allowed ingredients (low sodium milk, egg, low sodium baking powder)	All commercial desserts and dessert mixes; homemade desserts except specially prepared low sodium; plain unflavored gelatin
Fats	2 tablespoons unsalted butter or margarine; vegetable oils; hydrogenated shortening; unsalted salad dressings or mayonnaise	Salted butter or margarine; bacon; commercial salad dressings or mayonnaise with salt
Fruits and Fruit Juices	Fresh, frozen or canned fruit juices, apples, apricots, banana, blueberries, sweet or sour cherries, grapfruit, grapes, lemon, lime, nectarine, orange, peaches, pears, pineapple, plums, strawberries, tangerine, water-melon; frozen juices to be reconstituted with distilled water	Dried fruits processed with sodium compounds; cantaloupe; fruit cocktail; glazed fruits; fruit-flavored drinks
Meat, Fish, Poultry, Cheese and Eggs	1 unsalted egg and 4 ounces of fresh, unsalted meat, poultry or boneless fish daily—beef, veal, lamb, pork, liver, turkey, chicken, catfish, cod, drum, flounder, haddock, halibut, ocean perch, red snapper, low sodium canned tuna or salmon; low sodium cheese	Canned, salted, smoked or processed meats, poultry or fish, chipped or corned beef, frankfurters, ham, luncheon meats, sausage, frozen fish fillets; clams, crabs, lobster, oysters, scallops, shrimp; all other types of cheese
Potatoes or Substitutes	Fresh unsalted white potatoes; fresh, frozen or low sodium canned corn; unsalted macaroni, noodles, rice, spaghetti; dried beans cooked without salt	Sweet potatoes; corn chips; potato chips; pretzels; other party chips; canned or frozen potato products; pork and beans

Foods	Foods Allowed	Foods to Avoid
Soups	Homemade specially prepared low sodium soups or broth made from allowed ingredients	Bouillon cubes; any commercial, canned or dehydrated soups containing salt, monosodium glutamate or other sodium compounds
Sweets	Honey; pure maple syrup; hard pure sugar candy; granulated sugar; jam or jelly not to exceed three tablespoons per day	Sweets with salt or sodium compounds added; molasses; marmalades; brown sugar; corn syrup; marshamallows
Vegetables and Vegetable Juices	Fresh, unsalted or low sodium canned asparagus, broccoli, brussel sprouts, cauliflower, onions, green pepper, lima beans, green beans, wax beans, squash, green peas, tomatoes, pumpkin, cucumber, eggplant, okra, lettuce, tomato juice	All other fresh, canned or frozen vegetables
Miscellaneous	Cocoa powder; pure herbs and spices; vinegar; and unsalted popcorn; low sodium catsup; low sodium chili sauce; low sodium pickles; low sodium peanut butter; low sodium mustard; unsalted white sauce made with allowed low sodium milk; unsalted nuts (not recommended for the young child)	*Black pepper; Dutch processed chocolate; baking chocolate; baking powder; gravy; horseradish; meat tenderizers; prepared mustard; olives; pickles; relishes; seasoning salts; catsup; chili sauce; soy sauce; steak sauces; baking soda; monosodium glutamate; commercial peanut butter; salted nuts

* Coffee and black pepper usually are not served unless specifically requested.

Suggested Meal Pattern

Breakfast	Lunch	Dinner
Orange Juice	2 ounces Unsalted Broiled Beef Patty	2 ounces Unsalted Broiled Chicken
1 unsalted Scrambled Egg	Baked Potato	Unsalted Buttered Rice
Unsalted Cream of Wheat	Unsalted Buttered Green Beans	Unsalted Buttered

Breakfast	Lunch	Dinner
Unsalted Toast Unsalted Butter Sugar 1 tablespoon Jelly 1 cup low sodium Milk	Unsalted Bread Unsalted Butter Chopped Lettuce with unsalted French Dressing Sliced Peaches ½ cup low sodium Milk 1 tablespoon Jelly	Yellow Squash Unsalted Bread Unsalted Butter Fresh Fruit Salad on Lettuce Unsalted Sugar Cookies ½ cup low sodium Milk 1 tablespoon Jelly

500 Milligram Sodium Infant Diet

Foods	Foods Allowed	Foods to Avoid
Beverages	Similac PM 60/40 or SMA (20 calories per ounce) not to exceed 26 ounces per day (prepared with tap water)	All other infant formulas; whole or skim milk
Cereals	6 tablespoons per day of strained barley, high protein, mixed, oatmeal or rice cereal; 1 piece of zwiebach	Strained mixed cereal with bananas, strained oatmeal with bananas, strained rice cereal with strawberries; all other teething biscuits or crackers
Fruits and Fruit Juices	Strained applesauce, applesauce and apricots, applesauce with pineapple, peaches, pears, pears and pineapple, plums with tapioca (not to exceed 3 jars a day); 1 can daily of a strained fruit juice	Strained apricots with tapioca, bananas with tapioca; bananas with pineapple and tapioca, prunes with tapioca
Meat, Poultry and Eggs	Unsalted pureed beef, chicken, lamb, liver, turkey, veal (not to exceed 14 tablespoons per day); 1 egg	Ham; all strained meats and egg yolks with salt
Vegetables	Fresh unsalted or canned low sodium pureed green beans, green peas, yellow squash, corn, carrots, beets	All other fresh, canned or strained vegetables

Food Category		Milligrams of Sodium
Beverages	26 ounces per day Similac PM 60/40 or SMA (20 calories per ounce) prepared with tap water	157

Food Category		Milligrams of Sodium
Breads		—
Cereals	6 tablepsoons per day strained cereals	19
Desserts	1 piece Zwiebach	—
Fats		—
Fruits and Fruit Juices	3 jars Strained Fruit per day 1 can Strained Fruit Juice	17
Meat, Fish, Poultry, Cheese, and Eggs	Unsalted Pureed Meat (7 oz) 1 unsalted Egg	140 66
Potatoes or Substitutes		—
Soups		—
Sweets		—
Vegetables and Vegetable Juices	Unsalted Pureed Vegetables	82
Miscellaneous		—
	Total	**481**

500 Milligram Sodium Diet (22 mEq)

Foods	Foods Allowed	Foods to Avoid
Beverages	Two cups whole, skim or chocolate milk, 1 cup low sodium milk per day**; tea, distilled water to be used for drinking and food preparation	*Coffee; buttermilk; prepared or instant milk-based beverages; carbonated beverages; tap water
Breads	Low sodium bread; low sodium crackers; low sodium melba toast; unsalted biscuits, corn-bread, muffins, all made with allowed ingredients (low sodium baking powder, low sodium milk, egg); unsalted yeast rolls	All enriched, whole grain breads; quick breads or yeast rolls prepared with salt; all other crackers; commercial bread mixes; self-rising flour
Cereals	Cooked unsalted cereals; puffed wheat, puffed rice, shredded wheat, low sodium cornflakes	Instant cereals; all other ready-to-eat cereals

* Coffee and black pepper usually are not served unless specifically requested.

** Lonolac powder prepared by Mead Johnson is a low sodium milk containing 7 milligrams of sodium per cup when reconstituted with distilled water. Use only with physician's order.

Foods	Foods Allowed	Foods to Avoid
Desserts	Low sodium gelatins; homemade unsalted puddings, pies, cakes, cookies, all made with allowed ingredients (low sodium milk, egg, low sodium baking powder)	All commercial desserts and dessert mixes; homemade desserts except specially prepared low sodium; plain unflavored gelatin
Fats	3 tablespoons unsalted butter or margarine; vegetable oils; hydrogenated shortening; unsalted salad dressings or mayonnaise	Salted butter or margarine; bacon; commercial salad dressings or mayonnaise with salt
Fruits and Fruit Juices	Fresh, frozen or canned fruit juices, apples, apricots, banana, blueberries, sweet or sour cherries, grapefruit, grapes, lemon, lime, nectarine, orange, peaches, pears, pineapple, plums, strawberries, tangerine, watermelon; frozen juices to be reconstituted with distilled water	Dried fruits processed with sodium compounds; cantaloupe; glazed fruits; fruit-flavored drinks
Meat, Fish, Poultry, Cheese, and Eggs	1 unsalted egg and 4 ounces of fresh, unsalted meat, poultry or boneless fish daily—beef, veal, lamb, pork, liver, turkey, chicken, catfish, cod, drum, flounder, haddock, halibut, ocean perch, red snapper; low sodium canned tuna or salmon; low sodium cheese	Canned, salted, smoked or processed meats, poultry or fish, chipped or corned beef, frankfurters, ham, luncheon meats, sausage, frozen fish fillets; clams, crab, lobster, oysters, scallops, shrimp; all other types of cheese
Potatoes or Substitutes	Fresh unsalted white potatoes; fresh, frozen or low sodium canned corn; unsalted macaroni, noodles, rice, spaghetti; dried beans cooked without salt; fresh sweet potatoes	Corn chips; potato chips; pretzels; other party chips; canned or frozen potato products; pork and beans
Soups	Homemade specially prepared low sodium soups or broth made from allowed ingredients	Bouillon cubes; any commercial, canned or dehydrated soups containing salt, monosodium glutamate or other sodium compounds

Foods	Foods Allowed	Foods to Avoid
Sweets	Honey; pure maple syrup; hard pure sugar candy; granulated sugar; jam or jelly not to exceed three tablespoons per day	Sweets with salt or sodium compounds added; molasses; marmalades; brown sugar; corn syrup; marshmallows
Vegetables and Vegetable Juices	Fresh, unsalted or low sodium canned asparagus, broccoli, brussel sprouts, cauliflower, onions, green pepper, lima beans, green beans, wax beans, squash, green peas, tomatoes, pumpkin, cucumber, eggplant, okra, lettuce, tomato juice	All other fresh, canned or frozen vegetables
Miscellaneous	Cocoa powder; pure herbs and spices; vinegar; unsalted popcorn; low sodium catsup; low sodium chili sauce; low sodium pickles; low sodium peanut butter; low sodium mustard; unsalted white sauce made with allowed low sodium milk; unsalted nuts (not recommended for the young child)	*Black pepper; Dutch processed chocolate; baking chocolate; baking powder; gravy; horseradish; meat tenderizers; prepared mustard; olives; pickles; relishes; seasoning salts; catsup; chili sauce; soy sauce; steak sauces; baking soda; monosodium glutamate; commercial peanut butter; salted nuts

* Coffee and black pepper usually are not served unless specifically requested.

500 Milligram Sodium Diet (22 mEq)

Food Category		Milligrams of Sodium
Beverages	2 cups Milk	240
	1 cup Low Sodium Milk	7
Breads	3 slices Low Sodium Bread	3
Cereals	1 serving Low Sodium Cereal	2
Desserts	Low Sodium Bakery Items	12
Fats	3 Tablespoons Unsalted Butter	
	Unsalted Salad Dressing	9
Fruits and Fruit Juices		10

Food Category		Milligrams of Sodium
Meat, Fish, Poultry, Cheese, and Eggs	4 ounces Unsalted Meat	100
	1 Unsalted Egg	66
Potatoes or Substitutes		10
Soups	Low Sodium Homemade with Allowed Ingredients	—
Sweets		10
Vegetables and Vegetable Juices	Low Sodium Vegetables	15
Miscellaneous		5
Distilled Water must be used for drinking and food preparation		—
	Total	**489**

Suggested Meal Pattern

Breakfast	**Lunch**	**Dinner**
Orange Juice	2 ounces Unsalted Broiled Beef Patty	2 ounces Unsalted Broiled Chicken
1 Unsalted Scrambled Egg	Baked Potato	Unsalted Buttered Rice
Unsalted Cream of Wheat	Unsalted Buttered Green Beans	Unsalted Buttered Yellow Squash
Unsalted Toast	Unsalted Bread	Unsalted Bread
Unsalted Butter	Unsalted Butter	Unsalted Butter
Sugar	Chopped Lettuce with unsalted French Dressing	Fresh Fruit Salad on Lettuce
1 tablespoon Jelly	Sliced Peaches	Unsalted Sugar Cookies
1 cup Milk	½ cup Milk	½ cup Milk
	1 tablespoon Jelly	1 tablespoon Jelly

800 Milligram Sodium Diet (35 mEq)

Food Category		Milligrams of Sodium
Beverages	2½ cups Milk	300
	8 ounces Carbonated Beverage	28
Breads	3 slices Low Sodium Bread	3
	6 unsalted Crackers	33
Cereals	1 serving Low Sodium Cereal	2

Food Category		Milligrams of Sodium
Desserts	Low Sodium Bakery Items	12
	2 Popsicles	10
	½ cup Ice Cream	42
Fats	3 Tablespoons Unsalted Butter	
	Unsalted Salad Dressing	9
Fruits and Fruit Juices		10
Meat, Fish, Poultry, Cheese, and Eggs	4 ounces unsalted Meat	100
	1 unsalted Egg	66
Potatoes or Substitutes		15
Soups	Low Sodium Homemade with allowed ingredients	—
Sweets		10
Vegetables and Vegetable Juices	Unsalted Vegetables	70
Miscellaneous		5
Tap Water	3 cups	75
	Total	**795**

800 Milligram Sodium Diet (35 mEq)

Foods	Foods Allowed	Foods to Avoid
Beverages	2½ cups whole, skim or chocolate milk; tea, eight ounces carbonated beverage	*Coffee; buttermilk; prepared or instant milk-based beverages
Breads	Low sodium bread; low sodium crackers; unsalted crackers; low sodium melba toast; unsalted biscuits, cornbread, muffins, all made with allowed ingredients (low sodium baking powder, milk, egg); unsalted yeast rolls	All enriched, whole grain breads, quick breads or yeast rolls prepared with salt; all other crackers; commercial bread mixes; self-rising flour
Cereals	Cooked unsalted cereals; puffed wheat, puffed rice, shredded wheat, low sodium cornflakes	Instant cereals; all other ready-to-eat cereals

* Coffee and black pepper usually are not served unless specifically requested.

Foods	Foods Allowed	Foods to Avoid
Desserts	Low sodium gelatins; fruit-flavored ices; popsicles; ice cream or sherbet (only ½ cup per day); homemade unsalted puddings, pies, cakes, cookies, all made with allowed ingredients (milk, egg, low sodium baking powder)	All commercial desserts and dessert mixes; homemade desserts except specially prepared low sodium
Fats	3 tablespoons unsalted butter or margarine; vegetable oils; hydrogenated shortening; unsalted salad dressings or mayonnaise	Salted butter or margarine; bacon; commercial salad dressings or mayonnaise with salt
Fruits and Fruit Juices	Fresh, frozen or canned fruit juices, apples, apricots, banana, blueberries, cantaloupe, sweet or sour cherries, grapefruit, grapes, fruit cocktail, lemon, lime, nectarine, orange, peaches, pears, pineapple, plums, strawberries, raisins (only ¼ cup per day), tangerine, watermelon; frozen juices to be reconstituted with tap water	Dried fruits processed with sodium compounds; glazed fruits and commercially prepared fruit-flavored drinks
Meat, Fish, Poultry, Cheese, and Eggs	1 unsalted egg and 4 ounces of fresh, unsalted meat, poultry or boneless fish daily—beef, veal, lamb, pork, liver, turkey, chicken, catfish, cod, drum, flounder, haddock, halibut, ocean perch; red snapper; low sodium canned tuna or salmon; low sodium cheese	Canned, salted, smoked or processed meats, poultry or fish—chipped or corned beef, frankfurters, ham, luncheon meats, sausage, frozen fish fillets; clams, crab, lobster, oysters, scallops, shrimp; all other types of cheese
Potatoes or Substitutes	Fresh unsalted white or sweet potatoes; fresh, frozen or low sodium canned corn; unsalted macaroni, noodles, rice, spaghetti; dried beans cooked without salt	Corn chips; potato chips; pretzels; other party chips; canned or frozen potato products; pork and beans

Foods	Foods Allowed	Foods to Avoid
Soups	Homemade specially prepared low sodium soups or broth made from allowed ingredients	Bouillon cubes; any commercial, canned or dehydrated soups containing salt, monosodium glutamate or other sodium compounds
Sweets	Honey; pure maple syrup; hard pure sugar candy; granulated sugar; brown sugar (only 2 tablespoons per day); jam or jelly not to exceed three tablespoons per day; marshmallows (only 2 per day)	Sweets with salt or sodium compounds added; molasses; marmalades; corn syrup
Vegetables and Vegetable Juices	Fresh, frozen, canned unsalted low sodium asparagus, broccoli, brussel sprouts, cabbage, carrots, collards, cauliflower, kale, mustard greens, turnip greens, onions, green pepper, lima beans, green beans, wax beans, squash, green peas, tomatoes, pumpkin, cucumber, eggplant, okra, lettuce, radishes, rhubarb, tomato juice; only one of the following per day: fresh, unsalted or low sodium canned spinach, celery, beets	All other fresh or canned vegetables. Also avoid frozen peas, lima beans, mixed vegetables and succotash
Miscellaneous	Cocoa powder; pure herbs and spices; vinegar; unsalted popcorn; low sodium catsup; low sodium chili sauce; low sodium pickles; low sodium peanut butter; low sodium mustard; unsalted nuts (not recommended for the young child)	*Black pepper; Dutch processed chocolate; baking powder; gravy; horseradish; meat tenderizers; prepared mustard; olives; pickles; relishes; seasoning salts; catsup; chili sauce; soy sauce; steak sauces; baking soda; monosodium glutamate, commercial peanut butter; salted nuts

* Coffee and black pepper usually are not served unless specifically requested.

Suggested Meal Pattern

Breakfast	Lunch	Dinner
Orange Juice 1 unsalted Scrambled Egg Unsalted Cream of Wheat Unsalted Toast Unsalted Butter Sugar 1 tablespoon Jelly 1 cup Milk	2 ounces Unsalted Broiled Beef Patty Baked Potato Unsalted Buttered Green Beans Unsalted Bread Chopped Lettuce with unsalted French Dressing Sliced Peaches 1 tablespoon Jelly ½ cup Milk	2 ounces Unsalted Broiled Chicken Unsalted Buttered Rice Unsalted Buttered Carrots Unsalted Bread Unsalted Butter Fresh Fruit Salad on Lettuce Unsalted Sugar Cookies 1 tablespoon Jelly 1 cup Milk

1000 Milligram Sodium Diet (44 mEq)

Food Category		Milligrams of Sodium
Beverages	3 cups Milk	360
	8 ounces Carbonated Beverage	28
Breads	3 slices Low Sodium Bread	3
	6 Unsalted Crackers	33
Cereals	1 serving Low Sodium Cereal	2
Desserts	Low Sodium Bakery Items	12
	1 cup Flavored Gelatin	92
	2 Popsicles	10
	1 cup Ice Cream	83
Fats	3 Tablespoons Unsalted Butter Unsalted Salad Dressing	9
Fruits and Fruit Juices		15
Meat, Fish, Poultry, Cheese and Eggs	4 ounces Unsalted Meat	100
	1 Unsalted Egg	66
Potatoes or Substitutes		15
Soups	Low Sodium Homemade with Allowed Ingredients	—
Sweets		10

Food Category		Milligrams of Sodium
Vegetables and Vegetable Juices	Unsalted Vegetables	70
Miscellaneous		5
Tap Water	3 cups	75
	Total	988

1000 Milligram Sodium Diet (44 mEq)

Foods	Foods Allowed	Food to Avoid
Beverages	Three cups whole, skim or chocolate milk; tea; eight ounces carbonated beverage	*Coffee; buttermilk; prepared or instant milk beverages
Breads	Low sodium bread; low sodium crackers; low sodium melba toast; unsalted biscuits, cornbread, muffins, all made with allowed ingredients (low sodium baking powder, milk, egg); unsalted yeast rolls	All enriched, whole grain breads, quick breads or yeast rolls prepared with salt; all other crackers; commercial bread mixes; self-rising flour
Cereals	Cooked unsalted cereals; puffed wheat, puffed rice, shredded wheat, low sodium cornflakes	Instant cereals; all other ready-to-eat cereals
Desserts	Fruit-flavored gelatins (only two ½ cup servings per day), unflavored gelatin; fruit-flavored ices; popsicles; ice cream or sherbet (only 1 cup per day); homemade unsalted puddings, pies, cakes, cookies all made with allowed ingredients (milk, egg, low sodium baking powder	All commercial desserts and dessert mixes; homemade desserts except specially prepared low sodium
Fats	3 tablespoons unsalted butter or margarine; vegetable oils; hydrogenated shortening; unsalted salad dressings or mayonnaise	Salted butter or margarine; bacon; commercial salad dressings or mayonnaise with salt
Fruits and Fruit Juices	Fresh, frozen or canned fruit juices, apples, apricots, banana, blueberries, cantaloupe, sweet	Dried fruits processed with sodium compounds; glazed

* Coffee and black pepper usually are not served unless specifically requested.

Foods	Foods Allowed	Foods to Avoid
	or sour cherries, grapefruit, grapes, fruit cocktail, lemon, lime, nectarine, orange, peaches, pears, pineapple, plums, strawberries, raisins (only ¼ cup per day), tangerine, watermelon; frozen juices to be reconstituted with tap water	fruits and commercially prepared fruit flavored drinks
Meat, Fish, Poultry, Cheese, and Eggs	1 unsalted egg and 4 ounces of fresh, unsalted meat, poultry or boneless fish daily—beef, veal, lamb, pork, liver, turkey, chicken, catfish, cod, drum, flounder, haddock, halibut, ocean perch, red snapper; low sodium canned tuna or salmon; low sodium cheese	Canned, salted, smoked or processed meats, poultry or fish; chipped or corned beef; frankfurters, ham, luncheon meats, sausage, frozen fish fillets; clams, crab, lobster, oysters, scallops, shrimp; all other types of cheese
Potatoes or Substitutes	Fresh unsalted white or sweet potatoes; fresh, frozen or low sodium canned corn; unsalted macaroni, noodles, rice, spaghetti; dry beans cooked without salt	Corn chips; potato chips; pretzels; other party chips; canned or frozen potato products
Soups	Homemade specially prepared low sodium soups or broth made from allowed ingredients	Bouillon cubes; any commercial, canned, or dehydrated soups containing salt, monosodium glutamate or other sodium compounds
Sweets	Honey; pure maple syrup; hard pure sugar candy; granulated sugar; brown sugar (only 2 tablespoons per day); jam or jelly not to exceed three tablespoons per day; marshmallows (only 2 per day)	Sweets with salt or sodium compounds added; molasses; marmalades; corn syrup
Vegetables and Vegetable Juices	Fresh or frozen, unsalted, low sodium asparagus, broccoli, brussel sprouts, cabbage,	All other fresh, or canned vegetables. Omit frozen peas,

Foods	Foods Allowed	Foods to Avoid
	carrots, collards, cauliflower, kale, mustard greens, turnip greens, onions, green pepper, lima beans, green beans, wax beans, squash, green peas, tomatoes, pumpkin, cucumber, eggplant, okra, lettuce, radishes, rhubarb, tomato juice; only one of the following per day: fresh, unsalted or low sodium canned spinach, celery, beets	lima beans, mixed vegetables and succotash
Miscellaneous	Cocoa powder; pure herbs and spices; vinegar; unsalted popcorn; low sodium catsup; low sodium chili sauce; low sodium pickles; low sodium peanut butter; low sodium mustard; unsalted white sauce made with allowed milk; unsalted nuts (not recommended for the young child)	*Black pepper; Dutch processed chocolate; baking chocolate; baking powder; gravy; horseradish; meat tenderizers; prepared mustard; olives; pickles; relishes; seasoning salts; catsup; chili sauce; soy sauce; steak sauces; baking soda; monosodium glutamate; commercial peanut butter; salted nuts

* Coffee and black pepper usually are not served unless specifically requested.

Suggested Meal Pattern

Breakfast	Lunch	Dinner
Orange Juice	2 ounces Unsalted Broiled Beef Patty	2 ounces Unsalted Broiled Chicken
1 Unsalted Scrambled Egg	Baked Potato	Unsalted Buttered Rice
Unsalted Cream of Wheat	Unsalted Buttered Green Beans	Unsalted Buttered Yellow Squash
Unsalted Toast	Unsalted Bread	Unsalted Bread
Unsalted Butter	Unsalted Butter	Unsalted Butter
Sugar	Chopped Lettuce with unsalted French Dressing	Fresh Fruit Salad on Lettuce
1 tablespoon Jelly	Sliced Peaches	Unsalted Sugar Cookies
1 cup Milk	1 cup Milk	1 cup Milk
	1 tablespoon Jelly	1 tablespoon Jelly

1500 Milligram Sodium Diet (65 mEq)

Food Category		Milligrams of Sodium
Beverages	3 cups Milk	360
	8 ounces Carbonated Beverage	28
Breads	3 slices Regular Bread	360
	6 unsalted crackers	33
Cereals	1 serving under 100 mgs of Sodium	100
Desserts	Low Sodium Bakery Items	12
	1 cup Flavored Gelatin	92
	2 Popsicles	10
	1 cup Ice Cream	83
Fats	3 Tablespoons Unsalted Butter	
	Unsalted Salad Dressing	9
Fruits and Fruit Juices		15
Meat, Fish, Poultry, Cheese, and Eggs	4 ounces Unsalted Meat	100
	1 Unsalted Egg	66
Potatoes or Substitutes		15
Soups	Low Sodium Homemade with Allowed Ingredients	—
Sweets		10
Vegetables and Vegetable Juices	Unsalted Vegetables	70
Miscellaneous		5
Tap Water	3 cups	75
		50*
	Total	1493

* 1 teaspoon regular baking powder in quick breads and desserts increases the sodium value 35-50 milligrams per serving.

1500 Milligram Sodium Diet (65 mEq)

Foods	Foods Allowed	Foods to Avoid
Beverages	Three cups whole, skim or chocolate milk; tea; eight ounces carbonated beverage	*Coffee; buttermilk; prepared or instant milk beverages

* Coffee and black pepper usually are not served unless specifically requested.

Foods	Foods Allowed	Foods to Avoid
Breads	Three slices regular bread; low sodium bread, low sodium crackers; low sodium melba toast; unsalted biscuits, cornbread, muffins, all made with allowed ingredients (regular baking powder, milk, egg); unsalted yeast rolls	All enriched, whole grain breads made with salt, in excess of allowed amounts; quick breads or yeast rolls prepared with salt; all other crackers; commercial bread mixes, self-rising flour
Cereals	Cooked unsalted cereals; puffed wheat, puffed rice, shredded wheat, sugar pops, froot loops, sugar smacks, apple jacks, low sodium cornflakes	Instant cereals; all other ready-to-eat cereals
Desserts	Fruit-flavored gelatins (only two ½ cup servings per day), unflavored gelatin; fruit-flavored ices; popsicles; ice cream or sherbet (only 1 cup per day); homemade unsalted puddings, pies, cakes, cookies all made with allowed ingredients (milk, egg, regular baking powder)	All commercial desserts and dessert mixes; homemade desserts except specially prepared without salt
Fats	3 tablespoons unsalted butter or margarine; vegetable oils; hydrogenated shortening; unsalted salad dressings or mayonnaise	Salted butter or margarine; bacon; commercial salad dressings or mayonnaise with salt
Fruits and Fruit Juices	Fresh, frozen or canned fruit juices, apples, apricots, banana, blueberries, cantaloupe, sweet or sour cherries, grapefruit, grapes, fruit cocktail, lemon, lime, nectarine, orange, peaches, pears, pineapple, plums, strawberries, raisins (only ¼ cup per day), tangerine, watermelon; frozen juices to be reconstituted with tap water	Dried fruits processed with sodium compounds; glazed fruits and commercially prepared fruit-flavored drinks
Miscellaneous	Cocoa powder; pure herbs and spices; vinegar; unsalted popcorn; low sodium catsup;	*Black pepper; Dutch processed chocolate; baking chocolate;

* Coffee and black pepper usually are not served unless specifically requested.

Foods	Foods Allowed	Foods to Avoid
	low sodium chili sauce; low sodium pickles; low sodium peanut butter; low sodium mustard; unsalted white sauce made with allowed milk; unsalted nuts (not recommended for the young child) ; regular baking powder	baking soda; gravy; horseradish; meat tenderizers; prepared mustard; olives; pickles; relishes; seasoning salts; catsup; chili sauce; soy sauce; steak sauces; monosodium glutamate; commercial peanut butter; salted nuts
Meat, Fish, Poultry, Cheese, and Eggs	1 unsalted egg and 4 ounces of fresh, unsalted meat, poultry or boneless fish daily—beef, veal, lamb, pork, liver, turkey, chicken, catfish, cod, drum, flounder, haddock, halibut, ocean perch, red snapper; low sodium canned tuna or salmon; low sodium cheese	Canned, salted, smoked or processed meats, poultry or fish—chipped or corned beef, frankfurters, ham, luncheon meats, sausage, frozen fish fillets; clams, crab, lobster, oysters, scallops, shrimp; all other types of cheese
Potatoes or Substitutes	Fresh unsalted white or sweet potatoes; fresh, frozen or low sodium canned corn; unsalted macaroni, noodles, rice, spaghetti; dry beans cooked without salt	Corn chips; potato chips; pretzels; other party chips; canned or frozen potato products; pork and beans
Soups	Homemade specially prepared low sodium soups or broth made from allowed ingredients	Bouillon cubes; any commercial, canned or dehydrated soups containing salt, monosodium glutamate or other sodium compounds
Sweets	Honey; pure maple syrup; hard pure sugar candy; granulated sugar; brown sugar (only 2 tablespoons per day) ; jam or jelly not to exceed three tablespoons per day; marshmallows (only 2 per day)	Sweets with salt or sodium compounds added; molasses; marmalade; corn syrup

Foods	Foods Allowed	Foods to Avoid
Vegetables and Vegetable Juices	Fresh, frozen, unsalted or canned low sodium asparagus, broccoli, brussel sprouts, cabbage, carrots, collards, cauliflower, kale, mustard greens, turnip greens, onions, green pepper, lima beans, green beans, wax beans, squash, green peas, tomatoes, pumpkin, cucumber, eggplant, okra, lettuce, radishes, rhubarb, tomato juice; only one of the following per day: fresh, unsalted or low sodium canned spinach, celery, beets	All other fresh or canned vegetables. Omit frozen peas, lima beans, mixed vegetables and succotash.

Suggested Meal Pattern

Breakfast	Lunch	Dinner
Orange Juice	2 ounces Unsalted Broiled Beef Patty	2 ounces Unsalted Broiled Chicken
1 unsalted Scrambled Egg	Baked Potato	Unsalted Buttered Rice
1 cup Sugar Pops	Unsalted Buttered Green Beans	Unsalted Buttered Carrots
1 slice Regular Bread	1 slice Regular Bread	1 slice Regular Bread
Unsalted Butter	Unsalted Butter	Unsalted Butter
Sugar	Chopped Lettuce with unsalted French Dressing	Fresh Fruit Salad on Lettuce
1 tablespoon Jelly	Sliced Peaches	Unsalted Sugar Cookies
1 cup Milk	1 tablespoon Jelly	1 tablespoon Jelly
	1 cup Milk	1 cup Milk

2000 Milligram Sodium Diet (87 mEq)

Food Category		Milligrams of Sodium
Beverages	2 cups Milk	240
	8 ounces Carbonated Beverage	28
Breads	3 slices Regular Bread	360
Cereals	1 serving under 100 mgs of Sodium	100
Desserts	Low Sodium Bakery Items	12
	1 cup Flavored Gelatin	92
	2 Popsicles	10
	1 cup Ice Cream	83

Food Category		Milligrams of Sodium
Fats	3 Tablespoons Unsalted Butter Unsalted Salad Dressing	9
Fruits and Fruit Juices		15
Meat, Fish, Poultry, Cheese, and Eggs	4 ounces Unsalted Meat 1 unsalted Egg	100 66
Potatoes or Substitutes	½ cup lightly salted during food preparation	200
Soups	Low Sodium Homemade with Allowed Ingredients	—
Sweets		10
Vegetables and Vegetable Juices	2 servings salted vegetables	550
Miscellaneous		5
Tap Water	3 cups	75
		50*
	Total	**2005**

* 1 teaspoon regular baking powder in quick breads and desserts increases the sodium value 35-50 milligrams per serving.

2000 Milligram Sodium Diet (87 mEq)

Foods	Foods Allowed	Foods to Avoid
Beverages	Two cups whole, skim or chocolate milk; tea; eight ounce carbonated beverage	*Coffee; buttermilk; prepared or instant milk-based beverages
Breads	Three slices regular bread; low sodium bread; low sodium crackers; low sodium melba toast; unsalted biscuits, cornbread, muffins, all made with allowed ingredients (regular baking powder, milk, egg); unsalted yeast rolls	All enriched, whole grain breads made with salt, in excess of allowed amounts; quick breads or yeast rolls prepared with salt; all other crackers; commercial bread mixes; self-rising flour
Cereals	Cooked, unsalted cereals; puffed wheat, puffed rice, shredded wheat, sugar pops, froot loops, sugar smacks, apple jacks, low sodium cornflakes	Instant cereals; all other ready-to-eat cereals.

* Coffee and black pepper usually are not served unless specifically requested.

Foods	Foods Allowed	Foods to Avoid
Desserts	Allow one regular and one simple dessert/day Fruit-flavored gelatins (only two ½ cup servings per day), unflavored gelatin; fruit-flavored ices; popsicles; ice cream or sherbet (only 1 cup per day); homemade unsalted puddings, pies, cakes, cookies, all made with allowed ingredients (milk, egg, regular baking powder)	All commercial desserts and dessert mixes; homemade desserts except specially prepared without salt
Fats	3 tablespoons unsalted butter or margarine; vegetable oils, hydrogenated shortening; unsalted salad dressings or mayonnaise	Salted butter or margarine; bacon; commercial salad dressings or mayonnaise with salt
Fruits and Fruit Juices	Fresh, frozen or canned fruit juices, apples, apricots, banana, blueberries, cantaloupe, sweet or sour cherries, grapefruit, grapes, fruit cocktail, lemon, lime, nectarine, orange, peaches, pears, pineapple, plums, strawberries, raisins (only ¼ cup per day), tangarine, watermelon; frozen juices to be reconstituted with tap water	Dried fruits processed with sodium compounds; glazed fruits and commercially prepared fruit-flavored drinks
Meat, Fish, Poultry, Cheese, and Eggs	1 unsalted egg and 4 ounces of fresh, unsalted meat, poultry or boneless fish daily—beef, veal, lamb, pork, liver, turkey, chicken, catfish, cod, drum, flounder, haddock, halibut, ocean perch, red snapper; low sodium canned tuna or slamon; low sodium cheese	Canned, salted, smoked or processed meats, poultry or fish, chipped or corned beef, frankfurters, ham, luncheon meats, sausage, frozen fish fillets; clams, crab, lobster, oysters, scallops, shrimp; all other types of cheese
Potatoes or Substitutes	Only ½ cup per day of lightly salted (do not add salt at table) potatoes, corn, macaroni, noodles, rice, spaghetti, or cooked dried beans; servings in excess of ½ cup must be unsalted	Corn chips; potato chips; pretzels; other party chips; canned or frozen potato products; pork and beans

Foods	Foods Allowed	Foods to Avoid
Soups	Homemade specially prepared low sodium soups or broth made from allowed ingredients	Bouillon cubes; any commercial, canned or dehydrated soups containing salt, monosodium glutamate or other sodium compounds
Sweets	Honey; pure maple syrup; hard pure sugar candy; granulated sugar; brown sugar (only 2 tablespoons per day); jam or jelly not to exceed three tablespoons per day; marshmallows (only 2 per day)	Sweets with salt or sodium compounds added; molasses; marmalades; corn syrup
Vegetables and Vegetable Juices	Fresh (may be lightly salted during food preparation), frozen or canned asparagus, broccoli, brussel sprouts, cabbage, carrots, collards, cauliflower, kale, mustard greens, turnip greens, onions, green pepper, lima beans, green beans, wax beans, squash, green peas, tomatoes, pumpkin, cucumber, eggplant, okra, lettuce, radishes, rhubarb, spinach celery, beets, tomato juice	Sauerkraut; all other fresh, canned or frozen vegetables.
Miscellaneous	Cocoa powder; pure herbs and spices; vinegar; unsalted popcorn; low sodium catsup; low sodium chili sauce; low sodium pickles; low sodium peanut butter; low sodium mustard; unsalted white sauce made with allowed milk; unsalted nuts (not recommended for the young child)	*Black pepper; Dutch processed chocolate; baking chocolate; baking powder; gravy; horseradish; meat tenderizers; prepared mustard; olives; pickles relishes; seasoning salts; catsup; chili sauce; soy sauce; steak sauces; baking soda; monosodium glutamate; commercial peanut butter; salted nuts

* Coffee and black pepper usually are not served unless specifically requested.

Suggested Meal Pattern

Breakfast	**Lunch**	**Dinner**
Orange Juice	2 ounces Unsalted Broiled Beef Patty	2 ounces Unsalted Broiled Chicken
1 Unsalted Scrambled Egg	Baked Potato	½ cup Buttered Rice
1 cup Sugar Pops	Buttered Green Beans	Buttered Carrots
1 slice Regular Bread	Unsalted Bread	1 slice Regular Bread
Unsalted Butter	Unsalted Butter	Unsalted Butter
Sugar	Chopped Lettuce with unsalted French Drsg.	Fresh Fruit Salad on Lettuce
1 tablespoon Jelly	Sliced Peaches	Unsalted Sugar Cookies
1 cup Milk	1 cup Milk	1 cup Milk
	1 tablespoon Jelly	1 tablespoon Jelly

Information on Sodium Chloride—Conversion of Milliequivalents and Milligrams

Sodium Chloride
1 gram – molecule = 58.5 grams
Sodium 23 grams (one gram-atom)
Chloride 35.5 grams (one gram-atom)
Sodium Chloride in grams × 0.393 = grams sodium

Valence: Na = 1 Cl = 1
1 mEq. of sodium = 23 mg

$$\frac{\text{Weight of sodium in mg} \times \text{valence}}{23} = \text{mEq of sodium}$$

Sodium

1	mg	=	0.04 mEq
10	mg	=	0.44 mEq
100	mg	=	4.35 mEq
1000	mg	=	43.50 mEq
1	mEq	=	23 mg
10	mEq	=	230 mg
100	mEq	=	2300 mg

1 gram NaCl = 17.1 mEq of Na (400 mg) or Cl (600 mg)

$$10 \text{ grams NaCl} = \frac{10{,}000}{58.5} = 171 \text{ mEq of Na (400 mg) or CL (600 mg)}$$

1 level tsp. NaCl = 2300 mg Na
1 level tsp. Baking Soda = 1000 mg Na
1 level tsp. Regular Baking Powder = 370 mg Na

Potassium-Restricted Diet

Potassium is widely distributed in both animal and plant foods. Meat, leafy dark-green vegetables, whole grain cereals and breads and fruits are especially rich sources. The normal diet provides approximately 3 to 8 grams (77-205 mEq) of potassium daily, varying directly with caloric

Table XXIII

Average Daily Water and Electrolyte Losses per 100 Kilocalories Metabolized

	Usual			Range		
	H_2O ml	Na mEq	K mEq	H_2O ml	Na mEq	K mEq
Lungs	15	0	0	10—60	0	0
Skin	40	0.1	0.2	20—100	0.1— 3.0	0.2— 1.5
Stool	5	0.1	0.2	0—50	0.1— 4.0	0.2— 3.0
Urine	65	3.0	2.0	0—400	0.2—30	0.4—30
Total	125	3.2	2.4	30—610	0.4—37	0.8—34.5

intake. A diet restricted in potassium will automatically be low in protein; the sodium content will be low unless added during preparation. Water soluble vitamins will likely be low. Since potassium salts are water soluble, cooking water and that used in canning of both vegetables and fruits should not be consumed.

Protein is restricted to a level that will just be sufficient to prevent tissue catabolism—approximately 0.2-0.5 gm per kilogram in the adult. For infants, the protein allowances are based on the amount provided by the quantity of milk required to ensure a satisfactory rate of growth. This is estimated to be a 2-2.4 gm/Kg/day by the sixth month.[20] The maintenance protein requirement for children and adults is 20 mg of ideal protein (N $\times$ 6.25) per basal kcal. Sufficient carbohydrate and fat should be provided to spare the protein and prevent added solute load on the kidney as urea and potassium. The optimal "protein sparing" amount of carbohydrate is 60-75 gm/M^2/day of glucose. Sodium content is restricted to a minimum with none added. Fluid balance is carefully monitored. Total fluid intake is usually in the range of 500 to 1000 ml daily for the adult.

The infant expends about 100 kcal per kg body weight while the adult requires approximately 38 kcal/kg. Normal individuals of all ages require 100-150 ml of water for maintenance needs per 100 kcal metabolized. Losses are likewise accounted for—approximately 800 ml. daily in insensible perspiration; 50-150 ml in feces; measured amounts lost through vomiting, diarrhea, excessive perspiration and urinary loss in the adult patient. See Table XXIII.

Mitchell and Smith[21] have arranged food groups similar to the diabetic exchange lists to be used in planning diets restricted in potassium, sodium and protein. Each group contains foods of approximately similar amounts of potassium and protein.

20. *Food and Agricultural Organization/World Health Organization, 1973;* Food and Nutrition Board, in press.
21. Mitchell, Mary C. and Edwin J. Smith; "Dietary Care of the Patient with Chronic Oliguria," *American Journal Clinical Nutrition, 19*:163-169; 1966.

Michelson et al in a survey of teen-age and adult groups in various cities found an average intake of potassium of 4.6 gms (118 mEq) per day (1.5-7.7 gms) representing a dietary gram-atomic Na:k ratio of about 1.53.[22]

High values may be considered to represent abnormal losses. Endogenous water produced by oxidation of carbohydrate, protein and fat amounts to about 5-15 ml.

Infants and Children

Healthy infants consume fluid equivalent to 10-15 per cent of their weight per day while the adult consumes only 2-4 per cent of their body weight daily.

Approximately 0.5-3 per cent of the fluid intake is retained by children depending upon the rate of growth.

Approximate losses are estimated as:

Kidney	Somewhat less than 50%
Intestinal tract	3-10%
Lungs and Skin	40-50%

Only 1% of the filtrate of the kidneys enters the bladder.

Protein Diets
20 Grams

	Serving Quantity	Grams Protein
High Biological Value Protein Foods		
A. Egg, medium	1	6
B. Milk	½ cup	4
Starches		
A. 1.0 gram Protein	1	1
B. 2.0 gram Protein	2	4
Vegetables		
A. 0.5 grams Protein	2	1
B. 1.0 grams Protein	1	1
Fruits		
A. 0.5 grams Protein	4	2
B. 1.0 grams Protein	1	1
Free Foods	—	—
Total		20

22. Michelson, J., J. C. Thompson, Jr., B. W. Hess and C. L. Comas; "Radioactivity in Total Diet," *Journal of Nutrition, 78*:371-383; 1962.

40 Grams

	Serving Quantity	Grams Protein
High Biological Value Protein Foods		
A. Egg	1	6
B. Milk	1 cup	8
C. Meat	2 oz.	16
Starches		
A. 1.0 grams Protein	1	1
B. 2.0 grams Protein	2	4
Vegetables		
A. 0.5 grams Protein	2	1
B. 1.0 grams Protein	1	1
Fruits		
A. 0.5 grams Protein	4	2
B. 1.0 grams Protein	1	1
Free Foods	—	—
Total		40

60 Grams

	Serving Quantity	Grams Protein
High Biological Value Protein Foods		
A. Egg	1	6
B. Milk	1 cup	8
C. Meats	4 oz.	32
Starches		
A. 1.0 grams Protein	1	1
B. 2.0 grams Protein	4	8
Vegetables		
A. 0.5 grams Protein	2	1
B. 1.0 grams Protein	2	2
Fruits		
A. 0.5 grams Protein	4	2
B. 1.0 grams Protein	1	1
Total		61

80 Grams

	Serving Quantity	Grams Protein
High Biological Value Protein Foods		
A. Egg	1	6
B. Milk	1½	12
C. Meats	6	48
Starches		
A. 1.0 grams Protein	1	1
B. 2.0 grams Protein	4	8
Vegetables		
A. 0.5 grams Protein	2	1
B. 1.0 grams Protein	2	2
Fruits		
A. 0.5 grams Protein	3	1.5
B. 1.0 grams Protein	1	1
Free Foods	—	—
Total		80.5

Exchange Lists for Protein Restricted Diets

High Biological Value Protein Foods

	Amt.	Pro.	K+	Na+	Cal
Eggs—6 grams Protein					
Egg, chicken, whole	1 medium	6.2	62	59*	78
Milk—8 grams Protein					
Homogenized Milk	1 cup	8.5	352	122	159
Chocolate Milk	1 cup	7.3	**	102	205
Half & Half	1 cup	7.6	310	110	322
Meats—8 grams Protein					
Cheese:					
Cheddar	1 oz	7.0	23	197	112
American, processed	1 oz	6.5	22	318	107
Cottage, Creamed	¼ cup	7.6	48	128	60
Beef, med. fat	1 oz	7.3	127	13*	74
Lamb, med. fat	1 oz	6.2	111	18*	73
Pork	1 oz	7.0	64	9*	94
Veal	1 oz	8.1	150	17*	83
Chicken, Turkey	1 oz	9.5	110	39*	57
Fish, fresh	1 oz	7.6	164	42*	50
Liver, calf	1 oz	6.7	123	37*	62
Tunafish, packed in water	¼ cup	8.4	84	12*	38

Starches—Group A, 1 gram Protein

	Amt.	Pro.	K+	Na+	Cal
Grapenut Flakes	¼ cup	.9	**	**	37
40% Bran Flakes	¼ cup	1.0	46	47	23
Special K	¼ cup	1.2	8	56	21
Raisin Bran	¼ cup	1.1	73	48	33
Shredded Wheat Miniature	¼ cup	1.2	17	trace	35
Pep	¼ cup	.9	19	61	34
Rice Krispies	½ cup	1.0	14	131	54
Puffed Wheat	½ cup	.8	0	trace	22
Product 19	½ cup	1.3	3	135	54
Sugar Smacks	½ cup	.9	11	11	56
Froot Loops	⅔ cup	.9	11	43	77
Corn Flakes	⅔ cup	1.1	16	134	53
Sugar Frosted Flakes	⅔ cup	1.2	17	151	96
Sugar Pops	⅔ cup	.9	15	45	72
Cocoa Krispies	⅔ cup	.9	22	148	99
Apple Jacks	⅔ cup	.8	13	45	72
Puffed Rice	1 cup	.8	0	trace	51
Puffa Puffa Rice	1 cup	1.0	23	25	120

* no salt added during preparation
** no value listed

	Amt.	Pro	K+	Na+	Cal
Starches—Group B, 2 gram Protein					
Bread, White	1 slice	2.0	20	118	62
Bread, Raisin	1 slice	1.5	54	84	60
Doughnut (Cake Type—Plain)	1 med	1.5	29	160	125
Doughnut (yeast type)	1 med	1.9	24	70	124
Tortilla (Corn)	1 (6″ diam)	1.5	**	215	63
Noodles, Egg (cooked, enriched)	⅓ cup	2.2	23	1*	67
Macaroni (cooked, enriched)	⅓ cup	1.6	28	trace*	50
Spaghetti (cooked, enriched)	⅓ cup	1.7	31	trace*	55
Oatmeal, cooked	⅓ cup	1.8	43	trace*	49
Cream of Wheat (regular, cooked)	½ cup	2.3	**	trace*	67
Malt-O-Meal (cooked)	½ cup	2.1	11	trace*	67
Farina, (cooked, enriched)	½ cup	1.9	**	1*	70
Rice, white milled	⅔ cup	2.0	28	trace*	110
Potato, white	1 med	2.1	407	3*	76
Baked or boiled in skin		2.1	407	3*	76
French Fried (½″ × ½″ × 2″)	10 pcs	2.1	427	3*	137
Mashed w/milk & margarine	½ cup	2.1	250	331	94
Potato, sweet Baked in skin	1 med	2.1	300	12*	141
Lima Beans (canned)	3 T	2.3	96	102	41
Brussels Sprouts (raw, cooked)	⅓ cup	2.1	137	5	18
Broccoli (raw/cooked)	½ cup	2.3	200	8	20
Corn (canned, kernels, drained solids)	½ cup	2.2	81	196	70
(raw/cooked kernels on cob)	1 ear (2″)	1.7	98	trace	50
Green Peas (canned)	⅓ cup	2.0	48	118	33
Spinach (raw, cooked)	⅓ cup	1.8	198	31*	14
(canned)	⅓ cup	1.6	154	144	15
(frozen, chopped, cooked)	⅓ cup	2.0	226	35*	16

* no salt added during preparation
** no value listed

Vegetables

These vegetables may be fresh, frozen or canned. If there is a sodium restriction, the canned vegetables should be "dietetic" or "canned without salt".

Vegetables—Group A, 0.5 grams Protein

	Amt.	Pro	K+	Na+	Cal
Carrots	1 small, raw	.6	171	24*	11
	⅓ cup, raw/cooked	.5	111	17*	15
	⅓ cup canned	.4	60	118	15
Cucumber	½ medium	.5	80	3*	8
Lettuce, Iceberg raw, chopped	1 cup	.5	106	4*	6
Pepper, green, raw	½ shell	.6	107	7*	11
Pickles: Dill	1 large	.7	200	1428	11
Sweet	1 small	.7	*	*	146
Radishes	5 small	.5	161	9*	9
Sauerkraut (canned)	⅓ cup	.5	70	374	9
Turnips (raw, cooked)	⅓ cup	.4	94	17*	12

Vegetables—Group B, 1.0 grams

	Amt.	Pro	K+	Na+	Cal
Asparagus, canned	3 med spears	1.1	96	136	11
Beans, Snap, green raw/cooked	½ cup	1.0	95	3*	16
canned	½ cup	.9	55	148	15
Beans, wax, yellow canned	⅓ cup	.9	63	156	16
Beets, canned	½ cup	.8	138	196	31
Cabbage, raw	⅔ cup	.9	156	13*	16
raw/cooked	⅓ cup	.8	126	11*	15
Cauliflower, raw	⅓ cup	.9	98	4*	9
raw/cooked	⅓ cup	.9	80	4*	9
Eggplant, raw cooked	½ cup	1.0	150	1*	19
Okra, raw, cooked	4 pods, 3″	1.0	87	1*	15
Onions, raw/cooked	½ cup	1.2	110	7*	29
Squash, summer raw/cooked	½ cup	.9	141	1*	14
frozen/cooked	⅓ cup	1.0	114	2*	14
Squash, winter raw/baked	¼ cup	.9	231	1*	32
boiled/mashed	⅓ cup	.9	219	1*	32
frozen/cooked	⅓ cup	.8	141	1*	26
Tomatoes, fresh	1 small	1.1	244	3*	22
canned	½ cup	1.0	217	130	21
juice	½ cup	.9	227	200	19

* no salt added during preparation

Fruits—Group A, 0.5 Protein

	Amt.	Pro	K+	Na+	Cal
Apple, raw	1 large	.5	253	2	133
Blueberries, raw	½ cup	.5	57	1	44
canned/heavy syrup	½ cup	.5	66	1	121
frozen sweetened	⅔ cup	.6	66	1	105
Cantaloupe, raw, diced	⅓ cup	.5	205	10	24
Cherries, sweet, raw	6 large	.5	76	1	28
Figs, raw	1 large	.6	97	1	40
canned/heavy syrup	3 med + 2T syrup	.5	149	2	84
Fruit Cocktail canned/heavy syrup	½ cup	.4	161	5	76
Grapefruit, raw	½ med (4″ diam)	.5	135	1	41
canned in syrup	½ cup	.6	135	1	70
Grapes, seedless Thompson & Tokay	½ cup	.5	139	3	54
Mango, raw	½ med	.7	189	7	66
Nectarines, raw	2 med	.6	294	6	64
Papaya, raw	⅓ med or ⅓ cup	.5	199	3	33
Peach, raw	1 med	.6	202	1	38
raw, sliced	½ cup	.5	170	1	32
canned/heavy syrup	2 med halves + 2T syrup	.4	130	2	78
frozen, sliced, sweetened	½ cup	.5	155	2	110
Pear, raw	½ (3″ x 2½″)	.7	130	2	61
Pineapple raw, diced	¾ cup	.4	146	1	52
canned, juice pack	1 large slice	.4	147	1	58
frozen chunks, sweetened	½ cup	.5	133	2	113
Plums, purple, canned, heavy syrup	3 med + 2T syrup	.5	189	1	111
Raisins, seedless	2T	.6	152	6	58
Strawberries, raw	½ cup	.5	123	1	28
frozen, sliced, sugar added	½ cup	.6	143	1	140
Tangerine, raw	1 small	.4	63	1	23
Watermelon raw, balls, cubes	½ cup	.5	100	1	26

	Amt.	Pro	K+	Na+	Cal
Juices					
Apricot Nectar	½ cup	.4	186	1	70
Grapefruit Juice					
canned, unsweetened	⅓ cup	.5	122	3	26
canned, sugar added	⅓ cup	.5	115	1	60
Pear Nectar	⅔ cup	.5	65	1	87
Pineapple Juice, canned	½ cup	.5	186	1	69
Prune Juice, canned	½ cup	.5	294	3	96
Tomato Juice, canned	¼ cup	.6	142	125	12
Fruits—Group B,	**1.0 Gram Protein**				
Apricots, raw	2-3 med	1.0	281	1	51
canned, hvy syrup	5 med halves	1.0	390	2	143
Avocado, raw, peeled	¼ (¾" x 4")	1.1	302	2	84
raw, cubed	⅓ cup	1.1	307	2	85
Banana, raw, peeled	1 small (6")	1.1	370	1	85
Blackberries, raw	⅔ cup	1.1	164	1	56
canned/hvy syrup	½ cup	1.0	137	1	114
frozen, not sweetened	½ cup	.9	115	1	36
Dates, dried, pitted, cut	¼ cup	1.0	288	1	122
Honeydew Melon, raw	2" wedge (6½")	1.2	377	18	49
Orange, raw	1 small (2½")	1.0	200	1	49
segments	½ cup	1.0	194	1	47
Plums, prune, raw	4 medium	1.1	227	1	100
Prunes, dried, cooked (no sugar)	5 med + 2T juice	1.0	327	4	119
Raspberries, red, raw	⅔ cup	1.1	150	1	51
frozen, sugar added	⅔ cup	1.1	165	1	162
Juice					
Orange Juice					
frozen, diluted	½ cup	.9	233	1	56
fresh	½ cup	.8	208	1	56

Low Protein Free Foods—0.2 gram Protein or less

	Amt.	K	Na	Cal
Beverages:				
Apple Cider, sweet	1 cup	249	10	124
Apple Juice	¾ cup	187	2	87
Carbonated Beverage	1 cup	**	**	104
Cranberry Juice	1 cup	15	3	165
Grape Juice, bottled	⅓ cup	99	1	56
Frozen, diluted	⅓ cup	29	1	45
Koolaide, sweetened	1 cup	20	24	80
Lemonade, frozen, diluted	½ cup	20	trace	55
Limeade, frozen, diluted	1 cup	33	trace	103
Peach Nectar	⅓ cup	66	1	41
Fats:				
Butter, Margarine	1 teaspoon	1	49	36
Salt Free Margarine	1 teaspoon	1	0	36
Vegetable Oil	1 tablespoon	0	0	124
Vegetable Shortening	1 tablespoon	0	0	123
Bacon Fat	1 tablespoon	**	**	126
Mayonnaise	1 tablespoon	5	84	101
French Dressing	1 tablespoon	11	192	57
Italian Dressing	1 tablespoon	2	293	77
Thousand Island Dressing	1 tablespoon	16	98	70
Sweets				
Sugar, white	1 tablespoon	0	0	48
Sugar, brown	1 tablespoon	35	4	56
Sugar, powdered	1 tablespoon	0	0	42
Corn Syrup	1 tablespoon	**	**	57
Honey	1 tablespoon	**	**	64
Chocolate flavored Syrup	1 teaspoon	13	4	16
Maple Syrup	1 tablespoon	26	3	50
Molasses, light	1 tablespoon	300	16	50
Apple Butter	1 tablespoon	**	**	37
Jams, assorted	1 tablespoon	**	**	55
Jellies, assorted	1 tablespoon	**	**	50
Marmalade, Orange	1 tablespoon	9	4	56
Gum drops	8 small	**	**	33
Jelly Beans	10	**	**	66
Lollipop (2¼″ diam)	1 med	**	**	108
Marshmallow, plain	1 large (60 to 1 lb)	1	4	25
Miscellaneous				
Applesauce	⅓ cup	78	2	41
Celery	2 small inner stalks	68	25	3

* no salt added during preparation
** no value listed

	Amt.	K	Na	Cal
Cherries, Maraschino	6	**	**	58
Cranberry Sauce	1 tablespoon	6	1	29
Onion, fresh, chopped	1 tablespoon	16	1	4
Pears, canned in heavy syrup	2 small halves + 2T syrup	84	1	76
Popsicle	1	**	**	95
Tomato Catsup	2 teaspoon	42	119	12

Note: The following items can be used to increase calories and/or food palatability:
Cal Power, Controlyte, Polycose, low protein bread, low protein rusk, low protein pasta, low protein cookies, vinegar, cornstarch, wheat starch, dry tapioca granules.

Renal Solute Load

Renal solute load refers to the metabolic wastes that are dissolved in the urine. These solutes are largely nitrogenous end-products in the form of urea and electrolytes. They derive endogenously from catabolism (both normal and abnormal) and from dietary sources.

In estimating the renal solute load, it is assumed that all dietary protein is excreted as urea (1 gram dietary protein yielding approximately 5.7 mosmol urea). Nitrogen is calculated by dividing the protein by 6.25. Each mole of urea contains two atoms of nitrogen (atomic weight 14). It is further assumed that all of the sodium, potassium and chloride are excreted; these ions plus urea represent some 75-80% of renal solute load in infants. While milk is consumed in large proportions at this age and furnishes substantial amounts of calcium, very little calcium is excreted and thus is not included in the calculation. Similarly, while phosphorus accounts for about one tenth of the renal solute load from milk, other sources are quite small and thus it is not used in the estimation. These discrepancies are more or less balanced or offset by the amounts of sodium, potassium, chloride and nitrogen used for tissue growth and excretory losses. Other minerals, creatinine, ammonia or bicarbonate are not used in the calculations.

During the first two weeks of life, newborns may be capable of urinary concentration of approximately 700 mosmol/liter only; thereafter this figure rises to 1000 mosmol/liter or more. With severe renal impairment, this may be 300 mosmol/liter or less.

Normal, healthy infants with adequate intake of water and the usual intake of appropriate nutrients have no problem with excessive renal solute load. It can become significant in the face of renal impairment or gross deviation in intake or output of fluids or solids.

Calculation of Approximate Renal Solute Load[23]

23. Fomon, Samuel J., *Infant Nutrition,* W. B. Saunders Co., 1967.

* no salt added during preparation
** no value listed

$$\text{Urea (mosmol)} = \text{nitrogen (mg)} \times \frac{1 \text{ mosmol}}{28 \text{ mg nitrogen*}}$$

Sodium	1 mosmol = 1 meq = 23 mg		
Chloride	1 mosmol = 1 meq = 35 mg		
Potassium	1 mosmol = 1 meq = 39 mg		

* Two nitrogen atoms (atomic weight 14)

	Atomic Weight
Sodium	22.99
Potassium	39.10
Chloride	35.457
Calcium	40.08
Phosphorus	30.975
Magnesium	24.32

Example

Human Milk

Protein 12 Gms./liter

12 × 5.7 (mosmol urea/gm) = 68.4 mosmol urea

Sodium 7.0 mEq/liter)

Potassium 14.0 mEq/liter) × Valence (1)

Chloride 12.0 mEq/liter)

33.0

68.4 + 33.0 = 101.4 mosmol/liter

Acid Ash and Alkaline Ash Diets

Acidity or alkalinity of foods refers not to their native state but rather to the potential reaction they ultimately will yield after being oxidized in vivo. Acid ash residue is defined as the preponderance in a food of inorganic (fixed) acid radicals, chiefly chloride, sulfate and phosphate, which form acid ions (anions) in the body. The value is computed and expressed as the amount of 0.1 (tenth-normal) alkali which would be required for neutralization. The alkaline ash residue is similarly titrated with the amount of 0.1 N acid for neutralization and measures the inorganic constituents forming cations or basic ions in the body—sodium, potassium, calcium and magnesium.

An acid-forming diet is one in which the total anion-forming ash content of the foods eaten is equivalent to 10-20 ml. of 0.1 N acid in excess of the total cation-forming ash. In the normal diet allowing milk, vegetables and fruit, this would be equivalent to 30-35 ml. of 0.1 N alkali. For the alkali-forming diet, these figures would be 20 ml. and 25 ml. or less, respectively. Allowances for protein, minerals and vitamins should remain at normal levels.

Most proteins (meat, fish, poultry, eggs and cereals), when oxidized in the body, result in an acidic residue (phosphate, sulfate, chloride). Most fruits and vegetables contain organic acid radicals (malate, citrate) that may be oxidized completely to carbon dioxide and water or stored as glycogen or fat, leaving an alkaline residue (sodium, potassium). There are some organic acids that, not being so oxidized are acidic (benzoic, quinic). Benzoic acid and quinic acids are converted to hippuric acid and tetrahydroxy hippuric acid, respectively, in the liver; being eliminated as such, they lower the pH of the urine. Thus, cranberries, plums and prunes contribute an acid-ash residue.[24] Cranberries or cranberry juice, because of the vitamin C content, may be substituted for citrus fruit or tomatoes, both of which produce an alkaline-ash residue.

Milk, even though rich in protein, because of its high calcium content results in a basic residue. Molasses is strongly basic.

Fats, oils, refined sugars, cornstarch and tapioca contribute neither anions or cations.

The usual American mixed diet provides a good balance of acid-forming and base-forming foods. Also, the human body, under normal circumstances, is capable of a wide range of adaptability.

Gonick and co-workers reexamined the acid-ash content of several foods and diets with a review of analytical data since Sherman and Sinclairs' paper in 1907.[25] A direct titrimetric procedure using recently developed techniques was employed. Hospital diets with protein content varying from 63 to 100 grams were essentially neutral (−10.0 to +7.9 mEq. of ash-TA). Protein restriction to 40 grams increased the amount of excess alkaline ash; however, the 20 gram protein Giovannetti diet, in spite of the low ash-T.A. derived from protein, was neutral because of the concomitant restriction of alkaline-ash producing foods (fruits and vegetables). They advocated, therefore, the 40 gram protein diet as the most useful diet in the treatment and prevention of renal acidosis.

High Calorie Diet

The high calorie diet is selected for those desiring to gain weight. This is achieved by providing a caloric intake greater than that necessary for maintenance and activity to allow fat storage. The diet is adequate or above in all nutrients. In this situation, a thorough dietary history would reveal the source of the nutritive insufficiency regarding intake. Eliminating organic disease, the most common causes are socio-economic, ignorance, fads or possible religious cultism. At times, personal preferences are at fault. The history furnishes an excellent guide to rehabilitation, or educated guidance that could remedy the situation. Needless to say, a thorough physical examination with appropriate laboratory tests would be required initially to rule out pathologic etiology or metabolic disturbances.

One must consume approximately 500 calories per day in excess of maintenance and activity allowance in order to gain weight in the range of one pound per week. After carefully assessing the nutritional history, one at-

24. Kahn, Harriet D., Vincent A. Panarello, John Saeli, Janet R. Sampson and Ernest Schwartz; "Effect of Cranberry Juice on Urine," *J.A.D.A. 51*:251-254, 1967.
25. Gonick, Harrey C., Gussie Goldberg and Dorothy Mulcare; "Reexamination of the Acid-Ash Content of Several Diets," *Amer. J. Clin. Nutr.; 21*:898-903; 1968.

tempts first to bring all nutrients falling below recommended allowance levels up to an adequate amount and then provide the desired number of additional calories from any of the food groups. Foods should be selected that are acceptable to the patient and that are compatible with ethnic or religious food habits.

Table XXIV

Acid-Base Reaction of Foods

Potentially Acid-Ash Foods	Potentially Alkaline-Ash Foods
Meat and Milk	
Meat, fish, fowl, shellfish Cheese, all types Eggs Peanut Butter	Milk, Cream, Buttermilk
Fat	
Bacon Nuts: Brazil, filberts, peanuts walnuts	Nuts: Almonds, chestnuts coconut
Bread	
Breads, all types Crackers Macaroni, noodles, spaghetti	None
Vegetables	
Corn and Lentils	All types (except corn and lentils)
Fruits	
Cranberries Plums Prunes	All types (except cranberries, plums, prunes)
Desserts	
Cakes and cookies, plain	
Neutral Foods	
Sweets and Starch	
Candy, plain Sugar and syrup Arrowroot Cornstarch Tapioca	
Fats	
Butter or margarine Cooking fats and oils	

26. Pierpaoli, Paul G.; "Drug Therapy and Diet," *Drug Intelligence and Clin. Pharm; 6*, March, 1972.

The food for the day is usually distributed among the three regular meals plus two to three supplemental feedings.

Low-Calorie Diet

Obviously, the most common use of this diet modification is for weight reduction. Unfortunately, excess weight has become a fairly frequent problem among both younger and older children, as well as adults. While various endocrine abnormalities must be considered in terms of etiology, the most common cause of obesity is simply that of over-eating. In this situation, the individual is consuming more calories than required for maintenance and the performance of work done. One of the most important and essential steps is to first determine the reason for the over-eating. In the case of children, the cause can frequently be traced to parents who have over-emphasized the intake of food with a child who has recovered from a major illness, have ideas that the fat child is the healthy child, or have used food and sweets as bribes, etc. There are children who apparently turn to eating as a source of satisfaction and, having become obese, use their physical size as a defense mechanism.

In approaching the problem of obesity, with the hope of achieving any degree of success, we must first establish rapport with the patient and then carefully consider the following points:

1. The patient must truly *want* to lose weight.
2. A detailed and thorough nutritional history must be obtained.
3. The reason for overeating must be determined and the patient guided and helped in obtaining insight into his own situation. This may be achieved by wise nutritional counseling in milder cases, while professional aid may be required in severe cases. The latter may involve not only the patient but family members as well.
4. All members of the professional team must demonstrate understanding and the sincere desire to help the patient.
5. The dietitian must provide a nutritionally-wise dietary plan for the correction of the problem, yet one that is acceptable and practical for the patient. This is better accepted if it is simply referred to as "learning to eat intelligently" rather than coldly classified as a "diet".
6. Regular periodic follow-up visits to lend support, offer suggestions and answer questions that may arise concerning the patient or program are vitally important, especially for any long-term cooperation and success.
7. Genuine *motivation* must be provided (competitive sports, approval by peers, personal appearance, health, clothes).
8. Diet alone is not enough. There must be activity and/or exercise sufficient to create the necessary deficit in caloric intake. This may mean a considerable adjustment in some cases.

The most satisfactory means of effecting weight reduction while consuming a nutritionally adequate and otherwise well-balanced diet is a sharp curtailment of sources of concentrated food energy—fat, sugars and starches. This plan can be satisfying, provide adequate nutrients and be maintained for an indefinite period by merely adding calories from appropriate foods. The reducing diet, to be deficient in caloric value, must necessarily be low in carbohydrate and fat but provide a sufficiency of protein, vitamins and minerals and a satisfactory satiety value. Religious and ethnic preferences should be recognized as well as personal likes and dislikes.

It is important not to lose weight too rapidly. It is necessary to create a deficit of 500 calories daily in order to lose about one pound per week. This is a rate that can be well tolerated by the body and one that the patient can adjust to without drastic changes. A consistent weight loss is more encouraging to the patient than a rigid or severe regime that is very difficult to adhere to for any length of time.

Diets for children are usually less restricted than in the case of adults because of their relatively high energy requirements and the process of growth. Caloric requirements are influenced by stature, activity, rate of growth, previous dietary intake, etc. To insure adequate provision for growth of all tissues, in addition to maintenance and repair, the diet must contain liberal quantities of protein, vitamins and minerals. With carbohydrate and fat being reduced, the proportionate amount of calories furnished by protein will obviously be increased. There must be sufficient carbohydrate for the liberal protein allowance and actually only a small amount of fat. With inadequate caloric intake, the depot fat is mobilized and may be completely oxidized giving rise to acidosis or ketosis. This is prevented with a higher intake of carbohydrate.

After the desired amount of weight has been lost, the diet can be planned with a small increase in calories to allow the patient to maintain his weight and yet not gain weight.

In planning the diet, the four basic food groups are used in the same manner as with the normal diet modified by reducing the total caloric intake. The exchange lists are used in planning the diet for the calorie-restriction desired.

Suggestions Regarding Preparation and Flavor

Older children may use reasonable amounts of condiments and herbs to add flavor to bland foods to make them more acceptable. These may include salt or salt substitutes, pepper, onion, garlic, horse-radish, green pepper, mushrooms, artificial sweetners extracts, vinegar, lemon, herbs and spices. Special salad dressings may be used. Mineral oil should not be used because the fat soluble vitamins and carotene are soluble in the hydrocarbon and thus the body is deprived of these nutrients. It interferes likewise with the absorption of calcium and phosphorous.

Attractive desserts may be prepared from junket, plain gelatin, egg white or fresh fruit without adding many calories.

The Ketogenic Diet

In clinical pediatrics today, the ketogenic diet has two primary uses. The first of these is as a provocative test for children suspected of having ketotic hypoglycemia. The second use is in children with epilepsy who have been uncontrolled by medication.

The Provocative Ketogenic Diet for Hypoglycemia.[27]

Ketotic hypoglycemia is probably the most common form of hypoglycemia in the young child. The age of onset is between 14 months and five and one-half years, and attacks almost always occur between 6-10 a.m. The children's symptoms are usually related to the central nervous system, ranging from apathy and listlessness to coma and convulsions. Clinical manifestations usually clear with the ingestion of food, or may clear spontaneously. The frequency of the episodes vary from intervals of a few months to a year or more. The fasting blood sugar levels in these patients are frequently within normal limits, even after an overnight fast of 12-14 hours. The blood sugars obtained during one of the episodes will frequently be below 40 mg%, and the urine test will be strongly positive for acetone. The child who is suspected of having ketotic hypoglycemia may then be given the provocative ketogenic diet. To do this the child is first given a high carbohydrate diet (50% of total calories) for three to five days. After an overnight fast, a low calorie ketogenic diet is given. This diet consists of 1200 calories per 1.73/meter^2 and contains 67% fat. The remaining calories of the diet are composed of 16% carbohydrate and 17% protein. This diet is divided into three equal portions and no other food is given between meals. Prior to starting the diet, blood sugar and plasma free fatty acid levels are obtained and blood sugars and fatty acid levels are measured every four hours throughout the day and night. The majority of children will develop acetonuria in eight to twelve hours, and in the susceptible child a fall in blood sugar and clinical manifestations of hypoglycemia will occur in another four to twelve hours. At the time of clinical manifestations, blood sugar and free fatty acid levels should be obtained as well as an insulin level. When the child is symptomatic, a Glucagon tolerance test should be done. (Glucagon dose = 0.3 mg/kg IV or IM, not to exceed 1 mg.) The response of the child with ketotic hypoglycemia to Glucagon is usually negligible.

The therapy for this type of hypoglycemia includes more frequent feedings including a bedtime snack, and the elimination of most sources of fat within the diet. If acetone is detected in the urine at bedtime or on arising, or during an acute illness, the child should be given sweetened drinks or candy to elevate the blood sugar level.

27. Cornblath, M. and Schwartz, R. *Disorders of Carbohydrate Metabolism in Infancy*, W. B. Saunders Company, 1966.

The Ketogenic Diet for Control of Epilepsy.[28]

Early in this century, attempts were made to control epilepsy by fasting the patient. This reportedly reduced the number of seizures for a short period of time. Since most of our current drug armamentarium was not available in the 20's, attempts were made to control epilepsy through the use of the ketogenic diet. Patients with akinetic, myoclonic, or petit mal epilepsy were best controlled by the ketogenic diet. Those with grand mal focal motor and psychomotor seizures were less well controlled, however. Today, the ketogenic diet is still used in those patients who are unresponsive to the usual regimen of drugs. The exact mechanism by which the ketogenic diet works has not been established. Recently, however, it has been found that the brain is able to use fats as a source of energy in anaerobic metabolism to a limited degree. This may be playing some role in the control of seizures in some patients. The diet itself is composed primarily of fats with the ratio of fats to carbohydrate and protein being 3:1 or 4:1. The patient must be hospitalized before the diet is begun, and fasted for a period of two to three days, or until his urine shows the presence of ketone bodies (Ketostix-positive). Once the child is in ketosis, the diet is started. The diet is calculated by calories. The child's caloric requirements are estimated. These are the techniques of calculating the diet. (P = protein, C = carbohydrate).

3:1 ratio

1 gm. fat = 9 calories × 3 = 27 calories
1 gm. P+C = 4 calories × 1 = 4 calories
31 calories per unit

4:1 ratio

1 gm. fat = 9 calories × 4 = 36 calories
1 gm. P+C = 4 calories × 1 = 4 calories
40 calories per unit

Example: 17 kg. weight × 70 calories per kg = 1,190 or 1,200 calories daily.

4:1 ratio (40 calories per unit)

1. Divide calorie unit (40) into total calories (1,200) = 30 units
2. Fat: multiply number of units (30) × 4 = 120 gm
3. P + C: multiply number of units (30) × 1 = 30 gm
4. P: 1 gm per kg (17 × 1) = 17 gm
5. C: Subtract number of grams P in diet from the total number of dietary units P + C (30-17) = 13 gm

The diet prescription is then:

Fat	120 gm	or 40 gm per meal
Protein	17 gm	or 5.66 gm per meal
Carbohydrate	13 gm	or 4.45 gm per meal

An alternate method for rapid calculation of 4:1 ratio diet follows: The number of grams of fat is 1/10 the number of calories needed daily.

28. Mike, E. M. "Practical Guide and Dietary Management of Children with Seizures using the Ketogenic Diet", *Am. J. Clin. Nutrition,* 17:399-409, 1965.

1. 1/10 of 1200 calories = 120 gm. fat
2. 1 gm. of fat = 9 calories; therefore, 120 × 9 = 1080 calories
3. Subtract this from total number of calories; 1200 − 1080 = 120 calories supplied by protein and carbohydrate
4. Both protein and carbohydrate = 4 calories/gm; therefore, 120 divided by 4 = 30 gm. of protein and carbohydrate.
5. Protein (1 gm. per kg.) subtracted from total grams protein and carbohydrate; therefore, 30 − 17 = 13 gm.

Ketogenic Diet Table of Calculations

Calories	3:1 (gm.)		4:1 (gm.)	
	F	C + P	F	C + P
800	78	26	80	20
900	87	29	90	23
1,000	96	32	100	25
1,100	108	36	110	28
1,200	117	39	120	30
1,300	129	43	130	33
1,400	135	45	140	35
1,500	144	48	150	38
1,600	156	52	160	40
1,700	165	55	170	43
1,800	174	58	180	45
1,900	183	61	190	48
2,000	198	66	200	50
2,100	204	68	210	53
2,200	213	71	220	55
2,300	222	74	230	58
2,400	231	77	240	60
2,500	243	81	250	63

When this diet is introduced to the child he may initially reject it, but eventually will usually accept it. Because of the high fat content, however, vomiting is a frequent problem. In addition, this diet usually contains inadequate vitamin B complex and vitamin C. Therefore, aqueous multivitamin preparation in a dose of 0.6 ml/day is suggested. Also, one must be careful that the calcium content of the diet is enough to provide 0.5 gm. calcium daily. If insufficient quantities of calcium are present, supplementary calcium must be added. Iron supplement is also indicated to provide 7-10 mg. elemental iron if the diet is inadequate in this element. No medication given to the child may contain carbohydrate of any kind lest this bring the child out of ketosis.

Once the child accepts the diet, the parents should be taught how to measure the food and adequately prepare the diet with the dietitian's help. They should be given a list of foods allowed on the ketogenic diet and recipe suggestions. They should also be warned that the introduction of any glucose or sugar in addition to the dietary restrictions may cause the child to escape from ketosis and cause recurrence of seizures. The child's urine is checked three to four times daily by the parents with Ketostix and should be continuously positive. The dose of medications the child is on may be reduced during the time of fasting, and further reduced as the diet is accepted. The child should be continued on the diet for a period of six weeks before it is abandoned if it appears to be ineffective. Usually, children remain on the diet for one to three years and then the diet is slowly discontinued. If seizures should recur, the diet is reinstituted. Children who are unable to accept the diet or develop severe vomiting must be taken off the diet.

Recently, a variation on the ketogenic diet has been introduced in the form of the medium chain triglyceride ketogenic diet. In this diet, medium chain triglyceride is used in place of the normal saturated fats. This diet becomes more palatable and since medium chain triglycerides are more completely absorbed, lower total quantities of fats are given to the patient. This diet is still in the experimental stages but seems to be an effective tool in controlling seizures.

Dietary Therapy of Inborn Errors of Metabolism

Introduction

There are a large number of hereditary disorders of intermediary metabolism where dietary therapy is a consideration. These disorders involve a deficiency of a particular enzyme in intermediary metabolism and the inheritance is generally autosomal recessive with a few X-linked recessive disorders. Dietary therapy is often aimed at reducing the intake of a particular precursor where a degradative metabolic pathway is blocked by enzyme deficiency. A number of the enzymes utilize co-factors which are derived from vitamins in the diet. In some of these instances, administration of high doses of vitamins facilitates the function of the small remaining amount of enzyme activity to an extent that the clinical manifestations of the disorder are relieved. In other conditions, the hereditary defect is actually in the enzyme steps involved in the conversion of the dietary vitamin to the enzyme co-factor. Thus, there are a number of conditions which are described as being vitamin responsive, that is, that administration of high doses of vitamins returns biochemical disturbances to normal and relieves clinical symptoms.[29,30]

Table XXV is a summary of some hereditary conditions divided according to efficacy of dietary therapy. The table includes dietary therapy under a very broad definition and is by no means intended to be absolutely complete. An additional table (Table XXVI) is provided summarizing some of the disorders in which high-dose vitamin therapy is of proven value (Scriver and Rosenberg, 1973).[31]

29. Stanbury, J. B. et al., *The Metabolic Basis of Inherited Disease,* 3rd Ed., McGraw Hill, 1972.
30. Synderman, S. E., *"The Dietary Therapy of Inherited Metabolic Diseases," Prog. in Food and Nutr. Sci.* 1:507, 1975.
31. Scriver, C. R. and Rosenberg, L. E., *Amino Acid Metabolism and Its Disorders,* W. B. Saunders Co., 1973.

Table XXV

Summary of Some Hereditary Conditions Divided According to Efficacy of Dietary Therapy

Metabolic Disorders in Which Dietary Therapy is Helpful

Diseases	Comments
Diabetes mellitus	reduce intake—? particularly carbohydrates
Hereditary fructose intolerance	eliminate fructose
Glycogen storage disease I. III, VI	frequent or continuous feeding
Galactosemia	eliminate galactose
Galactokinase	eliminate galactose
Phenylketonuria	reduce phenylalanine
Hereditary tyrosinemia	reduce phenylalanine and tyrosine
Urea cycle disorders:	
Carbamyl phosphate synthetase def.	keto acid therapy and reduced protein intake
Ornithine transcarbamylase def.	
Argininosuccinic aciduria	
Citrullinemia	
Arginase def.	
Hyperlysinemia I, II	reduce lysine
Homocystinuria	some patients responsive to pyroxidine
Maple syrup disease and variant	reduce leucine, isoleucine and valine
Propionic acidemia	reduce protein
Methylmalonic acidemia	some B_{12} reponsive, other reduce protein
Refsum's disease	reduce phytanic acid
Orotic aciduria	increased pyrimidines
Wilson's disease	reduce copper
Hypokalemic periodic paralysis	increase potassium, decrease sodium
Hyperkalemic periodic paralysis	carbohydrate feedings
Normokalemic periodic paralysis	increase sodium chloride
Pseudohypoparathyroidism	increase calcium and Vitamin D
Lactase deficiency	eliminate lactose
Vitamin D resistant rickets	pharmacologic vitamin D $\pm$ increased phosphate
Renal tubular acidosis	increase citric acid, calcium, Vitamin D
Vasopressin—resistant diabetes insipidus	increase water $\pm$ decrease solute
Cystinosis and Fanconi syndrome	alkalinizing diet, increase Vitamin D, cystine-free diet probably not helpful
Cystic Fibrosis	pancreatic enzymes, Vitamins A and D, medium chain triglycerides
Cystinuria	increase fluid intake, ? penicillamine

Continued on next page

Table XXV (cont.)

Metabolic Disorders in Which Dietary Therapy May be Helpful

Diseases	Comments
Glycogen storage disease V (McArdle)	increase glucose and fructose with exercise
Primary hyperoxaluria I, II	pharmacologic doses of pyridoxine
Hyperphenylalaninemia	? benign
Histidinemia	? reduce histidine
Hyperprolinemia I, II	reduce proline, probably helpful in type I
Cystathionuria	may be benign
Isovaleric acidemia	? reduce leucine
Nonketotic hyperglycinemia	? reduce glycine, ? increase methionine
Abetalipoproteinemia	fat intolerance, ? medium chain triglyceride and Vitamin A useful
Hyperliproteinemia I-V	typing system and value of therapy for each under investigation
Xanthinuria	? reduced purines
Hartnup disease	? increase nicotinamide, ? increase protein
Alcaptonuria	many unsuccessful attempts, possibly ascorbic acid

Metabolic Disorders in Which Dietary Therapy is Not Helpful

Diseases	Comments
Iminoglycinuria	benign
Pentosuria	benign
Essential fructosuria	benign
Glycogen storage disease II, IV	——
Multiple types of familial goiter	replacement therapy
Albinism, three types	——
Hydroxyprolinemia	unsuccessful attempts
Tangier disease	——
Familial lecithin cholesterol acyl transferase deficiency	——
Lysosomal storage diseases generally	——
Disorders of adrenocortical biogenesis	——
Gout	generally not useful compared to drugs
Lesch-Nyhan syndrome	unsuccessful attempts
Hemochromatosis	——
Porphyrias	——
Hyperbilirubinemias:	
Dubin—Johnson, Gilberts, Crigler—Najar	——
Hypophosphatasia	——

Table XXVI
Summary of Same Disorders of Metabolism in Which High-Dose Vitamin Therapy is of Proven Value
The Vitamin-Responsive Disorders of Amino Acid Metabolism

Vitamin	Disorder	Therapeutic Dose	Biochemical Basis
Thiamine (B_1)	Lacticacidosis	5-20 mg	Pyruvate carboxylase deficiency
	Branched-chain aminoacidopathy (MSUD variant)	5-20 mg	Branched-chain ketoacid decarboxylase deficiency
Pyridoxine (B_6)	Infantile convulsions	10-50 mg	Glutamic acid decarboxylase deficiency
	Hypochromic anemia	>10 mg	Unknown
	Cystathioninuria	100-500 mg	Cystathionase deficiency
	Xanthurenicaciduria	5-10 mg	Kynureninase deficiency
	Homocystinuria	25-500 mg	Cystathionine synthase deficiency
	Hyperoxaluria	100-500 mg	Glyoxylate:α-ketoglutarate carboligase deficiency
Cobalamin (B_{12})	Juvenile pernicious anemia	<5 μg	IF deficiency or defective ileal transport
	Transcobalamin II deficiency	>100 μg	Deficiency of transcobalamin II
	Methylmalonicaciduria	>250 μg	Defective synthesis of Ad—B_{12} coenzyme
	Methylmalonicaciduria homocystinuria and hypomethininemia	>500 μg	Defective synthesis of Ad—B_{12} and CH_3—B_{12} coenzymes
Folic acid	Megaloblastic anemia	<0.05 mg	Defective intestinal absorption of folate
	Formiminotransferase deficiency	>5 mg	Formiminotransferase deficiency
	Homocystinuria and hypomethioninemia	>10 mg	N^5, N^{10}-methylenetetrahydrofolate reductase deficiency
	Congenital megaloblastic anemia	>0.1 mg	Dihydrofolate reductase deficiency
Biotin	Propionicacidemia	10 mg	Propionyl-CoA carboxylase deficiency
Niacin	Hartnup disease	40-200 mg	Defective intestinal and renal transport of tryptophan and other "neutral" amino acids

Adapted from Scriver and Rosenberg, "Amino Acid Metabolism and Its Disorders," by W. B. Saunders Company, 1973.

Dietary Management of Childhood Diabetes Mellitus

by Leighton Hill, M.D.

There are important differences in the management of childhood diabetes and adult diabetes in regard to diet. Some of the differences in emphasis are due to the following facts:

1. Many adult patients can be managed with diet alone, whereas, this is almost always not the case in the insulin-dependent growth onset diabetes.
2. Most adults with diabetes are overweight. Children with diabetes are usually not overweight and are often underweight at the time of diagnosis.
3. Most children, including those with diabetes, show variations in appetite from day to day. No defect in the appetite mechanisms of children with diabetes has been demonstrated. In addition, children have rather strong likes and dislikes as far as various foods are concerned and this must be recognized.
4. Most children expend more energy than adults and, of course, must grow and develop.

Keeping these points in mind and the fairly well-accepted ideas as to the pathogenesis of atherosclerosis and hypertension, the followng basic aims of dietary therapy can be stated:

1. The diet should be a well balanced and nutritious one. This is by far the most important.
2. The times of meals and snacks and the approximate amount eaten at each meal should be similar from day to day (within reason).
3. If at all possible, the child should not be allowed to become obese. Calorie restriction may be necessary if excess weight gain begins to occur.
4. The intake of free sugar should be limited, but not banned. Fruits should be emphasized as desserts and snacks. The best time to allow "treats" of candy, soda pops, etc., is during heavy exercise.
5. The person with childhood diabetes should avoid getting into the habit of using large amounts of salt on his food.
6. The child or adolescent with diabetes should limit his or her intake of eggs to 3 to 4 per week, should use a low-fat milk, and generally should avoid large amounts of animal fat (bacon, sausage, fat attached to lean pork, beef, etc.).
7. Artificially sweetened drinks should be used in moderation, no more than the equivalent of 1-2 sugar-free soda pops per day.

It should be noted that this approach to diet is considered to be too liberal by some clinicians and researchers who work with children with diabetes, and more restrictive and concise dietary plans are available.

*Orientation Notes on Childhood Diabetes**

L. Leighton Hill, M.D.

General Information

Diabetes Mellitus occurs when the pancreas ceases to produce enough *insulin.* Normally, sugars and starches in food are absorbed from the intestine and appear in the blood in the form of a sugar called glucose. A certain amount of glucose is always present in the blood and is used by the body to meet its energy needs. Glucose is the principal energy fuel for the body. To insure a continuous supply of this vital sugar, glucose is stored in the muscles and the liver and is released as needed. Both the *use* and *storage* of sugar by the body depends on the *presence of insulin.*

In the absence of insulin the body cannot store glucose or use it as fuel in the cells of the body. Glucose then begins to build up in the blood and in the fluid *outside* of the cells of the body. When it reaches a certain level in the blood, it starts to spill over into the urine. (Normally, there is no spill of the sugar in the urine). The kidney acts as a dam holding the sugar in the body until it reaches the spill level. At first, small amounts appear as the spill level is passed, but as the blood sugar continues to rise, more and more sugar is spilled into the urine. Since sugar cannot be excreted by the kidney as a solid, it must be accompanied by large amounts of water. This causes the large urine volume these young people have and accounts for the bedwetting that is often seen. The patient must drink a lot of water to replace the water lost in the urine to avoid getting dehydrated (dried out). The patient is excreting some of the food he eats in the urine so that weight loss may occur despite an increased appetite. These are the principal symtoms of diabetes: weight loss, large urine volume, large water intake and increased appetite.

Giving insulin reverses all of this. The patient begins to burn and store sugar in the body cells. The blood sugar falls and the spill of sugar in the urine lessens and may stop if the blood sugar goes below the level of the dam (kidney). The heavy urination ceases so water drinking decreases and the patient begins to gain weight as he utilizes all of the types of foods ingested.

Only 5% of the total number of diabetics are under 14 years of age at the time of diagnosis. The great majority of diabetics have the adult type. There are many differences between childhood diabetes and adult diabetes: Adult type: Patients are usually overweight and can often be treated by weight reduction and diet alone. The adult has only partial diabetes; that is, he continues to produce ½, ⅔ or even ¾ of his own insulin. Oral medications that reduce the blood sugar are often effective in the adult patient. The adult is generally less active than the child and tends to have more regular habits.

Childhood type: Patients are seldom overweight and may be underweight and it should therefore be obvious that weight reduction diets are out of

* Reprinted from special handout to parents of diabetic children, Baylor College of Medicine—Texas Children's Hospital.

the question. It should be emphasized that in children, unlike many adults, diabetes cannot be managed by diet alone. Children have *total diabetes*—they completely stop making insulin and therefore all naturally require insulin injections. The diabetic drugs taken by mouth are not effective. The child has less regular habits, much more variation in activity and many more dietary prejudices. He also has increased nutritional requirements during periods of rapid growth, particularly at puberty.

The tendency to diabetes is inherited, but as yet unknown environmental factors must also be present to "bring out" complete diabetes. The inheritance pattern suggests that the tendency to diabetes is inherited from both parents, not just one.

Our principal aim is that your child should lead a completely normal life with the diabetes interfering as little as possible. Foremost is our desire for him or her to grow up to be a well-adjusted, emotionally normal and productive person. Acceptance of the reality of the diagnosis is important. It is also important to put diabetes in the proper perspective. We don't want the family life to totally revolve around the diabetes. The management of diabetes should be handled as any habit such as bathing, brushing the teeth, etc. Do a good conscientious job but don't overdo it. We do not place any particular restrictions on your child but good health habits (balanced diet, regular exercise, recreation, adequate rest, etc.) should be encouraged. Obviously, it is important to learn as much as you can about the condition. A well-informed child or parent usually acts in a more confident manner and does not harbor anxieties or secret fears.

Insulin. Insulin is required by all persons with the childhood type of diabetes. It must be taken by injection into the fatty tissues between the skin and muscle. The actions of insulin are discussed under Part A of this section. Types of insulin you will use are:

1. Regular insulin—also called crystalline insulin. This insulin is quick acting, producing some effect in 30 minutes, peaking at two hours, and lasting for about 6 hours. This insulin is clear; it looks like water.
2. NPH insulin—this insulin is long-acting and is cloudy in appearance. After injection, the peak of activity is between 8 and 12 hours and the total duration of activity is 24-26 hours.
3. Lente insulin—another long-acting insulin, similar to NPH in its action and duration and sometimes used instead of NPH.

We recommend the use of U-100 strength insulin whether regular, NPH, or Lente. U-100 means 100 units per cc. or syringeful. You must use U-100 syringes with your U-100 insulins. We recommend the use of disposable syringes. The needle size should be #26 or #27 and ½-inch in length. These are very small needles.

Urine Tests for Sugar. The urine is tested for sugar to crudely estimate the blood sugar level. We do not use blood tests for sugar in the management of the child with diabetes (this is another point that contrasts with the management of the adult patient).

As stated previously, the kidney can be thought of as a dam and as long as the blood sugar is below a certain level (the level of the dam) there is no spill of sugar in the urine and the urine and the urine test is negative. If the blood sugar level is a little over the dam (the kidney) then trace amounts of sugar appear. As the blood sugar rises further, then you have 1+, then 2+, 3+, 4+ and 5+ positive urine sugar tests. Again we use urine testing for sugar to estimate the blood sugar level several times per day. Routinely, we will request that you test the urine 3 times daily: before breakfast, after school (or before supper), and at bedtime. We recommend the use of the 2-drop Clinitest method for testing sugar and urge you to do the test just as the instructions on the color chart indicate.

Significance of Urine Acetone Tests. When your child goes home, we will ask you to check his or her urine for acetone each time it is 4+ or 5+ for sugar. (Acetone is not significant in diabetes unless it is accompanied by heavy sugar spill.) We generally ignore small amounts of acetone and consider only moderate and large amounts as being significant.

The presence of significant acetone (along with 4 or 5+ sugar) in the urine constitutes an emergency. It indicates an extreme need for insulin. Acetone is a by-product of burning body fat for energy purposes instead of carbohydrate and signifies the presence of large quantities of keto-acids in the body. If not treated with extra insulin, then the accumulation of these acids can cause a severe acidosis and diabetic coma can result. Acetone in the urine is the first step in the sequence of events leading to complete breakdown of diabetic control—diabetic coma. Acetone is most likely to show up during infections or other stresses. Infections or stresses tend to block the action of insulin and may produce an added requirement for insulin. If acetone is looked for under appropriate circumstances (4+ or 5+ sugar spill, infections, injuries, emotional stress, etc.) and treated promptly, then your child should never have diabetic acidosis and coma.

Treatment

Day to Day Control of Diabetes. Long-acting insulin (usually NPH) is used for the day to day control. In the majority of instances, only one insulin injection per day is required. The urine tests for sugar are used to determine if the amount of insulin is correct. We will therefore ask you to keep records of those tests. A sample form usually set up in a composition book as shown: (Remember that three tests per day are recommended.)

Date	Dose of Insulin	A.M. Test	Afternoon Test	Bedtime Test	Remarks
6/14/74	20	0	1+	0	
6/15/74	20	tr	0	1+	
6/16/74	20	2+	0	2+	

The remarks column is for recording unusual changes in the diet, insulin reactions, positive tests for acetone or anything that has a bearing on the interpretation of the tests. Our aim of control will be:

½ of the urine tests—negative to trace)
roughly
½ of the urine tests—positive (1+ through 5+))

The dose of insulin can be raised or lowered by 2 units depending on the urine tests. If the spill is too heavy, indicating that the blood sugar is too high, then the dose is raised. If most of the urines are negative for sugar, then the dose of insulin is decreased. The change in dosage is made whenever it is *clearcut* to decrease the dosage after only one day. There are day to day unexplained fluctuations in the insulin requirement and we try to average these out to some extent by making infrequent adjustments in dosage (unless, of course, it appears clearcut to make a change). Generally speaking, we try not to change the dose of insulin too often.

After your child has had diabetes for awhile, we may recommend mixing in some regular or quick-acting insulin with the long-acting insulin given each morning. This is to provide a faster start as far as insulin activity is concerned. The amount of regular would be between ⅛ and ¼ of the total dose. We will talk to you in more detail about this if we decide it is indicated in the management of your child.

There may also be times when it is unwise to give the long-acting insulin. For example, if your child is vomiting, you may not want to commit yourself to 24 hours of insulin activity. We may want to use small repeated doses (¼ of usual daily dose) of quick-acting or regular insulin on such days. You would not even give these small amounts unless the child is spilling 2+ or above sugar.

Diet. Three facts are important in contrasting the emphasis placed on diet in the management of the adult patient vs. the childhood patient:

1. Many adult patients can be managed with diet alone, whereas, this is almost always impossible in the childhood diabetic.
2. Most adults with diabetes are overweight. Children with diabetes are not usually overweight and are often underweight at the time of diagnosis.
2. Most children do show a change in food intake from day to day and have rather strong likes and dislikes as far as food is concerned.

In regard to #1 above, it should be apparent that since the child with diabetes cannot be managed with diet alone, we might place less emphasis on the diet in diabetic control. It is also obvious (re: #2 above) that weight reduction diets are unneeded and, in fact, are out of the question because children must continue to gain weight and to grow. In regard to #3 above, you cannot make your child adopt adult attitudes toward foods and eating habits by command, and thus a certain amount of flexibility on your part is vital.

Our major aims as to diet are as follows:

1. The diet should be a well-balanced and nutritious one. This is by far the most important aim.

2. The times of the meals and the approximate amount eaten at each meal should be similar from day to day (within reason).
3. The young person with diabetes should not be allowed to become obese (fat).
4. The intake of sugar (table sugar, candy, soda pop, etc.) should be limited to some extent. They should not be completely banned. The best time to allow "treats" of candy, etc. is during heavy exercise.
5. We also feel that it is good for any child, including one with diabetes, to avoid getting into the habit of using large amounts of salt on his food.
6. Similarly we feel that any child, including one with diabetes, should limit his or her intake of eggs to 3-4 per week, should use a low-fat milk and generally should avoid large amounts of animal fat (bacon, sausage, etc.).

Your child must be given adequate food for normal growth and development and sufficient energy foods (carbohydrates or starches) to meet his energy needs. He should eat what the rest of the family eats (that is, if the rest of the family eats a good well-balanced diet). It is not necessary to prepare special foods for him and *no* foods should be completely forbidden. A few words might be in order to explain why we want the diet to be similar from day to day. The person without diabetes provides enough insulin to handle the food he eats. If he eats no food, he makes little insulin; if he eats moderate amounts of food, he makes moderate amounts of insulin; and if he eats huge quantities of food, his body provides enough insulin to metabolize the food. The food intake and insulin are always balanced and the blood sugar level does not change very much. In the diabetic, however, the situation is reversed since he takes a "shot" of insulin in the morning and this insulin must be balanced by his intake of food. You can easily see, then, that he must eat relatively constant amounts of food from day to day in order to maintain the balance between insulin and food intake. The times of meals should be fairly regular and the size of meals from day to day should be similar. In other words, he or she should not be given a half slice of toast for breakfast one morning and the next morning be given juice, eggs, toast, cereal, bacon, jelly, hashbrown potatoes and milk. This is an exaggeration, but in general, breakfast from day to day should be similar in size. Again, this is a goal to shoot for, but we realize that in dealing with children, especially small children, this is often difficult.

Exercise. Exercise is very important to your child. Insulin is helped by exercise so that the more a child gets (all other factors being equal), the less insulin he requires. Frequent regular exercise will lead to better control of the diabetes and will improve the long-term outlook. We would like to see all of our children with diabetes become athletes, if this is possible. Exercise, in excess of the usual, will necessitate a somewhat greater intake of food to avoid insulin reactions. As pointed out previously, this is a good time to allow a sugar treat.

Emergencies (Very important section—you *must* know this information.

1. Too much insulin: (insulin reaction, insulin shock, hypoglycemia). Since insulin and exercise help the body burn up sugar, an insulin reaction (too much insulin) can occur if:

too much insulin is given
a meal is skipped or skimped
there is excessive exercise without extra snacks

The first two causes are obvious since the food intake and insulin administration must balance. If either the food intake is cut or too much insulin is given, you may wind up with too much insulin effect and an imbalance. Exercise causes insulin to work better and with exercise in excess of the usual, blood sugar may fall unless extra food (sugar) is given. The signs and symptoms of an insulin reaction or low blood sugar are: hunger, weakness, shakiness, paleness, increased sweating, headache, pounding of heart, stomach-ache, starry-eyed, irritability, change in personality, sleepiness, deep sleep and finally convulsions. All of these signs and symptoms can be produced by other things but with a true insulin reaction *several* of these signs, not just one, appear. Usually it is progressive—first one sign, then another, then several more, etc. The exact pattern of the above signs and symptoms changes from child to child.

Insulin reactions can be treated by giving sugar or sugar containing liquids (coke, orange juice, etc.). The earlier the low blood sugar reaction is treated, the easier it is to treat. Whenever your child has any signs or symptoms of an insulin reaction, then give sugar without regard to the urine test. (Urine tests are not reliable for judging reactions because reactions can come on rapidly and the bladder often stores the urine produced over a 6-8 hour period.) If your child is unconscious from his insulin reaction or for any reason cannot take sugar by mouth, then glucagon can be administered by injection. Glucagon will temporarily raise the blood sugar, making it possible to get in sugar by mouth. Remember, that glucagon will only give a temporary rise in blood sugar and that administration of sugar by mouth is *always* the primary treatment. (Glucagon is a hormone which stimulates the liver to release sugar. It comes in a one-dose vial but must be mixed with a diluting solution, which is provided, before giving the whole amount. The method of injection is the same as for insulin.

2. Too little insulin or diabetic ketosis*: Whenever the urine is 4+ or 5+ for sugar, then it should be tested for acetone. A moderate or strongly positive acetone test is an indication for the immediate administration of *quick-acting* insulin. *This is an emergency!* The presence of acetone along with heavy sugar spill is the first step in a chain of events that can lead to keto-acidosis and diabetic coma. Regular or quick-acting insulin is given at a dose of ¼ *of the total usual daily morning insulin dose.* For example, if your boy or girl has been receiving 24 units of insulin as his daily dose, then you would give 6 units of regular insulin. The urine is then checked every 3 hours for sugar and if it is 4+ or 5+, it is tested for acetone. The ¼ dose of regular can be repeated then every 3 hours until the acetone is

* This is the most important information in this whole handout—Vital!!

gone. The acetone is most likely to show up during periods of stress (significant infections, emotional upsets, injury, etc.). However, you do not have to guess about this—the urine test for acetone can always be depended on.

When a moderate or large amount of acetone is present, along with 4+ or 5+ sugar, an emergency exists. Giving fast-acting insulin when this is first discovered will prevent a serious situation (keto-acidosis). If acetone is not treated early, is is more difficult to correct—many times leading to the inconvenience and expense of hospitalization. Severe keto-acidosis is a very serious situation.

Summary

Do not let your concern for details obscure your major objectives. There are two major objectives:

Day to Day Control

1. Check and record urine test for sugar 3 times daily. Check for acetone when sugar test is 4+ or 5+ positive for sugar.
2. The NPH insulin is given once daily in the A.M. The dosage is changed as necessary to try to keep about ½ of the tests negative to trace for sugar. Do not change the dose too often. The insulin dose cannot be skipped.
3. Diet. A well-balanced diet with meals at about the same time every day and similar amounts from day to day.
   Avoid: a. getting overweight
   b. lots of sugar (candy, cokes, icings, etc.)
   c. lots of animal fat (eggs, fatty meats, bacon, cream)—use low fat milk
   d. salting foods heavily

Emergencies (2)

1. Too much insulin—"insulin reaction". Diagnose by symptoms and treat with sugar.
2. Too little insulin—4+ and 5+ urine sugar with moderate to large acetone. Rx: Give regular insulin (¼ of usual morning daily dose) and repeat every 3-4 hours until acetone is gone.

Important: If your child is vomiting profusely for more than 2-3 hours, and has heavy sugar and acetone, call a doctor IMMEDIATELY.

Above all, your child's emotional and psychological development should be of primary concern, for this factor in the long run will likely have a far greater effect on his/her control than anything else we have talked about.

Galactosemia

Galactosemia, first described in 1935 by Mason and Turner, usually refers to the disorder of galactose-1-phosphate uridyl transferase deficiency.

Another more benign disorder, galactokinase deficiency, is associated with increased blood galactose and premature cataracts but will not be further discussed. Galactosemia is an autosomal recessive disorder with pan-ethnic occurrence and an incidence of 2-5 per 100,000 live births. In addition to the deficient allele of galactosemia, another allele for the transferase, the Duarte variant, occurs with 50% of normal activity per gene. Heterozygotes for the galactosemia gene and Duarte gene occur at about 1% to 10% of the population respectively. The deficient enzyme represents the second step in metabolism of galactose to glucose whereby galactose-1-phosphate and UDP glucose are converted to UDP galactose and glucose-1-phosphate. The defect results in increased galactose in blood and the presence of galactose in urine. Galactose-1-phosphate and galactitol are increased in blood and tissues.

The clinical findings in galactosemia include failure to thrive, vomiting, diarrhea, impaired liver function, cataracts and mental retardation. Untreated patients often do not survive although partial treatment through empirical formula changes is not rare. Susceptibility to neonatal meningitis and septicemia has been found as well as occasional hypoglycemia. The diagnosis will be accomplished increasingly by newborn screening programs, which either detect increased blood galactose, thus requiring adequate milk intake, or detect the red cell enzyme deficiency independent of intake.

When the diagnosis is suspected clinically the Benedict's test for reducing substance in the urine may be positive although the glucose oxidase Glucostix test will be negative. Lactose intake must be present for the test to be meaningful. The enzyme deficiency is readily demonstrated in red blood cells and in cultured skin and amniotic cells for definitive diagnosis. Investigations of the pathogenesis of galactosemia have centered on the role of accumulated galactitol and galactose-1-phosphate. The conclusion seems clearest in the lens where galactitol causes inhibition of water and many secondary changes with cataract formation. The pathogenesis of the other manifestations is less certain although the role of galactose-1-phosphate might be more significant since these manisfestations are absent in galactokinase deficiency where galactose-1-phosphate does not accumulate.

The optimal management of galactosemia is the elimination of galactose (usually as lactose) from the diet. The elimination may be complete since galactose is readily synthesized from glucose and thus non-essential. The elimination should include the diet of the prospective mother at risk for galactosemic children since protection *in utero* appears inadequate. Children are occasionally born with cataracts and there is evidence to suggest better mental outcome when prenatal galactose restriction is added to postnatal-restriction.

Dietary therapy can be accomplished with any of numerous galactose free formulas including the soy formulas although they contain some nondigestible galactose oligosaccharides. Such formulas can be substituted for milk in many baked goods. Dietary restriction should be continued for life although permission to include some baked goods should be considered in older patients. Occult sources of lactose are many as this is a commonly used filler, e.g. in many medications. The beneficial effect of dietary therapy on survival, liver damage, cataracts and growth is well documented. Because many "untreated" patients had some dietary restriction, because of the variability of the mental retardation, and because of the lack of prenatal treatment in first born cases, the effect of therapy on mental function has been beneficial but not overwhelming. Although prenatal treatment offers reason for optimism, this could only be achieved for all patients if heterozygote screening of the general population were undertaken.

Galactose-Free Diet

Principle: The galactose-free diet is used in the treatment of galactosemia and is planned to prevent galactose from collecting in the body. Galactosemia is caused by the lack of galactose-1-phosphate uridyl transferase, an enzyme needed for the conversion of galactose to glucose in the liver. Lactose (milk sugar) is hydrolyzed in the intestine to galactose. Foods containing lactose or galactose are eliminated from the diet. Labels of all foods and medicine must be carefully checked to make certain they do not contain milk or milk products, lactose, casein, whey or curds.

Adequacy: The special formula is supplemented with vitamins and minerals; therefore, the infant and older child will receive the Recommended Daily Dietary Allowances for all nutrients, if the foods allowed are consumed in the suggested amounts.

Foods	**Foods Allowed**	**Foods to Avoid**
Beverages	Non-milk formulas such as Nutramigen or Pregestimil; carbonated beverages; tea; coffee*; soy-based formulas**; Meat Base Formula	All milk, milk drinks
Breads	Homemade bread or rolls made without milk, butter or milk-base margarine; French bread, Vienna bread; tortillas; some brands of crackers or saltines	Prepared mixes such as biscuits, muffins, pancakes and waffles; bread or rolls made with milk; zwieback. *Check all labels carefully*

* Coffee and pepper are not usually served unless specifically requested.

** Soy-based formulas contain alpha-galactosides raffinose and stachyose, which contain galactose. Research studies by Gitzelmann and Auricchio, 1965 and 1966, consider soy-based formulas safe, unless diarrhea is present; alpha-galactoside hydrolysis does occur during diarrhea with evidence of the free hexoses in the stool.

Foods	Foods Allowed	Foods to Avoid
Cereals	Cooked cereals such as oatmeal, grits, cream of wheat, cornmeal; prepared cereals such as cornflakes, sugar smacks, frosted flakes, rice krispies	Cooked or prepared cereals with dry milk solids or lactose listed as an ingredient, such as Instant Cream of Wheat, Special K, Total. *Check all labels carefully.*
Desserts	Fruit flavored ices, popsicles; gelatin desserts; angel food or chiffon cakes; icing made with corn syrup, egg whites, sugar and water; homemade cookies, puddings or fruit pies made without milk or milk products	Sherbet; ice cream; milk custards and puddings; pies, cakes and cookies made with milk or milk products; any dessert made with chocolate
Fat	Margarine without milk solids (i.e., mar-parv, Soft Chiffon Diet Imitation, Kraft's Soft Diet Parkay-imitation, Kosher margarines†); shortening; cottonseed, safflower, corn, peanut oils; mayonnaise; salad dressings without cheese, milk, or milk products; crisp bacon; bacon fat; lard; some cream substitutes (check labels carefully).	Margarine; butter; cream; salad dressings containing cheese, milk or milk products; cream cheese
Fruits and Fruit Juices	All fresh, canned, or frozen prepared without lactose.	Artificial fruit juices containing lactose or glutamate. *Check all labels carefully.*
Meat, Fish, Poultry, Cheese and Egg	Beef, veal, poultry, fish; eggs prepared without milk or milk products. Cooking method for beef, veal, fish or poultry may be baking, roasting, stewing, broiling or frying with allowed oils, shortening or bacon fat	Creamed or breaded meats, fish, and fowl; all cheese; all organ meats such as liver, heart or brain; shellfish; luncheon meats; sausage; frankfurters; yogurt

† Kosher-type or soft imitation-type margarines do not contain dry milk solids; these may be purchased in some supermarkets or stores specializing in Kosher foods.

Foods	Foods Allowed	Foods to Avoid
Potatoes or Substitutes	White or sweet potatoes; corn; macaroni; noodles; spaghetti; rice	Mashed potatoes with milk or milk products; instant or dehydrated potato products containing milk, lactose, or glutamate
Soups	Beef base soups such as bouillon, broth, consomme; vegetable soups without peas or lima beans	Cream soups; chowders; commercially prepared soups with lactose
Sweets	Hard candy; honey; jams or jellies, marmalade; cane sugar, brown sugar; molasses; syrup gum drops, marshmallows *(check all labels carefully)*	Chocolate; cocoa; beet sugar or molasses; candy made with milk or lactose, such as caramels.
Vegetables and Vegetable Juices	All fresh, frozen or canned except those listed under foods to avoid	Any creamed, breaded, or buttered vegetable; beets, lima beans, peas, soybeans[††]
Miscellaneous	Salt, spices; flavoring without lactose or glutamate; catsup, mustard; pickles, vinegar; peanut butter; popcorn with special margarine	Chewing gum; artificial sweeteners with lactose; monosodium glutamate; agar; gum arabic (arcacia); carrageenin. Check all labels carefully

Birth to One Year: Baby foods are introduced in the same manner as to the normal child. Special formula is substituted for milk base formulas; organ meats, strained peas and beets are also eliminated.

†† Lima beans, beets, peas and soybeans contain stachyose, a tetrasaccharide. There is some questions as to whether stachyose is hydrolyzed to galactose and for this reason it is best to eliminate these vegetables.

Sources: Robinson's *Normal and Therapeutic Nutrition,* 1972, 14th Edition, pp. 609-610, 637-638
Lillian Hoagland Meyer, *Food Chemistry,* Reinhold Publishing Corporation, New York, 1960, pp. 95-99.

Suggested Meal Pattern
(1 year and older)

Breakfast
Orange Juice
Hard-cooked Egg
French Bread
Grape Jelly
Oatmeal
Sugar
Special Formula

Snack
Banana

Lunch
Broiled Beef Patty
Diced Potatoes
Green Beans
Peach Halves
Cherry Popsicle
Iced Tea, Sugar, Lemon
Special Formula

Snack
Grape Juice

Dinner
Roasted Chicken
Steamed Rice
Cooked Carrots
Pear Halves
Fruit Flavored Ice
Coke
Special Formula

Snack
French Bread and Jelly Sandwich

Phenylketonuria

Phenylketonuria is a classic autosomal recessive inborn error of metabolism in which phenylalanine hydroxylase deficiency results in markedly increased levels of blood phenylalanine. With the inability to convert phenylalanine to tyrosine, phenylalanine is metabolized by a number of secondary pathways to compounds such as phenylpyruvic acid, phenylacetic acid, phenyllactic acid and others. These compounds are present in excess in the urine and give rise to the positive ferric chloride or dinitrophenylhydrazine screening test as well as accounting for the "mousy" odor of the disease.

Clinically, the disease is primarily one of severe mental retardation with impairment of brain growth. Microcephaly and seizures are common and patients frequently have IQs in the range of 20, thus being profoundly handicapped and requiring extensive nursing care. The incidence of classical PKU in the United States is 1:10,000-15,000 with a much lower incidence in American blacks. It has now been clearly proven that dietary reduction of phenylalanine intake will result in a marked lowering of blood phenylalanine levels and in a marked improvement in mental development. The exact molecular basis by which hyperphenylalaninemia causes mental retardation remains unknown.

In practical application, virtually all newborns in the United States are screened for PKU by collecting a dried blood sample immediately prior to discharge from the nursery. The phenylalanine content of the blood is measured using the Guthrie bacteriologic assay. Patients with elevated phenylalanine levels should be evaluated immediately for the presence of PKU, although the screening test does result in some false positive results in an attempt to avoid false negatives.

Occasional patients with PKU may escape detection, particularly if milk intake is inadequate prior to the time of obtaining the sample. Patients with serum phenylalanones documented above 20 mg./dl are considered to have classical PKU and are subjects for dietary therapy. Therapy is instituted using the commercial formula, Lofenalac, which is normal except for protein content that has been made deficient in phenylalanine. Phenylalanine is an essential amino acid and Lofenalac alone will produce phenylalanine deficiency with anemia, poor growth and even death. Therefore, other sources of protein are added to the diet to achieve an intake of phenylalanine, which is approximately twenty per cent of the usual amount. Serial blood phenylalanine blood determinations are used to adjust dietary intake with an attempt to maintain blood phenylalanine between 3 to 6 mg./dl.

The beneficial effects of early dietary treatment have been well documented and there is evidence that patients should be on dietary therapy by three weeks of age if optimal results are to be obtained. In patients treated from a very early age, the resultant IQs are not significantly different from the unaffected siblings. Dietary therapy is commonly discontinued at age 4 or 5 years, based on the evidence that IQ does not significantly deteriorate when this is accomplished. There are a number of patients who have lesser degrees of phenylalanine hydroxylase deficiency and these patients have been described as variant forms, as transient forms, and as patients with hyperphenylalaninemia. The need for therapy in patients with blood phenylalanies between 10 and 20 mg./dl is uncertain and patients with phenylalanines greater than 20 mg./dl are routinely treated. A less common form of phenylketonuria due to deficiency of dihydropteridine reductase has been described. It is important to identify patients with this condition since dietary treatment will return blood phenylalanine to normal but patients appear to develop mental retardation despite this.

An additional problem is that of the teratogenic effect on fetuses for mothers affected with phenylketonuria. Offspring of women with blood phenylalanine levels greater than 20 mg./dl have been retarded in 99 per cent of the cases and are frequently affected with multiple congenital malformations. Although the outcome may be slightly improved by such women returning to dietary therapy at the time of pregnancies, there is no indication that this therapy will completely prevent the risk of serious harm to the fetus and pregnancy is not advised for women affected with PKU. If such women are pregnant and the pregnancy is to continue, careful dietary treatment is advised.

Phenylalanine Content of Lofenalac

Powder		Beverage (Normal Dilution) 1 Measure: 2 oz. H_2O	
Measures	**Phenylalanine mg.**	**Ounces**	**Phenylalanine mg.**
1	7.5	1	3.8
2	15	2	7.6
3	22.5	3	11.4

Phenylalanine Content of Lofenalac

Powder		Beverage (Normal Dilution) 1 Measure: 2 oz. H_2O	
Measures	Phenylalanine mg.	Ounces	Phenylalanine mg.
4	30	4	15.2
5	37.5	5	19
6	45	6	22.8
7	52.5	7	26.6
8	60	8	30.4
9	67.5	9	34.2
10	75	10	38
11	82.5	11	41.8
12	90	12	45.6
13	97.5	13	49.4
14	105	14	53.2
15	112.5	15	57
16 (1 cup)	120	16	60.8
17	127.5	17	64.6
18	135	18	68.4
19	142.5	19	72.2
20	150	20	76
21	157.5	21	79.8
22	165	22	83.6
23	172.5	23	87.4
24	180	24	91.2
25	187.5	25	95
26	195	26	98.8
27	202.5	27	102.6
28	210	28	106.4
29	217.5	29	110.2
30	225	30	114
31	232.5	31	117.8
32	240	32 (1 quart)	121.6
33	247.5		
34	255		
35	262.5		
36	270		

Research Foundation, Children's Hospital, Cincinnati 29, Ohio, (B. Umbarger)

Dietary Management of Phenylketonuria

Most states now routinely perform a Guthrie screening test on newborn infants, designed to detect elevations of blood phenylalanine. This blood test depends on adequate intake of protein to elevate the phenylalanine in infants affected with PKU. False negative tests may occur if blood is drawn early after birth or if protein intake is decreased due, for example, to poor feeding. For this reason it is recommended that the Guthrie test be routinely repeated at the time of the first pediatric visit at four to six weeks of age.

In an attempt to avoid false negative tests, the criteria for interpretation result in a modest number of false positive tests. This means that there may be only a 20% or so chance that an infant with a positive screening tests will have PKU. In the event of a positive screening test, a quantitative serum phenylalanine should be obtained immediately. The need for immediate follow-up of positive Guthrie screening tests cannot be over-emphasized since early institution of dietary therapy, preferably within two to three weeks, is essential for optimal mental prognosis. This result should be obtained in one or two days and the patient need not be started on dietary therapy until the follow-up test result is available.

There is increasing concern that institution of dietary therapy in unaffected infants and over-restriction of phenylalanine in affected infants may result in brain damage. For this reason, no infant should be started on Lofenalac in whom the diagnosis has not been confirmed and no affected infant should be given a diet of Lafenalac alone. The Lofenalac formula must be supplemented with other dietary sources to prevent phenylalanine deficiency. Newborn infants with classical PKU usually require a formula mixture of approximately five parts of Lofenalac with one part of whole cow's milk. Dietary management, however, is based on monitoring of blood phenlylalanine levels and not on the administration of pre-determined amounts of phenylalanine, which should be used rather only as guidelines.

The object of dietary treatment in phenylketonuria is to restrict the intake of the offending phenylalanine and consequently lower the circulating level. Normal serum phenylalanine levels are from 1-3 mg/ml; phenylketonurics have from 15-60 mg. or more (as high as 10 to 50 times normal). Since phenylalanine is an essential amino acid, a certain amount that will maintain normal growth and development must be provided. Synderman et al (J. Nutr. *56*:253, 1955) found this requirement for normal infants to be from 60 to 90 mg/kg/day. The specific amount required appears to be an individual factor and varies from person to person. Age is also a factor in this requirement, the younger infant requiring relatively more than the older child or adult. The phenylalanine level in the cord blood at birth is normal. Within a few days, as the infant begins to consume milk (either breast or cow's milk), the serum phenylalanine level rises and phenylpyruvic acid appears in the urine.

Dietary treatment is not initiated until there is confirmation of the diagnosis of "classical" PKU. The following criteria are usually used:

1. Serum phenylalanine level over 15 mg/100 ml
   (Normal: 1-4 mg/100 ml)
2. Serum tyrosine level less than 5 mg/100 ml
   (Normal: less than 5 mg/100 ml)
3. Urine phenylalanine excretion over 100 mcg/ml
   (Normal: 10-75 mcg/ml)

4. Urine orthohydroxyphenylacetic acid (oHPAA) over 10 mcg/ml (Normal: 0)

These determinations are performed weekly during the first three months, twice per month from 3 to 6 months and then monthly. If serum phenylalanine levels are persistently below 2 mg/100 ml. or there is inadequate weight gain, additional phenylalanine may be given in small amounts of milk (evaporated or regular cow's milk). For satisfactory results, serum phenylalanine levels are best maintained between 2 and 5 mg/100 ml.

Lofenalac (Mead-Johnson Company) is a specially-prepared formula (enzymic casein hydrolysate) low in phenylalanine (0.06 to 0.1%) combined with fat and carbohydrate and the addition of vitamins, minerals and three purified amino acids (L-Methionine, L-Tryptophan and L-Tyrosine), providing otherwise total nutrient composition. For complete composition, see Table I.

The diet is prescribed and calculated on an individual basis in terms of the patient's nutritional needs for protein, carbohydrate, fat, fluid, etc. Since the phenylalanine content of foods is estimated to be about 5% of the total protein, it is obvious that there necessarily will be severe restriction of high-protein foods. Lofenalac serves as the basis of the diet and the remainder is chosen from selected low-protein vegetables, fruits, bread and cereals, fats, desserts and free foods. All high-phenylalanine foods are avoided. This diet is prescribed in terms of total daily phenylalanine allowance or mg/kg/day. After one has determined the protein requirement for the individual, the phenylalanine content is reduced to about 14 to 17% that of a normal diet. This level is further adjusted to the individual on the basis of his or her blood and urine determination.

Phenylalanine requirements increase rapidly in the infant due to the rapid rate of growth and must be adjusted or there is the problem of phenylalanine deficiency. Some workers in the field prefer the lower limit of 3 mg. because of having experienced such difficulty with the narrow margin allowed by 2 mg./100 ml. They likewise allow upper limits of 8-10 mg% because of apparently successful therapy and no noticeable untoward effects (Berry et al., Amer. J. Dis. Child. *113*:2-5, 1967).

As the infant grows and the nutritional requirements increase, the Lofenalac may be used in a more concentrated form. It is difficult to achieve adequate intake of the liquid form by about a year of age to meet these requirements, and low-phenylalanine natural foods are included.

To help mothers understand, plan and administer the diet, "equivalent lists", similar to those used in the diabetic diet planning, were devised. Foods are listed in definite amounts that are one or more equivalents of phenylalanine, one equivalent representing 15 mg. phenylalanine. Thus it is easier for them to plan, substitute and make allowances for deviations from the planned diet.

Information Needed for Calculation of PKU Diet

NRC Allowances (1974) — **Phenylalanine Rec'd for PKU Children**

Age	**Weight kg**	**Weight lbs**	**Energy kcal**	**Protein gms**	**Phenylalanine**
0-6 mos.	6	14	kg × 117	kg × 2.2	80-50
6 mo-1 yr.	9	20	kg × 108	kg × 2.0	50-30
1-3 yrs	13	28	1300	23	35-20
4-6 yrs	20	44	1800	30	30-15

1. Age and weight
2. Prescribed protein, kilocalorie and phenylalanine intake per kg/day
3. Lofenalac
   1 measure (1T) provides:
   7.5 mg phenylalanine
   1.4 gm protein
   43 kilocalories
4. When milk is given, *mix with* Lofenalac
   1 oz. evaporated milk supplies:
   2.2 gm protein
   107 mg phenylalanine
   44 kilocalories
5. **Exchange**

	Avg kilcalories
1 vegetable	10
1 fruit	80
1 bread	10

Example of Calculation

4 yr. old child   Weight: 20 kg (44 lbs.)

Allowances:

Kilocalories	(90/kg)	1800
Protein	(1.5 gm/kg)	30 gms
Phenylalanine	(20 mg/kg)	400 mgs

$$\frac{\text{30 gms protein}}{\text{1.4 gms/1 T Lofenalac}} = \text{21.5 measures Lofenalac}$$

21.5 (T) × 43 (kcal) = 925 kcal from Lofenalac

21.5 (T) × 7.5 (mg phenylalanine) = 161 mg phenylalanine from Lofenalac

400 mg (allowance) less 161 mg (from Lofenalac) = 239 mg. phenylalanine to come from other food. Each exchange is equivalent to 15 mg phenylalanine, thus 239 divided by 15 = 16 food exchanges.

Total daily kilocalories		1800
From Lofenalac		925
From other food		875
5 bread	50	
4 vegetable	40	
7 fruit	560	650
From free foods		225

Exchanges	mg Phenylalanine	kilocalories
5 bread	75	50
4 vegetable	60	40
7 fruit	105	560
Total	240	650

Phenylalanine Content of Gerber Baby Foods as Purchased

All data given have been determined by direct analysis.

Unless otherwise indicated, data for jarred foods apply to both strained and junior textures.

These data are representative of Gerber Baby Foods only. Other brands could have appreciably different phenylalanine contents.

(January, 1967)

Address inquiries on nutritional data to:

Professional Relations Department
Gerber Products Company
Fremont, Michigan 49412

	Phenylalanine	
Formulas	**mg per 100 gm**	**mg per tablespoon**
MBF (Meat Base Formula)	290	45.3
Dry Cereals		
Barley Cereal	442	10.6
High Protein Cereal	1655	39.8
Mixed Cereal	465	11.2
Oatmeal	729	17.5
Rice Cereal	256	6.2
Cereals With Fruit (in jars)		
Mixed cereal with Applesauce and Bananas	27.5	3.9
Oatmeal with Applesauce and Bananas	22.9	3.3
Rice Cereal with Applesauce and Bananas	15.2	2.2
Fruits		
Applesauce	9.8	1.4
Applesauce & Apricots	10.5	1.5
Applesauce with Pineapple	10.4	1.5
Apricots with Tapioca	8.4	1.2
Bananas with Tapioca	7.2	1.0
Bananas with Pineapple & Tapioca	10.0	1.4
Peaches	9.5	1.4
Pears	6.8	1.0
Pears and Pineapple	8.5	1.2
Plums with Tapioca	9.7	1.4
Prunes with Tapioca	8.3	1.2
Vegetables		
Beets (strained only)	17.2	2.5

Vegetables—*(Continued)*	Phenylalanine mg per 100 gm	mg per tablespoon
Carrots	13.7	2.0
Creamed Corn	27.4	3.9
Creamed Spinach	44.8	6.4
Garden Vegetables (strained only)	66.7	9.5
Green Beans (Strained only)	34.2	4.9
Mixed Vegetables	34.6	4.9
Peas (strained only) (too variable to average data)	Range 69.4-109.0	9.9-15.6
Squash	22.2	3.2
Sweet Potatoes	25.2	3.6
Meats and Egg Yolks		
Beef	563	80.4
Beef with Beef Heart (strained only)	606	86.6
Beef Liver (strained only)	586	83.7
Chicken	562	80.3
Chicken Sticks (junior only)	377	53.9
Egg Yolks (strained only)	434	62.0
Egg Yolks with Ham (strained only)	378	54.0
Ham (strained only)	432	61.7
Lamb	503	71.9
Meat Sticks (junior only)	592	84.6
Pork	538	76.9
Turkey (strained only)	443	63.3
Veal	515	73.6
High Meat Dinners and Cheese Foods		
Beef with Vegetables	262	37.4
Chicken with Vegetables	219	31.3
Creamed Cottage Cheese with pineapple (strained only)	298	42.6
Ham with Vegetables	212	30.3
Turkey with Vegetables	199	28.4
Veal with Vegetables	226	32.3
Dinners		
Beef and Egg Noodles	28.2	4.0
Cereal, Egg Yolks & Bacon	10.5	1.5
Chicken Noodle Dinner	16.7	2.4
Cream of Chicken Soup	78.0	11.1
Vegetables & Bacon	27.6	3.9
Vegetables & Chicken	23.3	3.3
Vegetables & Ham with Bacon	34.6	4.9
Vegetables & Lamb	28.3	4.0
Vegetables & Liver with Bacon	66.0	9.4
Vegetables & Turkey	31.0	4.4

Desserts	Phenylalanine mg per 100 gm	Phenylalanine mg per tablespoon
Cherry Vanilla Pudding	5.2	0.7
Chocolate Flavored Custard Pudding	96.5	13.8
Dutch Apple Dessert	5.9	0.8
Fruit Dessert with Tapioca	10.8	1.5
Orange Pudding (strained only)	26.3	3.8
Vanilla Custard Pudding	85.5	12.2
Apple Gel	4.8	0.7
Cherry Gel	4.7	0.7
Orange Gel	7.1	1.0
Raspberry Gel	4.5	0.6

Phenylalanine Exchange List
Vegetables

Each serving as listed is one equivalent or 15 mg phenylalanine

Food	Amount	Phenyl-alanine mg	Protein gm	Calo-ries
Baby and Junior				
Beets	7 Tbsp	15	1.1	35
Carrots	7 Tbsp	15	0.7	28
Creamed Spinach	1 Tbsp	16	0.4	6
Green Beans	2 Tbsp	15	0.3	7
Squash	4 Tbsp	14	0.4	14
Table Vegetables				
Asparagus, cooked	1 stalk	12	0.6	4
Beans, green, cooked	4 Tbsp (1/4 cup)	14	0.6	9
Beans, yellow, wax, cooked	4 Tbsp (1/4 cup)	15	0.6	9
Bean Sprouts, mung, cooked	2 Tbsp	18	0.6	5
Beets, cooked	8 Tbsp (1/2 cup)	14	0.8	34
Beet greens, cooked	1 Tbsp	14	0.2	3
Broccoli, cooked	1 Tbsp	11	0.3	3
Brussels Sprouts, cooked	1 medium	16	0.6	5
Cabbage, raw, shredded	8 Tbsp (1/2 cup)	15	0.7	12
Cabbage, cooked	5 Tbsp (1/3 cup)	16	0.8	12
Carrots, cooked	8 Tbsp (1/2 cup)	17	0.5	23
Carrots, raw	1/6 large (1/4 cup)	16	0.5	16
Cauliflower, cooked	3 Tbsp	18	0.6	6
Celery, cooked, diced*	4 Tbsp (1/4 cup)	15	0.4	6
Celery, raw*	1-8 inch stalk	16	0.5	7
Chard leaves, cooked	2 Tbsp	19	0.6	6
Collards, cooked	1 Tbsp	16	0.5	5

* Phenylalanine calculated as 3.3% of total protein.

Food	Amount	Phenyl-alanine mg.	Protein gm.	Calo-ries
Cucumber slices, raw	8 slices, 1/8″ thick	16	0.7	12
Eggplant, diced, raw	3 Tbsp	18	0.4	9
Kale, cooked	2 Tbsp	20	0.5	5
Lettuce*	3 small leaves	13	0.4	5
Mushrooms, cooked*	2 Tbsp	14	0.4	35
Mushrooms, fresh*	2 small	16	0.5	3
Mustard greens, cooked	2 Tbsp	18	0.6	6
Okra, cooked*	2-3″ pods	13	0.4	7
Onion, raw, chopped	5 Tbsp (1/3 cup)	14	0.5	20
Onion, cooked	4 Tbsp (1/4 cup)	14	0.5	19
Onion, young scallion	5-5″ long	14	0.5	23
Parsley, raw, chopped*	3 Tbsp	13	0.4	5
Parsnips, cooked, diced*	3 Tbsp	13	0.3	18
Peppers, raw, chopped*	4 Tbsp	13	0.4	12
Pickles, Dill	8 slices, 1/8″ thick	16	0.7	12
Pumpkin, cooked	4 Tbsp (1/4 cup)	14	0.5	16
Radishes, red, small*	4	13	0.4	8
Rutabagas, cooked	2 Tbsp	16	0.3	10
Peas	1 Tbsp	16	0.6	7
Spinach, cooked	1 Tbsp	15	0.4	3
Squash, summer, cooked	8 Tbsp (1/2 cup)	16	0.6	16
Squash, winter, cooked	3 Tbsp	16	0.6	14
Tomato, raw	1/2 small	14	0.5	10
Tomato, cooked	4 Tbsp (1/4 cup)	15	0.6	10
Tomato Juice	4 Tbsp (1/4 cup)	17	0.6	12
Tomato Catsup	2 Tbsp	17	0.6	34
Turnip Greens, cooked	1 Tbsp	18	0.4	4
Turnips, diced, cooked	5 Tbsp (1/3 cup)	16	0.4	12
Soups				
Beef Broth (Campbell's condensed)	1 Tbsp	14	0.5	3
Celery (Campbell's condensed)	2 Tbsp	18	0.4	19
Minestrone (Campbell's condensed)	1 Tbsp	17	1.5	25
Mushroom (Campbell's condensed)	1 Tbsp	11	0.2	17
Onion (Campbell's condensed)	1 Tbsp	14	0.6	8
Tomato (Campbell's condensed)	1 Tbsp	11	0.2	11
Vegetarian Vegetable Soup (Campbell's condensed)	1 1/2 Tbsp	17	0.4	14

Food	Amount	Phenyl-alanine mg	Protein gm	Calories
Fruits				
Each serving as listed is one equivalent or 15 mg phenylalanine				
Baby and Junior				
Applesauce and apricots	16 Tbsp (1 cup)	15	0.6	205
Applesauce and pineapple	16 Tbsp (1 cup)	11	0.5	176
Apricots with tapioca	16 Tbsp (1 cup)	16	0.6	187
Bananas	8 Tbsp (½ cup)	14	0.6	97
Bananas with pineapple	16 Tbsp (1 cup)	18	0.6	187
Peaches	10 Tbsp	15	0.7	124
Pears	12 Tbsp (¾ cup)	16	0.5	106
Pears and pineapple	16 Tbsp (1 cup)	17	1.0	166
Plums with tapioca	12 Tbsp (¾ cup)	16	0.5	163
Prunes with tapioca	12 Tbsp (¾ cup)	16	0.5	152
Fruit Juices				
Apricot nectar	6 oz (¾ cup)	14	0.6	102
Cranberry juice	12 oz (1½ cup)	15	0.6	39
Grape juice	4 oz (½ cup)	14	0.5	80
Grapefruit juice	8 oz (1 cup)	16	1.2	104
Orange juice	6 oz (¾ cup)	16	1.2	84
Peach nectar	5 oz (⅔ cup)	15	0.5	75
Pineapple juice	6 oz (¾ cup)	16	0.6	90
Prune juice	4 oz (½ cup)	16	0.5	84
Table Fruits				
Apple, raw	4 small 2½″ diam.	16	0.8	176
Applesauce	16 Tbsp (1 cup)	12	0.6	192
Apricots, raw	1 medium	12	0.5	25
Apricots, canned	2 medium, 2 Tbsp syrup	14	0.6	80
Avocado, cubed or mashed*	5 Tbsp (⅓ cup)	16	0.6	80
Banana, raw, sliced	4 Tbsp (¼ cup)	15	0.4	32
Blackberries, raw*	5 Tbsp (⅓ cup)	14	0.6	25
Blackberries canned in syrup*	5 Tbsp (⅓ cup)	13	0.5	55
Blueberries, raw or frozen*	12 Tbsp (¾ cup)	16	0.6	60
Blueberries, canned in syrup*	10 Tbsp	16	0.6	140
Boysenberries, frozen, sweet*	8 Tbsp (½ cup)	16	0.6	72
Cantaloupe	5 Tbsp (⅓ cup)	16	0.4	15
Cherries, sweet, canned in syrup*	8 Tbsp (½ cup)	16	0.6	104
Dates, pitted, chopped	3 Tbsp	18	0.7	96
Figs, raw*	1 large	18	0.7	40

* Phenylalanine calculated as 2.6% of total protein.

Food	Amount	Phenyl-alanine mg	Protein gm	Calo-ries
Figs, canned in syrup*	2 figs, 4 tsp. syrup	16	0.6	90
Figs, dried*	1 small	16	0.6	40
Fruit Cocktail*	12 Tbsp. (¾ cup)	16	0.6	120
Grapes, American type	8 grapes	14	0.5	24
Grapes, American slipskin	5 Tbsp. (⅓ cup)	16	0.6	25
Grapes, Thompson seedless	8 Tbsp (½ cup)	13	0.8	64
Guava, raw*	½ medium	13	0.5	35
Honeydew melon*	¼ small 5″ melon	13	0.5	32
Mango, raw*	1 small	18	0.7	66
Nectarines, raw	1-2″ high, 2″ diameter	15	0.4	45
Oranges, raw	1 medium 3″ diameter or ⅔ cup sections	15	1.1	60
Papayas, raw*	¼ medium or ½ cup	14	0.6	36
Peaches, raw	1 medium	15	0.5	46
Peaches, canned in syrup	2 medium halves	18	0.6	88
Pears, raw	1-3″ x 2½″	14	1.3	100
Pineapple, raw*	16 Tbsp (1 cup)	16	0.6	80
Pineapple, canned in syrup*	2 small slices	13	0.5	93
Plums, raw	½-2″ plum	12	0.3	15
Plums, canned in syrup	3-2 Tbsp. syrup	16	0.5	91
Prunes, dried	2 large	14	0.4	54
Raisins, dried, seedless	2 Tbsp	14	0.5	54
Raspberries, raw*	5 Tbsp. (⅓ cup)	13	0.5	25
Raspberries, canned in syrup*	6 Tbsp.	14	0.5	78
Strawberries, raw*	8 large	16	0.6	32
Strawberries, frozen*	6 Tbsp	14	0.5	108
Tangerines	1½ large	15	1.2	66
Watermelon*	½ cup cubes	13	0.5	28

Breads and Cereals

Each serving as listed is two equivalents or 30 mg phenylalanine

Food	Amount	Phenyl-alanine mg	Protein gm	Calo-ries
Baby and Junior				
Cereals, ready to serve				
Barley	3 Tbsp	32	0.8	24
Oatmeal	2 Tbsp	34	0.8	16
Rice	5 Tbsp (⅓ cup)	30	0.6	40
Wheat	2 Tbsp	30	0.6	17
Creamed Corn	3 Tbsp	30	0.5	27
Sweet Potatoes (Gerber's)	3 Tbsp	32	0.5	31
Table Foods				
Cereals, cooked				
Cornmeal	4 Tbsp (¼ cup)	29	0.6	29

* Phenylalanine calculated as 2.6% of total protein.

Food	Amount	Phenyl-alanine mg	Protein gm	Calo-ries
Cream of Rice	4 Tbsp (¼ cup)	35	0.7	34
Cream of Wheat	2 Tbsp	27	0.6	16
Farina	2 Tbsp	25	0.5	18
Malt-o-meal	2 Tbsp	27	0.5	17
Oatmeal	2 Tbsp	32	0.7	18
Pettijohns	2 Tbsp	24	0.5	19
Ralstons	2 Tbsp	34	0.7	18
Rice, brown or white	4 Tbsp (¼ cup)	35	0.7	34
Wheatena	2 Tbsp	27	0.5	19
Cereals, ready to serve				
Alpha bits	4 Tbsp (¼ cup)	32	0.6	28
Cheerios	3 Tbsp	32	0.6	20
Corn Chex	4 Tbsp (¼ cup)	29	0.6	32
Cornfetti	5 Tbsp (⅓ cup)	31	0.6	46
Cornflakes	5 Tbsp (⅓ cup)	29	0.6	30
Crispy Critters	4 Tbsp (¼ cup)	30	0.6	28
Kix	5 Tbsp (⅓ cup)	31	0.6	31
Krumbles	3 Tbsp	32	0.7	26
Rice Chex	6 Tbsp	32	0.7	49
Rice Flakes	5 Tbsp (⅓ cup)	33	0.6	32
Rice Krispies	6 Tbsp	30	0.6	40
Rice, puffed	12 Tbsp (¾ cup)	30	0.6	38
Sugar Crisp, puffed wheat	4 Tbsp (¼ cup)	30	0.6	46
Sugar Sparkled Flakes	5 Tbsp (⅓ cup)	29	0.6	55
Wheat Chex	10 biscuits	30	0.6	22
Wheaties	3 Tbsp	26	0.5	20
Wheat, puffed	6 Tbsp	30	0.6	16
Crackers				
Barnum Animal	5	30	0.6	45
Graham (65/lb.)	1	26	0.5	30
Ritz (no cheese)	2	24	0.5	34
Saltines (140/lb.)	2	29	0.6	28
Soda (63/lb.)	1	36	0.7	30
Wheat Thins (248/lb.)	5	30	0.6	45
Corn, cooked	2 Tbsp	32	0.7	17
Hominy	2 Tbsp	32	0.7	17
Macaroni, cooked	1½ Tbsp	31	0.7	20
Noodles, cooked	3 Tbsp	32	0.7	20
Popcorn, popped	5 Tbsp (⅓ cup)	31	0.6	17
Potato Chips	4-2″ diameter	30	0.6	44
Potato, Irish, cooked	3 Tbsp	33	0.8	31
Spaghetti, cooked	1 Tbsp	24	0.5	14
Sweet Potato, cooked	2 Tbsp	25	0.4	31
Tortilla, corn	1½-6″ diameter	30	0.8	31
White Bread	1 slice	79	2.0	50

* Phenylalanine calculated as 2.6% of total protein.

Food	Amount	Phenyl-alanine mg	Protein gm	Calories
Jolly Joan Bread	1 slice	9	.2	115

Fats

Each serving as listed contains 5 milligrams phenylalanine

Food	Amount	Phenyl-alanine mg	Protein gm	Calories
Butter	1 Tbsp	5	0.1	100
French Dressing, commercial	1 Tbsp	5	0.1	59
Margarine	1 Tbsp	5	0.1	100
Mayonnaise, commercial	½ Tbsp	5	0.1	30
Olives, green or ripe	1 medium	5	0.1	12

Desserts

Each serving as listed is two equivalents of 30 mg phenylalanine

Cake*	1/12 of cake
Cookies—Rice Flour*	2
Corn Starch*	2
Cookies, Arrowroot	1½
Ice Cream—Chocolate*	⅔ cup
Pineapple*	⅔ cup
Strawberry	⅔ cup
Jello	⅓ cup
Puddings*	½ cup
Sauce, Hershey	2 Tbsp
Wafers, sugar, Nabisco	5

Free Foods

Contain little or no phenylalanine, may be used as desired

Apple Juice
Beverages, carbonated
Gingerbread*
Guava Butter
Candy
  Butterscotch
  Cream Mints
  Fondant
  Gum Drops
  Hard
  Jelly Beans
  Lollipops
Cherries, Maraschino
Fruit Ices (if no more than ½ cup used daily)
Cornstarch
Jell-quick
Jellies
Kool Aide
Lemonade
Molasses
Oil
Strawberry Quik
Pepper, black, ground
Popsicles with artificial fruit flavor
Rich's Topping
Salt
Shortening, vegetable
Soy Sauce
Sugar, brown, white or confectioner's
Syrups, corn or maple
Tang
Tapioca

* Special recipe must be used—in Phenylalanine-Restricted Diet Recipe Book.

Phenylalanine Content of Foods (Gerber's)

One equivalent equals 15 milligrams (mg) phenylalanine.

	Amount	Phenyl-alanine mg	Protein gm	Calories
Cereals with Fruit (in jars)				
Mixed Cereal with Applesauce & Bananas	3.8 T.	= 15 mg PA	.7	44
Oatmeal with Applesauce & Bananas	4.5 T.	= 15 mg PA	.9	49
Rice Cereal with Applesauce & Bananas	6.8 T.	= 15 mg PA		
Fruits				
Applesauce	10.7 T.	= 15 mg PA	.3	128
Applesauce & Apricots	10 T.	= 15 mg PA	.6	128
Applesauce with Pineapple	10 T.	= 15 mg PA	.3	110
Apricots with Tapioca	12.5 T.	= 15 mg PA	.5	146
Bananas with Tapioca	15 T.	= 15 mg PA	1.1	182
Bananas with Pineapple & Tapioca	10.7 T.	= 15 mg PA	.4	125
Peaches	10.7 T.	= 15 mg PA	.8	132
Pears	15 T.	= 15 mg PA	.6	146
Pears and Pineapple	12.5 T.	= 15 mg PA	.7	130
Plums with Tapioca	10.7 T.	= 15 mg PA	.5	149
Prunes with Tapioca	12.5 T.	= 15 mg PA	.5	159
Vegetables				
Beets (strained only)	6 T.	= 15 mg PA	1.0	30
Carrots	7.5 T.	= 15 mg PA	.8	30
Creamed Corn	3.8 T.	= 15 mg PA	.6	34
Creamed Spinach	2.3 T.	= 15 mg PA	.9	13
Garden Vegetables (strained only)	1.5 T.	= 15 mg PA	.5	7
Green Beans (strained only)	3 T.	= 15 mg PA	.5	11
Mixed Vegetables	3 T.	= 15 mg PA	.6	17
Peas (strained only)	1 T.	= 15 mg PA	.6	7
Squash	4.6 T.	= 15 mg PA	.5	16
Sweet Potatoes	4 T.	= 15 mg PA	.7	45
Dinners (not high meat dinners)				
Beef and Egg Noodles	4 T.	= 15 mg PA	1.4	27
Cereal, Egg Yolks, & Bacon	10 T.	= 15 mg PA	3.4	104
Chicken Noodle Dinner	6 T.	= 15 mg PA	1.9	44
Cream of Chicken Soup	1.5 T.	= 15 mg PA	.6	13
Vegetables & Bacon	4 T.	= 15 mg PA	.9	60
Vegetables & Chicken	4.5 T.	= 15 mg PA	1.4	28
Vegetables & Ham with Bacon	3 T.	= 15 mg PA	.8	31
Vegetables & Lamb	4 T.	= 15 mg PA		
Vegetables & Liver with Bacon	1.5 T.	= 15 mg PA		
Vegetables & Turkey	3.4 T.	= 15 mg PA		

	Amount	Phenyl-alanine mg	Protein gm	Calories
Desserts				
Cherry Vanilla Pudding	21	T. = 15 mg PA	1.5	321
Chocolate Flavored Custard Pudding	1	T. = 15 mg PA	.3	13
Dutch Apple Dessert	18.8	T. = 15 mg PA		
Fruit Dessert with Tapioca	10	T. = 15 mg PA		
Orange Pudding (strained only)	3.9	T. = 15 mg PA	.4	46
Vanilla Custard Pudding	1.2	T. = 15 mg PA	.3	13
Gels				
Apple Gel	21	T. = 15 mg PA		
Cherry Gel	21	T. = 15 mg PA		
Orange Gel	15	T. = 15 mg PA		
Raspberry Gel	25	T. = 15 mg PA		
High Meat Dinners				
Beef with Vegetables	1	T. = 30 mg PA	1	13
Chicken with Vegetables	1	T. = 30 mg PA	1	12
Ham with Vegetables	1	T. = 30 mg PA	1	11
Turkey with Vegetables	1	T. = 30 mg PA	.8	10
Veal with Vegetables	1	T. = 30 mg PA	1	9
Meat and Egg Yolks				
Egg Yolks (strained only)	1½	T. = 30 mg PA	1.9	43
Egg Yolks with Ham (strained only)	1½	T. = 30 mg PA	2.4	42

Reprinted from California State Department of Public Health, 1972.

Maple Syrup Urine Disease (MSUD)

Branched chain ketoaciduria (BCKA) or MSUD has now been separated into classical, intermittent, mild and thiamine responsive forms. In 1954 Menkes and colleagues described the clinical features of the classic form. All forms of BCKA are autosomal recessive disorders with a pan-ethnic occurrence and a combined estimated frequency of 0.3 per 100,000 live births. Deficiency of branched chain ketoacid decarboxylase is the etiology in all forms, being most complete in the classic form. The deficient enzyme is a subunited (non-identical) structure catalysing multiple enzyme steps and involving thiamine pyrophosphate, acetyl Co^A. lipoic acid and NAD^+. The single gene defect causes the simultaneous inability to decarboxylate the respective α-keto acids of leucine, isoleucine and valine. The defect results in the accumulation of leucine, isoleucine, valine and alloisoleucine in the blood with the last of these previously mistaken as methionine. The amino acids are excreted in increased amounts but the α-keto acids are the predominant compounds in the urine.

Classic BCKA presents with feeding difficulties, vomiting, hypertonicity and a shrill cry in the first week or two of life. Flaccidity and apnea may occur with hypoglycemia. Loss of the Moro reflex, decreased deep tendon reflexes and convulsions are common. The hallmark odor is prominent and death usually occurs early with survivors being severely neurologically impaired. The intermittent form of BCKA presents later in infancy or childhood usually with catabolism associated with intercurrent illness. Clinical findings similar to the classical disease may appear abruptly. Mild BCKA implies a chronic state of metabolic imbalance with mental retardation without acute decompensation and may differ little from the intermittent disorder. Patients with thiamine responsive BCKA have partial enzyme deficiency and show clinical and biochemical improvement with large doses of thiamine. The diagnosis is often suspected from the odor although increasingly newborn screening programs will detect patients. The ferric chloride and dinitrophenylhydrazine (DNPH) reactions detect the ketoacids in urine. The serum amino acid elevations are definitive although the enzyme deficiency can be demonstrated in leukocytes, cultured skin fibroblasts and amniotic fluid cells.

Although the pathogenesis is uncertain, clinical experience suggests that toxic metabolites, possibly primarily of leucine, are responsible. Disturbances in myelinization, in protein synthesis and in serotonin levels have been reported, as well as inhibition of various enzymes *in vitro* by branched chain amino acids and ketoacids. The odiferous compound is unknown, but the odor is produced by feeding isoleucine but not leucine and valine.

Treatment of BCKA is the carefully regulated restriction of the intake of the essential amino acids; isoleucine, leucine and valine. This is accomplished initially with a usual formula base free of protein. To this is added an amino acid mix free of isoleucine, leucine and valine. The addition of a small amount of normal milk formula is regulated by frequent quantitative serum amino acid measurements. The diet is managed using leucine equivalents with requirements being 8-15 mg/kg/day. Although some solid foods, particularly fruits and vegetables, can be allowed later, the diet requires liberal use of free amino acids. Dietary therapy must be continued indefinitely. In times of acute toxicity, as at diagnosis or with infections, all branched chain intake is eliminated and exchange transfusion or dialysis may be required. All patients should be tested for thiamine responsiveness and treated if appropriate. Some patients with mild or intermittent BCKA may be managed with low leucine diet without the use of special formulas. Special formulas are available from a variety of suppliers, e.g., Mead Johnson formula base #80056* and General Biochemicals amino acid mix #71004.*

Dietary Management of Maple Syrup Urine Disease

The diagnosis of maple syrup urine disease of the classical form represents a life-threatening problem. Proper therapy involves the use of a synthetic formula composed of an amino acid mixture along with a usual source of carbohydrate, fat, vitamins and minerals. Special formulations are available for treatment of maple syrup urine disease but can be ob-

* Available for research purposes only

tained only with the approval of the Nutrition Committee of the American Academy of Pediatrics. Life-threatening complications of maple syrup urine disease can be treated with peritoneal or hemodialysis. Dietary management requires careful monitoring of blood amino acid levels and should generally be carried out in regional centers where facilities and experience are available for the management of this condition. No over-the-counter products are available for management of maple syrup urine disease.

Gylcogen Storage Diseases[32]

Glycogen storage disease refers to a group of conditions with diverse metabolic effects and only the most common disorders are discussed below.

Type II glycogen storage disease (Pompe's disease) is fatal, lysosomal storage disease with particular involvement of skeletal and cardiac muscle, normoglycemia and no effective dietary therapy.

Type IV glycogen storage disease is associated with deficiency of the glycogen branching enzyme and results in the formation of abnormal glycogen which causes cirrhosis and liver failure. This condition is fatal, results in normoglycemia and is not treatable by dietary therapy.

Type V glycogen storage disease (McArdle's) is associated with deficiency of muscle phosphorylase with symptoms of pain and muscle weakness on extended exercise. The disease usually presents in adulthood and is associated with normoglycemia and is not amenable to dietary therapy.

Glycogen storage diseases type I (von Gierke's disease, glucose-6-phosphatase deficiency), type III. (debrancher deficiency), type VI (hepatic phosphorylase deficiency) are all associated with inability to mobilize glucose from glycogen and are all associated with some degree of systemic hypoglycemia. The clinical picture varies somewhat among these diseases but symptoms of hypoglycemia, growth failure, hepatomegaly, systemic acidosis, anemia, hyperuricemia and hyperlipidemia all can occur. It has been demonstrated that continuous parenteral alimentation or continuous nasogastric alimentation which will maintain a normal or above normal blood sugar will relieve many, if not all, of the symptoms and secondary metabolic disturbances. It is felt that many of the metabolic disturbances are related to the excessive action of glucogon in the face of resistant hypoglycemia. One of the main benefits of such therapy is improved growth and some patients have been treated with 24 hour nasogastric infusion of a nutrient solution with the child wearing a continuous infusion pump in the form of a back-pack. Patients have also been treated with portocaval anastomosis with many reports of improvement in metabolic status and growth. The question has been raised as to the long-term efficacy of portocaval anastomosis, and the operative risk can be significant. The optimal diet for patients with this group of glycogen storage diseases has been debated. It is generally accepted that a diet with a relatively

32. Greene, H. L. et al. Continuous Nocturnal Nasogastric Feeding for Management of Type I Glycogen Storage Disease, *New Engl. J. Med. 294*:423, 1976.

low fat content is preferred. Diets high in protein content and diets high in carbohydrate content have been recommended at various times. Probably the frequency of feeding is more important than whether the frequent meals are of primarily carbohydrate or primarily protein content. In type I glycogen storage disease, the ability to convert sugars such as galactose (lactose) or fructose (sucrose) to glucose will be impaired because of the need to pass through glucose-6-phosphate before entering the blood stream, and it may be preferable to avoid these sugars in patients with type I glycogen storage disease.

One attractive mode of therapy under consideration is the use of nighttime nasogastric tube feeding and frequent daytime feeding for patients with glycogen storage disease types I, III, VI or hepatic phosphorylase kinase deficiency. Approximately 12 hours of nighttime nasogastric tube feeding is accomplished at home using a commercial preparation such as Vivonex* or Polycose.† The patients then eat approximately equally divided portions of a high carbohydrate diet every three hours during the daytime hours. Approximately 60 to 65% of the kilocalories are given during the daytime hours and 35 to 40% of the kilocalories in the form of the nighttime nasogastric infusion. In patients with type I glycogen storage disease, lactose and sucrose are avoided. The patient can be monitored at home using urinary ketones and blood sugars measured by Dextrostix as indices of adequacy of the treatment regimen during the daytime hours. It is attempted to maintain a blood sugar above 80 mg./dl at all times and to avoid ketosis. Many patients will show improved growth, improved exercise tolerance and reversal of chemical abnormalities on this program.

The Homocystinurias

Homocystinuria was described in 1962 in retarded, fair skinned, blond children who excreted large amounts of homocystine in urine. Although the most common disorder is associated with cystathionine synthase deficiency, acquired or inherited blocks in the methyltetrahydrofolatehomocystine methyltransferase reaction also cause homocystinuria. Cystathionine synthase deficiency, to be discussed first, is an autosomal recessive disorder with an uncertain incidence variously estimated at 1 in 30,000 to 1 in 200,000 live births. The deficient enzyme requires pyridoxal phosphate for its conversion of homocystine and serum to cystathionine. The defect results in increased serum homocystine and methionine with the former increased in the urine. Serum cystine and brain cystathionine are decreased.

Cystathionine synthase deficiency is variously manifested with dislocated lenses, mental retardation, growth failure, kyphoscoliosis, pectus excavatum and venous and arterial thromboses. The thrombotic episodes are thought to be caused by homocystine-induced endothelial injury with

* *Vivonex*—elemental diet by Eaton Laboratories

† *Polycose*—water and glucose polymers derived from controlled hydrolysis of corn starch by Ross Laboratories.

secondary increased platelet consumption. The pathogenesis of the mental retardation is unclear. The diagnosis of homocystinuria has been confused with Marfan's syndrome historically primarily due to the occurrence of dislocated lenses, skeletal abnormalities and vascular accidents in both. The diagnosis may be suspected clinically or through newborn screening. The urinary nitroprusside test is positive but other causes of sulfur amino aciduria must be distinguished. Increased homocystine and methionine are present in serum and the former in urine. The enzyme deficiency is demonstrable in biopsied liver or cultured skin or amniotic cells.

The most important aspect of treatment is determination of the responsiveness to vitamin B_6. A substantial portion of patients, probably with residual enzyme activity, have marked biochemical response to 250-500 mg. daily of B_6 with measurable increases in liver cystathionine synthase activity. Although long term experience is not yet available, B_6 does reduce platelet consumption in responsive patients and there is optimism for this physiological therapeutic approach. In patients unresonsive to B_6, diets low in methionine (20 to 40 mg. per kg. per day) but supplemented with Ca-cystinate (100 to 200 mg. per kg. per day) have been used with some success. Evaluation of this therapy is hampered by the inconstant manifestations of the disease, but serum homocystine can be reduced. Such a diet should be used in B_6 unresponsive patients.

Homocystinuria is also seen with intestinal malabsorption of vitamin B_{12}, with impaired intracellular metabolism of B_{12}, and with defective formation of N^5-methyltetrahydrofolate from its precursor, methylenetetrahydrofolate. These conditions all involve impaired activity of N^5-methyltetrahydrofolate methyltransferase which converts homocystine to methionine. Consequently they can be distinguished by the lack of serum methionine deviation. The various disorders must be evaluated individually as to whether they are acquired or inherited and whether absorptive or metabolic. Many of these cases will be responsive to B_{12} or folic acid therapy.

Appendix

Table A-1
More Common Carbohydrates in Foods per 100 gm. Edible Portion

Food	Mono-saccharides			Disaccharides			Polysaccharides					
	Fructose	Glucose	Reducing Sugars*	Lactose	Maltose	Sucrose	Cellulose	Dextrins	Hemicellulose	Pectin	Pentosans	Starch
Fruits												
	gm	gm	gm	gm	gm	gm	gm	gm	gm	gm	gm	gm
Agave juice	17.0		19.0	†								
Apple	5.0	1.7	8.3			3.1	0.4		0.7	0.6		0.6
Apple Juice			8.0			4.2						
Apricots	0.4	1.9				5.5	0.8		1.2	1.0		
Banana												
Yellow green			5.0			5.1						8.8
Yellow			8.4			8.9						1.9
Flecked	3.5	4.5				11.9						1.2
Powder			32.6			33.2		9.6				7.8
Blackberries	2.9	3.2				0.2						
Blueberry juice, commercial			9.6			0.2						
Boysenberries			5.3			1.1				0.3		
Breadfruit												
Hawaiian			1.8			7.7						
Samoan			4.9			9.7						
Cherries												
Eating	7.2	4.7	12.5			0.1				0.3		
Cooking	6.1	5.5	11.6			0.1						
Cranberries	0.7	2.7				0.1						
Currants												
Black	3.7	2.4				0.6						
Red	1.9	2.3				0.2						
White	2.6	3.0										
Dates												
Invert sugar, seedling type	23.9	24.9				0.3						
Deglet Noor			16.2			45.4						
Egyptian			35.8			48.5						3.0
Figs, Kadota												
Fresh	8.2	9.6				0.9						0.1
Dried	30.9	42.0				0.1						0.3
Gooseberries	4.1	4.4				0.7						
Grapes												
Black	7.3	8.2										
Concord	4.3	4.8	9.5			0.2						
Malaga			22.2			0.2						
White	8.1	8.1										
Grapefruit	1.2	2.0				2.9					1.3	
Guava			4.4			1.9						

Food	Mono-saccharides			Disaccharides			Polysaccharides					
	Fructose	Glucose	Reducing Sugars*	Lactose	Maltose	Sucrose	Cellu-lose	Dextrins	Hemi-cellu-lose	Pectin	Pento-sans	Starch
						Fruits, continued						
	gm.	gm.	gm.	gm.	gm	gm.	gm	gm	gm.	gm	gm	gm
Lemon												
Edible portion		1.3				0.2				3.0	0.7	
Whole	1.4	1.4				0.4						
Juice	0.9	0.5				0.1						
Peel			3.4			0.1						
Loganberries	1.3	1.9				0.2						
Loquat												
Champagne		12.0				0.8						
Thales		9.0				0.9						
Mango			3.4			11.6						0.3
Melon												
Cantaloupe	0.9	1.2	2.3			4.4				0.3		
Cassaba,												
Vine ripened			2.8			6.2						
Picked green			3.2			3.9						
Honeydew												
Vine ripened			3.3			7.4						
Picked green			3.6			3.3						
Yellow	1.5	2.1				1.4						
Mulberries	3.6	4.4										
Orange												
Valencia (Calif.)	2.3	2.4	4.7			4.2						
Composite values	1.8	2.5	5.0			4.6	0.3		0.3	1.3	0.3	
Juice												
Fresh	2.4	2.4	5.1			4.7						
Frozen, reconstituted			4.6			3.2						
Palmyra palm, tender kernel	1.5	3.2				0.4						
Papaw (Asimina triloba) (North America)			5.9			2.7						
Papaya (Carica papaya) (tropics)			9.0			0.5						
Passion fruit juice	3.6	3.6				3.8						1.8
Peaches	1.6	1.5	3.1			6.6		0.7		0.7		
Pears												
Anjou			7.6			1.9				0.7		
Bartlett	5.0	2.5	8.0			1.5				0.6		
Bosc	6.5	2.6				1.7				0.6		
Persimmon			17.7									
Pineapple												
Ripened on plant	1.4	2.3	4.2			7.9						
Picked green			1.3			2.4						
Plums												
Damson	3.4	5.2	8.4			1.0						
Green Gage	4.0	5.5				2.9						
Italian prunes			4.6			5.4				0.9		
Sweet	2.9	4.5	7.4			4.4		0.5		1.0	0.1	
Sour	1.3	3.5				1.5				1.0		
Pomegranate			12.0			0.6						
Prunes, uncooked	15.0	30.0	47.0			2.0	2.8		10.7	0.9	2.0	0.7
Raisins, Thompson seedless			70.0							1.0		
Raspberries	2.4	2.3	5.0			1.0				0.8		
Sapote	3.8	4.2		0.7								

Food	Mono-saccharides			Disaccharides			Polysaccharides					
	Fructose	Glucose	Reducing Sugars*	Lactose	Maltose	Sucrose	Cellulose	Dextrins	Hemicellulose	Pectin	Pentosans	Starch
Fruits, continued												
	gm	gm	gm	gm	gm	gm	gm	gm	gm	gm	gm	gm
Strawberries												
Ripe	2.3	2.6				1.4						
Medium ripe			3.8			0.3						
Tangerine			4.8			9.0						
Tomatoes	1.2	1.6	3.4				0.2		0.3	0.3		
Canned			3.0			0.3						
Seedless pulp			6.5			0.4	0.4			0.5		
Watermelon												
Flesh red and firm, ripe			3.8			4.0				0.1		
Red, mealy, overripe			3.0			4.9				0.1		
Vegetables												
Asparagus, raw			1.2						0.3			
Bamboo shoots			0.5			0.2	1.2					
Beans												
Lima												
Canned						1.4						
Fresh						1.4						
Snap, fresh			1.7			0.5	0.5	0.3	1.0	0.5	1.2	2.0
Beets, sugar						12.9	0.9		0.8			
Broccoli							0.9		0.9		0.9	1.3
Brussel Sprouts							1.1		1.5			
Cabbage, raw			3.4			0.3	0.8		1.0			
Carrots, raw			5.8			1.7	1.0		1.7	0.9		
Cauliflower		2.8				0.3	0.7		0.6			
Celery												
Fresh			0.3			0.3						
Hearts			1.7			0.2						
Corn												
Fresh		0.5				0.3	0.6	0.1	0.9		1.3	14.5
Bran									77.1		4.0	
Cucumber			2.5			0.1						
Eggplant			2.1			0.6			0.5			
Lettuce			1.4			0.2	0.4		0.6			
Licorice root		1.4				3.2						22.0
Mushrooms, fresh			0.1				0.9		0.7			2.5
Onions, raw			5.4			2.9			0.3	0.6		
Parsnips, fresh						3.5						7.0
Peas, green						5.5	1.1		2.2			4.1
Potatoes, white	0.1	0.1	0.8			0.1	0.4		0.3			17.0
Pumpkin			2.2			0.6			0.5			0.1
Radishes			3.1			0.3			0.3	0.4		
Rutabagas		5.0					1.3				0.8	
Spinach			0.2				0.4		0.8			
Squash												
Butternut	0.2	0.1				0.4						2.6
Blue Hubbard	1.2	1.1				0.4	0.7					4.8
Golden Crookneck			2.8			1.0						

Food	Mono-saccharides			Disaccharides			Polysaccharides					
	Fructose	Glucose	Reducing Sugars*	Lactose	Maltose	Sucrose	Cellu-lose	Dextrins	Hemi-cellu-lose	Pectin	Pento-sans	Starch
Vegetables, continued												
	gm	gm	gm	gm	gm	gm	gm	gm	gm	gm	gm	gm
Sweet potato												
Raw	0.3	0.4	0.8		1.6	4.1	0.6		1.4	2.2		16.5
Baked			14.5			7.2						4.0
Mature Dry Legumes												
Beans												
Mung												
Black gram						1.6						
Green gram						1.8						
Navy							3.1	3.7	6.4		8.2	35.2
Soy			1.6			7.2	2.6	1.4	6.6		4.0	1.9
Cow pea						1.5	5.4		4.8			
Garbanzo (chick peas)						2.4						
Garden pea (Pisum sativum)‡						6.7	5.0		5.1			38.0
Horse gram (Dolichos biplorus)						2.7						
Lentils						2.1						28.5
Pigeon pea (red gram)						1.6						
Soybean												
Flour						6.8						
Meal						6.8						
Milk and Milk Products												
Buttermilk												
Dry				39.9								
Fluid, genuine and cultured				5.0								
Casein		0.1		4.9								
Ice cream (14.5% cream)				3.6		16.6						
Milk												
Ass				6.0								
Cow				4.9								
Dried												
Skim				52.0								
Whole				38.1								
Fluid												
Skim				5.0								
Whole				4.9								
Sweetened, condensed				14.1		43.5						
Ewe				4.9								
Goat				4.7								
Human												
Colostrum				5.3								
Mature				6.9								
Whey				4.9								
Yogurt				3.8								
Nuts and Nut Products												
Almonds, blanched			0.2			2.3					2.1	
Chestnuts			2.2			3.6					1.2	18.0
Virginia			1.2			8.1		0.3			2.8	18.6
French			3.3			36.					2.5	33.1

Food	Mono-saccharides			Disaccharides			Polysaccharides					
	Fructose	Glucose	Reducing Sugars*	Lactose	Maltose	Sucrose	Cellu-lose	Dextrins	Hemi-cellu-lose	Pectin	Pento-sans	Starch
Nuts and Nut Products, continued												
	gm	gm	gm	gm	gm	gm	gm	gm	gm	gm	gm	gm
Coconut milk, ripe						2.6						
Copra meal, dried	1.2	1.2				14.3	15.6	0.6			2.2	0.9
Macadamia nut			0.3			5.5						
Peanuts			0.2			4.5	2.4	2.5	3.8			4.0
Peanut butter			0.9									5.9
Pecans						1.1					0.2	
Cereals and Cereal Products												
Barley												
Grain, hulled							2.6		6.0		8.5	62.0
Flour						3.1					1.2	69.0
Corn, yellow							4.5		4.9		6.2	62.0
Flaxseed							1.8		5.2			
Millet grain									0.9		6.5	56.0
Oats, hulled											6.4	56.4
Rice												
Bran			1.4			10.6	11.4		7.0		7.4	
Brown, raw			0.1			0.8		2.1			2.1	69.7
Polished, raw		2.0	trace#			0.4	0.3	0.9			1.8	72.9
Polish			0.7								3.8	
Rye												
Grain							3.8		5.6		6.8	57.0
Flour											4.1	71.4
Sorghum grain											2.5	70.2
Soya-wheat (cereal)											3.3	46.4
Wheat												
Germ, defatted						8.3					6.2	
Grain			2.0			1.5	2.0	2.5	5.8		6.6	59.0
Flour, patent			2.0		0.1	0.2		5.5			2.1	68.8
Spices and Condiments												
Allspice(pimenta)			18.0			3.0						
Cassia			23.3									
Cinnamon			19.3									
Cloves			9.0									2.7
Nutmeg			17.2									14.6
Pepper, black			38.6									34.2
Sirups and Other Sweets												
Corn sirup		21.2			26.4			34.7				
High conversion		33.0			23.0			19.0				
Medium conversion		26.0			21.0			23.0				
Corn sugar		87.5			3.5			0.5				
Chocolate, sweet dry						56.4						
Golden sirup			37.5			31.0						
Honey	40.5	34.2				1.9		1.5				
Invert sugar			74.0			6.0						
Jellies, pectin						40-65						
Royal jelly	11.3	9.8				0.9						
Jellies, starch						25-60						7-12
Maple sirup			1.5			62.9						
Milk chocolate				8.1		43.0						

Food	Mono-saccharides			Disaccharides			Polysaccharides					
	Fructose	Glucose	Reducing Sugars*	Lactose	Maltose	Sucrose	Cellu-lose	Dextrins	Hemi-cellu-lose	Pectin	Pento-sans	Starch
Sirups and Other Sweets, continued												
	gm	gm	gm	gm	gm	gm	gm	gm	gm	gm	gm	gm
Molasses	8.0	8.8				53.6						
Blackstrap	6.8	6.8	26.9			36.9						
Sorghum sirup			27.0			36.0						
Miscellaneous												
Beer			1.5					2.8			0.3	
Cacao beans, raw, Arriba	0.6	0.5	1.1			1.9						
Carob bean												
Pod			11.2			23.2				1.4		
Pod and seeds			11.1			19.4						
Soy sauce	0.9											

* Mainly monosaccharides plus the disaccharides, maltose and lactose.
† Blanks indicate lack of acceptable data.
‡ Also known as Alaska pea, field pea, and common pea.
# Trace = less than 0.05 gm.

Table A-2

Less Common Carbohydrates in Foods, per 100 gm. Edible Portion

Food	Carbohydrates		
	gm Arabinose	gm Araban	
Beet sugar	0.6	—	
Soybean meal	—	4.7	
Soybean flour	—	3.6	
Soy sauce	0.3	—	
	Galactose	Galactans	
Peach	0.2	—	
Sapote	0.6	—	
Beet sugar	0.3	—	
Rutabagas	—	0.3	
Navy bean	—	1.3	
Soybean	—	2.3	
Soybean flour	—	4.2	
Soybean meal	—	4.1	
Soybean sauce	0.4	—	
Casein	0.2	—	
Pear	0.2	—	
Apple	0.2	—	
	Glycogen (phytoglycogen)		
Corn, fresh	4.4		
Mushrooms, fresh	0.6		
	gm Mannose	gm Mannans	gm
Egg albumin	0.3	—	
Casein	0.1	—	
Brewer's yeast	—	14.0	
	Pentose		
Copra meal	2.4		
Corn kernel	0.2		

Food	Carbohydrates		
	Raffinose	Stachyose	Ver-bascose
Beans, black mung, dry	0.5	1.8	3.7
Beans, green mung, dry	0.8	2.5	3.8
Beans, soy, dry	1.9	5.2	—
Cacao seeds, raw	—	1.9	—
Copra meal	2.4	—	—
Cow pea	0.4	2.0	3.1
Field bean (Dolichos lablab)	0.5	2.1	3.6
Garbanzo (chick pea)	1.0	2.5	4.2
Horse gram	0.7	2.0	3.1
Lentils	0.6	2.2	3.0
Lima beans, canned	—	0.2	—
Molasses, beet	1.8	—	—
Pigeon pea	1.1	2.7	4.1
Wheat germ, defatted	6.6	—	—
	Sarbitol		
Apple	1.0		
Apple juice	0.3		
Apricot	1.0		
Hawthorn	4.7		
Hawthorn, English	7.6		
Loquat	0.2		
Pear, small green	2.4		
Pear, large green	1.9		
Pear, ripe	2.3		
Pear, Bosc	3.5		
Peach	0.2		
Plum, Kelsey	2.8		
Pyracantha berry	4.0		
Rowan berries (mountain ash)	8.7		
Toyon berry, green	2.5		

Hardinge, M. G., Swarner, J. B. and Crooks, H., "Carbohydrates in Foods," Journal of American Dietetic Association, 46:198-202; 1965.

Table A-3

Metric Equivalents

U.S. to Metric			
Length			
	1 inch	= 25 millimeters	(2.5 cm.)
	1 foot	= 0.3 meter	(30.5 cm.)
Mass			
	1 ounce (dry)	= 28.35 gm	
	1 pound	= 0.45 kilogram	
Volume			
	1 teaspoon	= 5 millimeters	
	1 tablespoon	= 15 millimeters	
	1 fluid ounce	= 29.574 millimeters	
	1 cup	= 0.24 liter	
	1 pint	= 0.47 liter	
	1 quart	= 0.95 liter	
Energy			
	1 calorie	= 4.18 joules	
Metric to U.S.			
Length			
	1 millimeter	= 0.04	inch
	1 meter	= 3.3	feet
	1 meter	= 1.1	yard
Mass			
	1 gram	= 0.035	ounce
	1 kilogram	= 2.2	pounds
Volume			
	1 milliliter	= 0.2	teaspoon
	1 milliliter	= 0.07	tablespoon
	1 milliliter	= 0.03	ounce
	1 liter	= 4.2	cups
	1 liter	= 2.1	pints
	1 liter	= 1.1	quarts
Energy			
	1 joule	= 0.24	calorie

metric scales

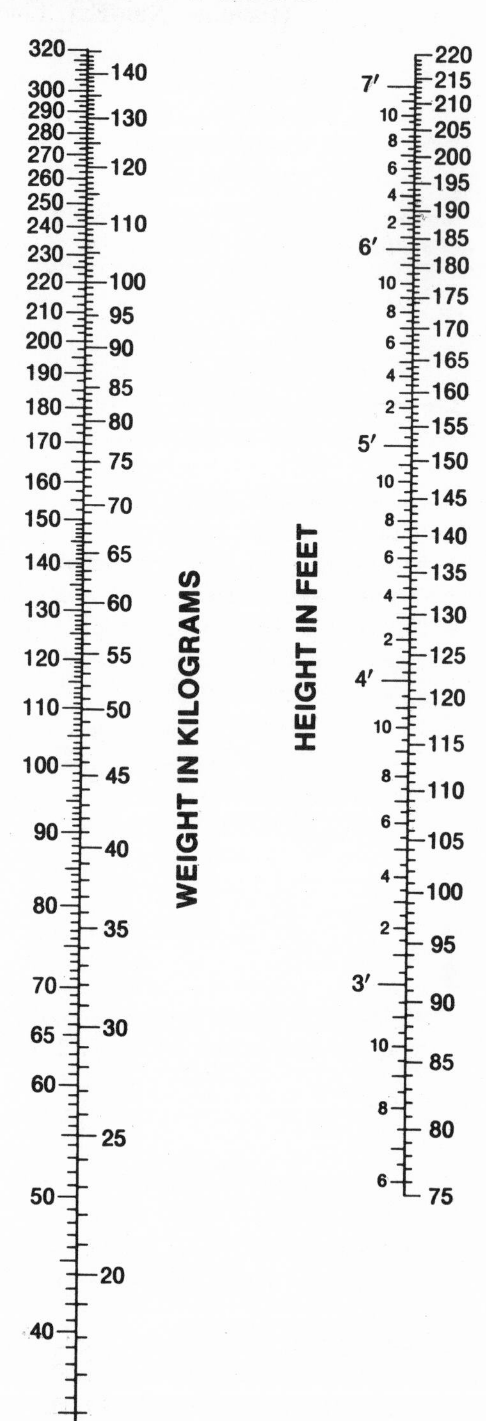

Exchange Lists For Meal Planning

Milk Exchanges

(Includes **Non-Fat,** Low-Fat, and Whole Milk)

One exchange of milk contains 12 grams of carbohydrate, 8 grams of protein, a trace of fat and 80 calories.

Milk is a basic food for your meal plan for very good reasons. Milk is the leading source of calcium. It is a good source of phosphorus, protein, some of the B-complex vitamins, including folacin and vitamin B_{12}, and vitamins A and D. Magnesium is also found in milk.

Since it is a basic ingredient in many recipes you will not find it difficult to include milk in your meal plan. Milk can be used not only to drink but can be added to cereal, coffee, tea and other foods.

This List shows the kinds and amounts of milk or milk products to use for one milk exchange. Those which appear in **bold type** are **non-fat.** Low-fat and whole milk contain saturated fat.

Non-Fat Fortified Milk	
Skim or non-fat milk	1 cup
Powdered (non-fat dry, before adding liquid)	⅓ cup
Canned, evaporated—skim milk	½ cup
Buttermilk made from skim milk	1 cup
Yogurt made from skim milk (plain, unflavored)	1 cup
Low-Fat Fortified Milk	
1% fat fortified milk (omit ½ Fat Exchange)	1 cup
2% fat fortified milk (omit 1 Fat Exchange)	1 cup
Yogurt made from 2% fortified milk (plain, unflavored) (omit 1 Fat Exchange)	1 cup
Whole Milk (Omit 2 Fat Exchanges)	
Whole milk	1 cup
Canned, evaporated whole milk	½ cup
Buttermilk made from whole milk	1 cup
Yogurt made from whole milk (plain, unflavored)	1 cup

Vegetable Exchanges

One exchange of vegetables contains about 5 grams of carbohydrate, 2 grams of protein and 25 calories.

The generous use of many vegetables, served either alone or in other foods such as casseroles, soups or salads, contributes to sound health and vitality.

Dark green and deep yellow vegetables are among the leading sources of vitamin A. Many of the vegetables in this group are notable sources of vitamin C—asparagus, broccoli, brussels sprouts, cabbage, cauliflower, collards, kale, dandelion, mustard and turnip greens, spinach, rutabagas, tomatoes and turnips. A number, including broccoli, brussels sprouts, beet greens, chard and tomato juice, are particularly good sources of potassium.

High folacin values are found in asparagus, beets, broccoli, brussels sprouts, cauliflower, collards, kale and lettuce. Moderate amounts of vitamin B_6 are supplied by broccoli, brussels sprouts, cauliflower, collards, spinach, sauerkraut and tomatoes and tomato juice. Fiber is present in all vegetables.

Whether you serve them cooked or raw, wash all vegetables even though they look clean. If fat is added in the preparation, omit the equivalent number of fat exchanges. The average amount of fat contained in a vegetable exchange that is cooked with fat meat or other fats is one fat exchange.

This list shows the kinds of **vegetables** to use for one vegetable exchange. One exchange is ½ cup.

Asparagus
Bean Sprouts
Beets
Broccoli
Brussels Sprouts
Cabbage
Carrots
Cauliflower
Celery
Cucumbers
Eggplant
Green Pepper
Greens:
- **Beet**
- **Chards**
- **Collards**
- **Dandelion**
- **Kale**
- **Mustard**
- **Spinach**
- **Turnip**

Mushrooms
Okra
Onions
Rhubarb
Rutabaga
Sauerkraut
String Beans, green or yellow
Summer Squash
Tomatoes
Tomato Juice
Turnips
Vegetable Juice Cocktail
Zucchini

The following **raw vegetables** may be used as desired:

Chicory
Chinese Cabbage
Endive
Escarole
Lettuce
Parsley
Radishes
Watercress

Starchy Vegetables are found in the Bread Exchange List.

Fruit Exchanges

One exchange of fruit contains 10 grams of carbohydrate and 40 calories.

Everyone likes to buy fresh fruits when they are in the height of their season. But you can also buy fresh fruits and can or freeze them for off-season use. For variety serve fruit as a salad or in combination with other foods for dessert.

Fruits are valuable for vitamins, minerals and fiber. Vitamin C is abundant in citrus fruits and fruit juices and is found in raspberries, strawberries, mangoes, cantaloupes, honeydews and papayas. The better sources of vitamin A among these fruits include fresh or dried apricots, mangoes, cantaloupes, nectarines, yellow peaches and persimmons. Oranges, orange juice and cantaloupe provide more folacin than most of the other fruits in this listing. Many fruits are a valuable source of potassium, especially apricots, bananas, several of the berries, grapefruit, grapefruit juice, mangoes, cantaloupes, honeydews, nectarines, oranges, orange juice and peaches.

Fruit may be used fresh, dried, canned or frozen, cooked or raw, as long as no sugar is added.

This list shows the kinds and amounts of **fruits** to use for one fruit exchange.

Fruit	Amount	Fruit	Amount
Apple	1 small	**Grape Juice**	¼ cup
Apple Juice	⅓ cup	**Mango**	½ small
Applesauce (unsweetened)	½ cup	**Melon**	
Apricots, fresh	2 medium	**Cantaloupe**	¼ small
Apricots, dried	4 halves	**Honeydew**	⅛ medium
Banana	½ small	**Watermelon**	1 cup
Berries		**Nectarine**	1 small
Blackberries	½ cup	**Orange**	1 small
Blueberries	½ cup	**Orange Juice**	½ cup
Raspberries	½ cup	**Papaya**	¾ cup
Strawberries	¾ cup	**Peach**	1 medium
Cherries	10 large	**Pear**	1 small
Cider	⅓ cup	**Persimmon, native**	1 medium
Dates	2	**Pineapple**	½ cup
Figs, fresh	1	**Pineapple Juice**	⅓ cup
Figs, dried	1	**Plums**	2 medium
Grapefruit	½	**Prunes**	2 medium
Grapefruit juice	½ cup	**Prune Juice**	¼ cup
Grapes	12	**Raisins**	2 tablespoons
		Tangerine	1 medium

Cranberries may be used as desired if no sugar is added.

Bread Exchanges

(Includes **Bread, Cereal** and **Starchy Vegetables**)

One exchange of bread contains 15 grams of carbohydrate, 2 grams of protein and 70 calories.

In this List, whole-grain and enriched breads and cereals, germ and bran products and dried beans and peas are good sources of iron and among the better sources of thiamin. The whole-grain, bran and germ products have more fiber than products made from refined flours. Dried beans and peas are also good sources of fiber. Wheat germ, bran, fried beans, potatoes, lima beans, parsnips, pumpkin and winter squash are particularly good sources of potassium. The better sources of folacin in this listing include whole-wheat bread, wheat germ, dried beans, corn, lima beans, parsnips, green peas, pumpkin and sweet potato.

Meat Exchanges—Lean Meat

One exchange of lean meat (1 oz) contains 7 grams of protein, 3 grams of fat and 55 calories.

All of the foods in the Meat Exchange Lists are good sources of protein and many are also good sources of iron, zinc, vitamin B_{12} (present only in foods of animal origin) and other vitamins of the vitamin B-complex.

Cholesterol is of animal origin. Foods of plant origin have no cholesterol.

Oysters are outstanding for their high content of zinc. Crab, liver, trimmed lean meats, the dark muscle meat of turkey, dried beans and peas and peanut butter all have much less zinc than oysters but are still good sources.

Dried beans, peas and peanut better are particularly good sources of magnesium; also potassium.

Your choice of meat groups through the week will depend on your blood lipid values. Consult with your diet counselor and your physician regarding your selection.

You may use the meat, fish or other Meat Exchanges that are prepared for the family when no fat or flour has been added. If meat is fried, use the fat included in the Meal Plan. Meat juices with the fat removed may be used with your meal or vegetables for added flavor. Be certain to trim off all visible fat and measure the meat after it has been cooked. A three-ounce serving of cooked meat is about equal to four ounces of raw meat.

To plan a diet low in saturated fat and cholesterol, choose only those exchanges in **bold type.**

This List shows the kinds and amounts of **lean meat** and other protein-rich foods to use for one low-fat meat exchange.

Beef:	**Baby Beef (very lean), Chipped Beef, Chuck, Flank Steak, Tenderloin, Plate Ribs, Plate Skirt Steak, Round (bottom, top), All cuts Rump, Spare Ribs, Tripe**	1 oz
Lamb:	**Leg, Rib, Sirloin, Loin (roast and chops), Shank Shoulder**	1 oz
Pork:	**Leg (Whole Rump, Center Shank), Ham, Smoked (center slices)**	1 oz
Veal:	**Leg Loin, Rib, Shank, Shoulder, Cutlets**	1 oz
Poultry:	**Meat without skin of Chicken, Turkey, Cornish Hen, Guinea Hen, Pheasant**	1 oz
Fish:	**Any fresh or frozen**	1 oz
	Canned Salmon, Tuna, Mackerel, Crab and Lobster,	¼ cup
	Clams, Oysters, Scallops, Shrimp,	5 or 1 oz
	Sardines, drained	3
Cheeses containing less than 5% butterfat		1 oz
Cottage Cheese, Dry and 2% butterfat		¼ cup
Dried Beans and Peas (omit 1 Bread Exchange)		½ cup

This List shows the kinds and amounts of **breads, cereals, starchy vegetables** and prepared foods to use for one bread exchange. Those which appear in **bold type are low-fat.**

Bread	
White (including French and Italian)	1 slice
Whole Wheat	1 slice
Rye or Pumpernickel	1 slice
Raisin	1 slice
Bagel, small	½
English Muffin, small	½
Plain Roll, bread	1
Frankfurter Roll	½
Hamburger Bun	½
Dried Bread Crumbs	3 Tbs
Tortilla, 6″	1
Cereal	
Bran Flakes	½ cup
Other ready-to-eat unsweetened Cereal	¾ cup
Puffed Cereal (unfrosted)	1 cup
Cereal (cooked)	½ cup
Grits (cooked)	½ cup
Rice or Barley (cooked)	½ cup
Pasta (cooked), Spaghetti, Noodles, Macaroni	½ cup
Popcorn (popped, no fat added)	3 cups
Cornmeal (dry)	2 Tbs.
Flour	2½ Tbs
Wheat Germ	¼ cup
Crackers	
Arrowroot	3
Graham, 2½″ sq.	2
Matzoth, 4″ x 6″	½
Oyster	20
Pretzels, 3⅛″ long x ⅛″ dia.	25
Rye Wafers, 2″ x 3½″	3
Saltines	6
Soda, 2½″ sq.	4
Dried Beans, Peas and Lentils	
Beans, Peas, Lentils (dried and cooked)	½ cup
Baked Beans, no pork (canned)	¼ cup
Starchy Vegetables	
Corn	⅓ cup
Corn on Cob	1 small
Lima Beans	½ cup
Parsnips	⅔ cup
Peas, Green (canned or frozen)	½ cup
Potato, White	1 small
Potato (mashed)	½ cup
Pumpkin	¾ cup
Winter Squash, Acorn or Butternut	½ cup
Yam or Sweet Potato	¼ cup
Prepared Foods	
Biscuit 2″ dia. (omit 1 Fat Exchange)	1
Corn Bread, 2″ x 2″ x 1″ (omit 1 Fat Exchange)	1
Corn Muffin, 2″ dia. (omit 1 Fat Exchange)	1
Crackers, round butter type (omit 1 Fat Exchange)	5
Muffin, plain small (omit 1 Fat Exchange)	1
Potatoes, French Fried, length 2″ to 3½″ (omit 1 Fat Exchange)	8
Potato or Corn Chips (omit 2 Fat Exchanges)	15
Pancake, 5″ x ½″ (omit 1 Fat Exchange)	1
Waffle, 5″ x ½″ (omit 1 Fat Exchange)	1

Fat Exchanges

One exchange of fat contains 5 grams of fat and 45 calories.

Fats are of both animal and vegetable origin and range from liquid oils to hard fats.

Oils are fats that remain liquid at room temperature and are usually of vegetable origin. Common fats obtained from vegetables are corn oil, olive oil and peanut oil. Some of the common animal fats are butter and bacon fat.

Since all fats are concentrated sources of calories, foods on this List should be measured carefully to control weight. Margarine, butter, cream and cream cheese contain vitamin A. Use of the fats on this List in the amounts on the Meal Plan.

This List shows the kinds and amounts of fat-containing foods to use for one fat exchange. To plan a diet low in saturated fat select only those exchanges which appear in **bold type.** They are **polyunsaturated.**

Margarine, soft, tub or stick*	1 teaspoon
Avocado (4" in diameter)**	1/8
Oil, Corn, Cottonseed, Safflower, Soy, Sunflower	1 teaspoon
Oil, Olive**	1 teaspoon
Oil, Peanut**	1 teaspoon
Olives**	5 small
Almonds**	10 whole
Pecans**	2 large whole
Peanuts**	
Spanish	20 whole
Virginia	10 whole
Walnuts	6 small
Nuts, other**	6 small
Margarine, regular stick	1 teaspoon
Butter	1 teaspoon
Bacon fat	1 teaspoon
Bacon, crisp	1 strip
Cream, light	2 tablespoons
Cream, sour	2 tablespoons
Cream, heavy	1 tablespoon
Cream Cheese	1 tablespoon
French dressing***	1 tablespoon
Italian dressing***	1 tablespoon
Lard	1 teaspoon
Mayonnaise***	1 teaspoon
Salad dressing, mayonnaise type***	2 teaspoons
Salt pork	3/4 inch cube

*Made with corn, cottonseed, safflower, soy or sunflower oil only
**Fat content is primarily monounsaturated
***If made with corn, cottonseed, safflower, soy or sunflower oil can be used on fat modified diet

Meat Exchanges—High-Fat Meat

For each exchange of high-fat meat omit 1 fat exchange.

This list shows the kinds and amounts of high-fat meat and other protein-rich foods to use for one high-fat meat exchange.

Beef:	Brisket, Corned Beef (Brisket), Ground Beef (more than 20% fat), Hamburger (commercial), Chuck (ground commercial), Roasts (Rib), Steaks (Club and Rib)	1 oz.
Lamb:	Breast	1 oz
Pork:	Spare Ribs, Loin (Back Ribs), Pork (ground), Country style Ham, Deviled Ham	1 oz
Veal:	Breast	1 oz
Poultry:	Capon, Duck (domestic), Goose	1 oz
Cheese:	Cheddar Types	1 oz
Cold Cuts		4½" x ⅛" slice
Frankfurter		1 small

Meat Exchanges—Medium-Fat Meat

For each exchange of medium-fat meat omit ½ fat exchange.

This list shows the kinds and amounts of medium-fat meat and other protein-rich foods to use for one medium-fat meat exchange.

Beef:	Ground (15% fat), Corned Beef (canned), Rib Eye, Round (ground commercial)	1 oz
Pork:	Loin (all cuts Tenderloin), Shoulder Arm (picnic), Shoulder Blade, Boston Butt, Canadian Bacon, Boiled Ham	1 oz
Liver, Heart, Kidney and Sweetbreads (these are high in cholesterol)		1 oz
Cottage Cheese, creamed		¼ cup
Cheese:	Mozzarella, Ricotta, Farmer's cheese, Neufchatel,	1 oz.
	Parmesan	3 tbs.
Egg (high in cholesterol)		1
Peanut Butter (omit 2 additional Fat Exchanges)		2 tbs.

Test Diets

Fecal Fat Excretion and Fat Balance Studies

Despite being somewhat cumbersome for the patient and laboratory personnel, quantitative analysis of fecal fat is the most sensitive test of digestive and absorptive function when a patient is suspected of having malabsorption. Adequate assessment of fat excretion requires a stool collection for at least three days, and if stools are infrequent, then collections must be continued for a longer period. Ideally, the patient should be on a normal diet with adequate fat content for three to four days before the beginning of the test, the amount of fat varying according to the child's age; for example, over twelve months of age, 25-30 grams per day; 1-3 years, 35 grams per day; over three years, 40 grams per day; 50-75 grams per day for teen-agers. This diet can be worked out with the aid of a dietitian. During the time of the study, a careful record of the actual intake must be made to insure adequate study. Three charcoal tablets are given to infants and young children, and six tablets to children older than six years, to mark the beginning and end of the collection. Two methods of interpretation are used. In an older child or adult, there should be no more than 5 grams of fat in the stool per day, when taking in adequate fat in the diet. For younger children, this value may vary somewhat, and therefore the coefficient of absorption is probably more accurate in determining adequate fat digestion and absorption. The coefficient of absorption is calculated as follows:

$$\frac{\text{Dietary fat—fecal fat}}{\text{Dietary fat}} \times 100 = \text{C.A.}$$

In children over the age of three years, the coefficient of absorption should be 95%; in the age group from 10 months to 3 years, 85-95%; in the newborn infant, 80-85%; and in premature infants, 60-75%.

Table A-5

Tube Feedings, Composition of 1500 mls. compared with R.D.A. for 7-10 years

COMPARISON OF 1500 mls. OF VARIOUS TUBE AND SUPPLEMENTARY FEEDINGS WITH THE R.D.A. FOR 7-10 YEAR OLDS (Approximately 1 kilocal/ml)	VITAMIN A (I.U.)	VITAMIN D (I.U.)	VITAMIN E (I.U.)	ASCORBIC ACID (mg)	VITAMIN B_1 (mcg)	VITAMIN B_2 (mcg)	NIACIN (mcg)	VITAMIN B_6 (mcg)	CALCIUM (mg)	PHOSPHORUS (mg)	IRON (mg)	PROTEIN (gm)
R.D.A. FOR 7-10 YEARS	3300	400	10	40	1200	1200	16000	1200	800	800	10	36
1500 mls. of the Tube Feedings												
COMPLEAT B	4605	375	27	55.5	1290	1560	9195	1845	1110	2025	16.5	58.5
ENSURE	3975	315	48	240.0	2550	2700	31800	3150	630	630	14.3	55.5
FLEXICAL	3750	300	23	75.0	1080	1200	13500	1500	780	660	7.5	33.0
FORMULA 2	750	345	32	75.0	1050	1800	15000	2250	1950	1650	22.5	57.0
ISOCAL	3900	315	59	234.0	3000	3375	39060	3870	945	780	14.1	51.0
MERITENE LIQUID	6255	495	38	124.5	2505	2505	12495	2505	2130	1875	25.1	90.0
NUTRI-1000	3960	315	24	79.5	1590	1590	11895	1590	1905	1425	9.5	51.0
PRECISION HN	3120	255	20	43.5	1245	1245	6255	1245	495	495	11.3	78.0
PRECISION LR	5205	420	32	73.5	2085	2085	10410	2085	840	840	18.8	43.5
SUSTACAL LIQUID	6960	555	42	84.0	2085	2505	29175	2910	1500	1380	25.1	90.0
SUSTAGEN	7935	630	72	475.5	6030	6825	79275	7935	5070	3810	28.5	166.5
*TCH MILK-BASED FEEDING	4395	300		106.5	1365	2340	10200	750	1155	1260	42.2	58.5
*TCH SOY-BASED FEEDING	5325	375	11	75.0	1635	2100	19050	1485	1080	1170	47.1	55.5

* Pre-prepared formulas are recommended due to the availability of complete nutritional analysis, sanitation and accurate dilution.

Foods which may be high in tyramine:

Cheeses as Brie, Camembert, *Cheddar,* Stilton and other ripe cheeses. Small amounts American processed cheese, cream cheese, and cottage cheese are allowed.
Chianti wine—may be desirable to avoid all wines, *beer,* etc.
Chicken livers
Fermented products and spoiled foods
Figs
Kippered or pickled herring
Meat extracts as Bovril and *Yeast extracts* as Marmite, Yex, Befit, Barmene, Yeastrel, etc. which are used as sandwich spreads or beverages in Britain and possibly Brewers Yeast when used in quantity as a health food.
Broad Bean Pods which are raised in Great Britain, Europe, and Canada but not in the United States for human food, should be avoided as they may contain the pressor principle dopa.

VMA (Vanillymandelic Acid) Test Diet

This diet is a screening test for the presence of a pheochromocytoma (chromaffin cell tumor).

The VMA Test Diet, when ordered for a period of forty-eight (48) hours (2 days), will exclude the following foods:

Vanilla
Coffee
Tea
Banana
Prepared Desserts (such as pie, cake, pudding, etc.)
Chocolate
Cola Drinks

Low Tyramine Diet

A low tyramine diet is usually ordered for patients receiving one of the monamine oxidase inhibitor drugs, i.e., the antihypertensive pargyline hydrochloride (Eutonyl) and nialamide (Niamid), phenelzine sulfate (Nardil) and tranylcypromine sulfate (Parnate), which are used as antidepressants. MAO inhibitors prevent the normal oxidation of tyramine and other pressor principles which may lead to a hypertensive crisis. Foods high in tyramine should be avoided for about a month after the drug has been discontinued.

A low tyramine diet may also be prescribed for certain patients suffering from migraine headaches, and an effort made to discover if foods high in tyramine may be a factor in triggering these headaches.

Index

All bold face page numbers signify that the information is in a Table.

Abetalipoproteinemia, **128**
Acid ash and alkaline ash diets, 118-119
Acid-base reaction of foods, **120**
Adrenocortical biogenesis, disorders of, **128**
Albinism, **128**
Alcaptonuria, **128**
Alkaline ash diet, 118-119
Alkalinizing diet, cystinosis, **127**
Allowances, daily dietary (NRC), 22, **24**
  caloric, children 1-10, **30**
  expressed in relation to energy need, **30**
Amino acids, "neutral," **129**
Anaerobic metabolism, 124
Anion-forming ash, 118-119
  in normal diet, 118
Arginase deficiency, **127**
Argininosuccinic aciduria, **127**
Ascorbic acid, **128**
Atomic weights, 118
Atwater conversion factors, 22-23

Baking powder,
  low-sodium, 81
  sodium content, 107
Baking soda,
  low-sodium, 81
  sodium content, 107
Biotin, **129**
Bouillon, 84
Branched chain ketoaciduria (BCKA). See Maple syrup urine disease (MSUD).
Brancher deficiency, type IV, GSD, 159
Bread exchanges, 171
Breast feeding, 25
Breast milk,
  composition, **7**
  protein content, 25
    efficiency of utilization, 25
    per cent of total kilocalories, 25
    sodium chloride
      consumption by infant, 81
      content, 81
    sodium content, 78
  renal solute load, **7**, 118
Broth, 84

Ca-cystinate, 161
Calcium,
  atomic weight, 118
  decreased absorption, mineral oil, 122
  ketogenic diet, 125
  pseudohypoparathyroidism, **127**
  renal solute load, 118
  renal tubular acidosis, **127**
  vitamin D resistant rickets, **127**
Carbamyl phosphate synthetase deficiency, **127**
Carbohydrate,
  allowance (NRC), **25**
  formulas
    composition, **7**
    sources, **8**
  inadequate intake, 25
  intolerance, 68-70
  minimum requirement, adult, 25
  oxidation (endogenous water), 109
  "protein-sparing," 108
  requirement, 25
  source of energy, 25
    versus fat, 25
  specific, composition of,
    less common carbohydrates in foods, **167**
    various foods, **162**
  storage, 25
  tube feedings, 45, **47**
    composition, **47**
    sources, **49**
Carbonated water, 84
Carotene,
  decreased absorption, mineral oil, 122
Cation-forming ash, in normal diet, 118
Celiac disease, 71-73
  gluten-free commercial products, 74-76
  gluten restricted diet, 73-74
Chloride,
  atomic weight, 118
  renal solute load, 118
CHO-Free, **7**, **8**, 11
Citric acid, renal tubular acidosis, **127**
Citrullinemia, **127**
Cobalamin. See vitamin B_{12}.
Coca Cola, 84
Coffee, 84
Compleat B, **47**, **49**, 53
Composition, nutrient, infant formulas, **7**
Congenital megaloblastic anemia, **129**
Consomme, 84
Copper, Wilson's disease, **127**
Cow's milk,
  composition, **7**
  sodium chloride,
    consumption by infants, 81
    content, 81
Cystathionase deficiency, **129**
Cystathionine, 160
Cystathionine synthase deficiency, **129**, 160
Cystathionuria, **128**, **129**
Cystic fibrosis, **127**
Cystine, **127**, 160
Cystinosis, **127**
Cystinuria, **127**

Debrancher deficiency, type III, GSD, 159
Diabetes insipidus, resistant, **127**
Diabetes mellitus, 130-137
  dietary management, childhood, 130
  metabolic disorder amenable to diet therapy, **127**
  orientation notes on childhood, 131
    diet, 134
    emergencies, 135-137
    exercise, 135
    general information, 131
    insulin, 132
    significance of urine acetone tests, 133
    summary, 137
    treatment, 133
    urine tests for sugar, 132
Diarrhea,
  carbohydrate intolerance, 68
  enzyme deficiency, 68
  lactose intolerance, 69
  Modular formula, use of, 14
  total parenteral nutrition (TPN), use of, 56
Diet,
  order, physician's, 1, 2(f)
      changes, 1, 2(f)
  renal acidosis, 119
  tests, 175, 177
Dietary analysis,
  request for, 3
  suggested meal pattern,
    chopped House diet, **29**
    regular House diet, **28**
Dietary procedures, 1-5
  caloric intake record, 3
  dietary analysis requests, 3
  dietary changes, 1, 2(f), 3
  diet instructions, 3
    in-patient, 3
    out-patient, 3
  formula room, 5
  in-between meal nourishment, 3
  infant dietary intake pattern, 4(f), 5
  meal service times, 3
  new admissions, 1
  physician's diet order sheet, 1, 2(f)
  selective computerized menus, 5
  therapeutic dietary products center (T.D.P.C.), 5
Dietary therapy,
  diabetes mellitus, 130-137
  galactosemia, 137-142
  glycogen storage diseases (GSD), 159-160
  homocystinurias, 160-161
  inborn errors of metabolism, 126-129
    introduction, 126
    summary, conditions according to efficacy of, **127**, **128**
    summary, same conditions, vitamin-responsive, **129**
  maple syrup urine disease (MSUD), 157-159
  phenylketonuria (PKU), 142-157
  renal acidosis, 119
Diets,
  infant, 6
  normal, 21-31
    basic principles, 21-31
    dietary allowances (NRC), **24**
    dietary pattern, planning, 22-31

House,
analysis vs. calculation, suggested meal pattern,
chopped, **29**
regular, **28**
recommended daily food intake patterns, children, **27**
major food groups, 22-23, **23**
nutritional needs, including growth, 21, 25, 30
standard, hospital, 32-44
chopped, 33-34
analysis vs. calculation, suggested meal patterns, children, **29**
recommended food intake patterns, **27**
dental soft, 36-37
recommended food intake patterns, children, **27**
elemental, **47, 49,** 50, 52
liquid, 37-43
clear, 37-40
Lytren, 40
Pedialyte, 40
Polycose, 38-39
full, 41-42
T & A, 42-44
T & A #1 soft, 42-44
T & A #2 soft, 42-44
regular (House), 32-33
analysis vs. calculation of suggested meal pattern, **28**
recommended food intake patterns, children, **27**
soft, 34-36
recommended food intake patterns, children, **27**
therapeutic, hospital, 63-161
acid ash and alkaline ash, 118-119
gluten restricted, 73-74
high calorie, 119-121
inborn errors of metabolism, 126-161
diabetes mellitus, 130-137
galactosemia, 137-142
glycogen storage diseases (GSD), 159-160
homocystinurias, 160-161
introduction, 126
maple syrup urine disease (MSUD), 157-159
phenylketonuria (PKU), 142, 157
low residue, 66-68
low sucrose, 77-78
milk-free, 70-71
minimum residue, surgical soft, 64-66
potassium restricted, 107-109
protein diets, 20 Gm, 40 Gm, 60 Gm, 80 Gm, 109-110
sodium restricted, 78-84
250 mg (11 mEq), 85-88
500 mg (22 mEq), infant, 88-89
500 mg (22 mEq), 89-92
800 mg (35 mEq), 92-96
1000 mg (44 mEq), 96-99
1500 mg (65 mEq), 100-103
2000 mg (87 mEq), 103-107
Dihydrofolate reductase deficiency, **129**
Disaccharidases, deficiency, 68-70
Disaccharides,
absorption, 68-70
deficiency, 68-70
digestion, 68-70

Elemental diets, 50, 52
disadvantages, 52
ingredient list, 55
nutrient composition, **47**
sources of protein, carbohydrate, fat, **49**
uses and advantages, 52
Energy (kilocalories), 22
content, national diet, 25
dietary allowances expressed in relation to, 30
expended,
adult, 108
infant, 108
fat, sources of, brain, 124
formulas, composition of, **7**
tube feedings, composition of, **47**
units, 22
Atwater conversion factors, 22, 23
joule, 22
kilocalorie, 22
Enfamil, **7, 8,** 11
Ensure, **47, 49,** 53
Enzyme deficiencies, 68-70
Epilepsy, ketogenic diet, 124
Exchange lists, 169

Fanconi syndrome, **127**
Fat,
daily allowances, **25**
digestion, 26
exchanges, 174
formulas,
composition, **7**
sources, **8**
intolerance, abetalipoproteinemia, **128**
per cent total kilocalories, 26
physiological role, 25
source of energy by brain, 124
storage, 26
tube feedings,
composition, **47**
sources, **49**
Fat soluble vitamins,
decreased absorption, mineral oil, 122
Fatty acids,
polyunsaturated (PUFA), 26
essential, 26. See linoleic acid
vitamin E: PUFA, 26
source of energy, 26
Flexical, **47, 49,** 53
Folic acid,
formiminotransferase deficiency, **129**
homocystinuria, 161
hypomethioninemia, **129**
megaloblastic anemia, **129**
Food,
acid-ash residue, 118-119
influence of protein, 119
acid-base reaction of, **120**
alkaline-ash residue, 118-119
effect on G-I tract, 63
intake patterns (NRC), children, **27**
Food Groups, 22
four major, 22, 23, **23**
Formiminotransferase deficiency, **129**
Formula 2, **47, 49,** 53
Formulas, infant, 6
dilutions of concentrated formulas, proportions for,
liquid, **9**
powdered, **10**
ingredient list, 6, 11-14
Bremil (Syntex), 6
CHO-Free (Syntex), 11
Enfamil (Mead-Johnson), 11
Isomil (Ross), 11
i-Soyalac (Loma Linda), 14
Lofenalac (Mead-Johnson), 11
Lonalac (Mead-Johnson), 11
Meat-Base (Gerber), 11
Mull-Soy (Syntex), 11
Neo-Mull-Soy (Syntex), 12
Nursoy (Wyeth), 12
Nutramigen (Mead-Johnson), 12
Portagen (Mead-Johnson), 12
Pregestimil (Mead-Johnson), 12
Probana (Mead-Johnson), 13
ProSobee (Mead-Johnson), 13
Similac PM 60/40 (Ross), 13
Similac (Ross), 13
Similac with iron (Ross), 13
Skim milk infant formula (Ross), 13
SMA (Wyeth), 13
Soyalac (Loma Linda), 14
Modular (Baylor Core), 14, 17-20
carbohydrate, 15, 17
complications, 18-20, **18**
composition,
compared with human milk and milk-based formulas, **16**
standard, **16**
fat, 15
indications, 18
preparation, method of, **15**
protein, 14
use of, 14, 17
vitamins, 17
nutrient composition, milk-based, soy-based, special, **7**
sources of protein, carbohydrate, fat, milk-based, soy-based, special, **8**
Fresca, 84
Fructose, GSD V, **128**
Fructosuria, essential, **128**
Fruit exchanges, 170

Galactan, 64
Galactitol, 138
Galactokinase deficiency, **127,** 138
Galactose, 64, 138
diet, free of, 139
Galactosemia, 64, **127,** 137-142
clinical features, 138
diagnosis, 138
diet, of prospective mother at risk, 138
dietary therapy,
beneficial effect, 139
duration, 138
Duarte variant, 138
incidence, 138
inheritance, 138
galactokinase deficiency, 138

galactose free diet, 139-142
galactose free formulas, 138
galactose-1-phosphate uridyl transferase deficiency, 137
management, 138
pathogenesis, 138
urine tests, 138
Galactose-1-phosphate uridyl transferase deficiency. See galactosemia.
Gastrointestinal disorders, 63-78
carbohydrate intolerance, 68-70
celiac disease, 71-73
enzyme deficiencies, 68-70
generalized, 63
low residue diet, 66-68
low sucrose diet, 77-78
milk-free diet, 70-71
specific, 64
Gingerale, 84
Glucagon,
glycogen storage diseases, 159
tolerance test, 123
Glucose,
GSD V, **128**
intolerance, 69
Glucose-6-phosphatase deficiency, 159
Glutamic acid decarboxylase deficiency, **129**
Gluten-free commercial products, 74-76
Gluten restricted diet, 73-74
Glycine, **128**
Glycogen storage diseases (GSD), **127**, **128**, 159-160
clinical features, 159
continuous alimentation,
infusion pump, 159
nasogastric, 159
parenteral, 159
diet, 159-160
monitoring, 160
portocaval anastomosis, 159
types,
I (von Gierke's disease), 159
II (Pompe's disease), 159
III (debrancher deficiency), 159
IV (branching deficiency), 159
V (McArdle's disease), **127**, 159
VI (hepatic phosphorylase deficiency), 159
Glyoxylate: alpha-ketoglutarate carboligase deficiency, **129**
Goiter, familial, **128**
Gout, **128**

Hartnup disease, **128**, **129**
Hemochromatosis, **128**
Hepatic phosphorylase deficiency (type VI GSD), 159
Hereditary disorders of intermediary metabolism, **127**, **128**
Hereditary fructose intolerance, **127**
High calorie diet, 119-121
Histidine, **128**
Histidinemia, **128**
Homocystine, 160
Homocystinurias, **127**, **129**, 160-161
clinical features, 160
defective formation of N^5-methyltetrahydrofolate, 161
diagnosis, 161
etiology, 160
impaired intracellular metabolism of B_6, 161
incidence, 160
inheritance, 160
malabsorption of B_6, 161
pyridoxal phosphate, 160
treatment, 161
B_6 responsive, **127**, **129**, 161
B_6 unresponsive, 161
Hydroxyprolinemia, **128**
Hyperalimentation. See total parenteral nutrition.
Hyperbilirubinemias, **128**
Hyperkalemic periodic paralysis, **128**
Hyperlipidemia, glycogen storage disease, 159
Hyperliproteinemia I-V, **128**
Hyperlysinemia, I, II, **127**
Hypernatremia, 48, 50
Hyperoxaluria, primary, I, II, **128**, **129**
Hyperphenylalanemia, **128**
Hyperprolinemia, I, II, **128**
Hypochromic anemia, **129**
Hypoglycemia,
glycogen storage diseases, 159
ketogenic diet, provocative, 123
ketotic, 123
malabsorption, 69
Modular formula, 14-20
TPN, 56-62
Hypokalemic periodic paralysis, **127**
Hypomethioninemia, **129**
Hypophosphatasia, **128**

Iminoglycinuria, **128**
Inborn errors of metabolism,
dietary therapy, 126-129
summary, efficacy of therapy, **127-128**
vitamin-responsive, **129**
Infantile convulsions, **129**
Insulin, 132
Isomaltose intolerance, 69
Isomil, **7**, **8**, 11
Isovaleric acidemia, **128**
i-Soyalac, **7**, **8**, 14

Jello water, 84
Joule, 22

Ketogenic diet, 123-126
calcium, 125
calculation, 124
duration, 126
epilepsy, 124
ketotic hypoglycemia, 123
MCT, 126
ratio of fats to carbohydrate and protein, 124
side effects, 125
supplementation, 125
table of calculations, 125
Ketotic hypoglycemia, 123
Kidney filtrate, bladder, 109
Kilocalorie, 22, 24, 30
Kool-aid, 84
Kynureninase deficiency, **129**

Lactase,
deficiency, 64, **127**
type I, GSD, 160
Lactase deficiency, 64, **127**
Lacticacidosis, **129**
Lecithin cholesterol acyltransferase deficiency, familial, **128**
Lesch-Nyhan syndrome, **128**
Linoleic acid, 26
deficiency, 26
physiological role, 26
requirement, 26
sources, 26
vitamin E ratio, 26
Lofenalac, **7**, **8**, 11
Lonalac, **7**, **8**, 11
Low calorie diet, 121, 122
Low residue diet, 66-68
Low sodium diets, 85-107
250 mg (11 mEq), 85-88
500 mg (22 mEq), 89-92
500 mg (22 mEq), infant, 88-89
800 mg (35 mEq), 92-96
1000 mg (44 mEq), 96-99
1500 mg (65 mEq), 100-103
2000 mg (87 mEq), 103-107
Low sucrose diet, 77-78
Lysosomal storage diseases, **128**
Lytren, 40, 84

Magnesium,
atomic weight, 118
renal solute load, 118
Malabsorption,
bowel resection, 64
carbohydrate intolerance, 69
Maltose intolerance, 69
Maple syrup urine diseases (MSUD), (branched chain ketoaciduria, BCKA),
alloisoleucine, 157
alpha-keto acids, 157
amenable to diet therapy, **127**
branched chain ketoacid decarboxylase, deficiency of, 157
clinical features, 157-158
classical, 157-158
intermittent, 158
mild, 158
thiamine responsive, 158
dialysis, hemo- and peritoneal, 159
dietary management, 158
monitoring, 159
incidence, 157
infections, 158
inheritance, 157
methionine, 157
pathogenesis, 158
thiamine, responsiveness, **128**, 158
toxicity, acute, 158
treatment, 158
dialysis, 158
diet, 158
special formulas, 158
duration, 158
monitoring, 158

transfusion, 158
types, 157
classical, 157, 158
intermittent, 157, 158
mild, 157, 158
thiamine responsive, 157, 158
urine tests,
dinitrophenylhydrazine (DNPH), 158
ferric chloride, 158
Marfan's syndrome, 160
McArdle's disease, (type V GSD), 159
Meal patterns,
analysis vs. calculation,
chopped diet, **29**
regular House diet, **28**
Meat-Base formula, **7, 8,** 11
Meat exchanges
high fat, 175
lean, 172
medium fat, 175
Medium chain triglycerides (MCT),
abetalipoproteinemia, **128**
cystic fibrosis, **127**
Megaloblastic anemia, **129**
Meritene, liquid, powder, **47, 49,** 54
Methionine, **128,** 161
Methylenetetrahydrofolate, 161
Methylmalonic acidemia, therapy, **127, 129**
Methylmalonic aciduria, **129**
Methyltetrahydrofolatehomocystine methyltransferase, 160
Metric equivalents and scales, 168
Milk, breast, cow, **7**
exchanges, 169
Milk free diet, 70-71
Milliequivalents, conversion to milligrams, 107
Milligrams, conversion to milliequivalents, 107
Mineral oil, adverse effect,
calcium, carotene, fat soluble vitamins, phosphorus, 122
Minimum residue diet, 64-66
Monosaccharides, deficiency (absorption, transport, unabsorbed), 68-70
Mull-Soy, **7, 8,** 11

Neo-Mull-Soy, **7, 8,** 12
Niacin, 129
Nicotinamide, **128**
N^5-methyltetrahydrofolate, 161
N^5-methyltetrahydrofolate methyltransferase, 161
N^5, N^{10}-methylenetetrahydrofolate reductase deficiency, 129
Nonketotic hyperglycinemia, **128**
Normal diets, 21
Normokalemic periodic paralysis, **127**
Nursoy, **7, 8,** 12
Nutramigen, **7, 8,** 12
Nutrient composition, infant formulas, **7**
Nutrient composition, tube, elemental, supplementary feedings, **47**
Nutri-1000, **47, 49,** 54

Organic acid radicals, 118-119
Ornithine transcarbamylase deficiency, **127**
Orotic aciduria, therapy, **127**

Pancreatic enzymes, **127**
Pedialyte, 40, 84
Pentosuria, **128**
Phenylketonuria (PKU), **127,** 142-157
classical, 143
clinical features, 142
diagnosis, 145-146
diet, low phenylalanine, 142, 143
dietary management, 144-148
diet calculation, 147
dihydropteridine reductase, deficiency, 143
exchange lists, 146, 150-155
Gerber foods, 156-157
hyperphenylalaninemia, **128,** 143 (variant forms, transient forms).
incidence, 142
inheritance, 142
Lofenalac, 143, 145, 146
composition, **7**
phenylalanine content, 143-144, 146
sources, protein, carbohydrate, fat, **8**
monitoring, 146
mothers with,
diet, 143
effect on fetus, 143
newborn screening, 142
orthohydroxyphenylacetic acid (oHPAA), urinary excretion, 146
phenylacetic acid, 142
phenylalanine,
blood levels,
cord blood, 145
criteria for therapy, 143
maintenance, 146
normal serum, 145
phenylketonurics, 145
content, Gerber baby foods, 148-150
deficiency, 143, 145, 146
essential amino acid, 143, 145
requirement, 145-146
urine levels, 145
phenylalanine hydroxylase deficiency, 142
phenyllactic acid, 142
phenylpyruvic acid, 142, 145
tests, 142
dinitrophenylhydrazine, 142
ferric chloride, 142
Guthrie, 142, 143, 144, 145
quantitative serum, 145
tyrosine, serum, 145
tyrosine, serum levels, 145
urine, excretion,
orthohydroxyphenylacetic acid oHPAA), 146
phenylalanine, 145
Phosphate, Vitamin D resistant rickets, **127**
Phosphorus,
atomic weight, 118
decreased absorption, mineral oil, 122
renal solute load, 118
Phytanic acid, **127**
Polycose,
composition, 38-39
glycogen storage diseases, 160
sodium and potassium values, 84
Polyunsaturated fatty acids (PUFA), vitamin E ratio, 26
Pompe's disease, type II, GSD, 159
Porphyrias, **128**
Portagen, **7, 8,** 12
Potassium,
atomic weight, 118
content,
beverages, electrolyte solutions, 84
exchange lists, 108, 111-117
hypokalemic periodic paralysis, **127**
intake,
average, 109
Na:K ratio, 109
loss, daily, per 100 kcal, 108
normal diet, 107
renal solute load, 118
restricted diet, 107
relation to fluid intake, 108
relation to protein, 108
relation to sodium, 108
sources, 107
Precision HN, **47, 49,** 54
Precision LR, **47, 49,** 54
Pregestimil, **7, 8,** 12
Probana, **7, 8,** 13
Proline, **128**
Propionic acidemia, therapy, **127, 129**
Propionyl-CoA carboxylase deficiency, **129**
ProSobee, **7, 8,** 13
Prostaglandins, essential fatty acid, precursor of, 26
Protein,
diets, restricted, 109-110 (20, 40, 60, 80 Gm)
exchange lists for, 108, 111-117
formulas,
content, **7**
sources, **8**
Hartnup disease, **128**
potassium restricted diet, 108
recommended dietary allowance, **24**
0-12 months, 25, 108
requirement,
adult, 108
children, 108
infant, 25
potassium restricted diet, 108
"sparing," 108
tube feedings, 45
content, **47**
sources, **49**
Pseudohypoparathyroidism, **127**
Purines, **128**
Pyridoxine. See vitamin B_6.
Pyrimidines, **127**
Pyruvate carboxylase deficiency, **129**

Raffinose, 64
Refsum's disease, therapy, **127**
Renal solute load, 117-118
Renal tubular acidosis, **127**
Requirements, daily dietary, 22
Root beer, 84

Salt. See sodium chloride.
Similac, **7, 8,** 13
Similac 60/40, **7, 8,** 13
Skim milk, 84
Skim milk formula, **7, 8**

SMA, **7**, **8**, 13
Sodium,
  allowance, mgs per each food category, **84**
  content,
    breast milk, 78, 80
    compounds, preparation, processing, preservation, 79
      drugs, 79
    junior foods, 82
    Lonalac (low sodium milk), 81
    meats, 82
      no salt added (Gerber), 83
    special solutions and products, 84
    strained baby foods, 82
    summary, infants, 83
  diets, restricted, 85-107. See low sodium diets.
  exchange lists, protein restricted diet, 108, 111-117
  hypokalemic periodic paralysis, **127**
  intake, average daily, infants, 82
  losses, 78, 80, 81
  potassium restricted diet, 108
  products, free of, 79
  requirement, 78
    infants, other than growth, 80
    per kilo new tissue, 80
  restricted diet, 78-107
    depletion, 81
    food groups, 79
    hemodialysis, 78-79
    indications, 78
    influence on other nutrients, 78
    objections to, 81
    supplements, 80
  sources, 79
  substitutes, 79, 81
Sodium chloride,
  content,
    baby foods, 80-82
    breast milk, 80, 81
    cow's milk, 81
    meats (Gerber), no salt added, 83
  conversion, mEqs and mgs, 107
  exchange lists, 108
  intake,
    average, 78-82
    infants, daily, 81
    summary, by infants, 83
  loss, daily, per 100 kcal, **108**
  normokalemic periodic paralysis, **127**
  requirement, daily, infant, 80
Sorbitol, 64
Soyalac, **7**, **8**, 14
Sprite, 84
Stachyose, 64
Standard hospital diets, 32
Sucrose,
  glycogen storage disease, type I, 160
  intolerance, 69
  low sucrose diet, 77-78
Sulfuramino aciduria, 160
Supplementary feedings,
  nutrient composition, **47**
  sources of protein, carbohydrate, fat, **49**
Sustacal, liquid, **47**, **49**, 54
Sustacal, powder, **47**, **49**, 55
Sustagen, **47**, **49**, 55

Tab, 84
Tangier disease, **128**
Tea, 84
Test diets, 175, 177
Total parenteral nutrition (TPN), 56-62
  complications, 59-60
    deficiency, nutrient, 60
    infections, 59
    mechanical, 59
    metabolic, 60
  indications, 56
  intralipid, 61-62
    essential fatty acid deficiency, 62
    indications, 61
    methods of administration, 61
    monitoring, 62
    solutions, 61
    suggested flow rates, 62
    supplements, 62
  Modular formula, 14, 17
  principles of infusion, 57
    monitoring, 58
    nutrient rate delivered, **59**
    rate of flow, 57
    supplements, 58
  solutions, currently stocked, 56
    composition,
      crystalline amino acid, **60**
      protein hydrolysate, **57**
  technique, 56
    catheter placement, 56
      care, 57
Transcobalamin II deficiency, **129**
Tryptophan, **129**
Tube feedings,
  analysis of,
    comparison of 1500 mls with R.D.A., **176**
    comparison of T.C.H. with R.D.A.,
      milk-based, **51**
      soy-based, **51**
  basic principles, 45
  blenderized, 45
  carbohydrate, 45
  commercially prepared, 46
    nutrient composition, **47**
    sources of protein, carbohydrate, fat, **49**
  fat, 46
  handling of, 50
  indications, 48
  ingredient list, 53-55
    Compleat-B, 53
    Ensure, 53
    Flexical, 53
    Formula 2, 53
    Isocal, 53
    Meritene, liquid, 54
    Meritene, powder, 54
    Nutri-1000, 54
    Precision HN, 54
    Precision LR, 54
    Sustacal, liquid, 54
    Sustacal, powder, 55
    Sustagen, 55
    Vivonex, 55
    Vivonex HN, 55
  protein, 45
Tyramine
  foods high in, 177
  low in diet, 177
Tyrosinemia, hereditary, **127**

Urea cycle disorder, **127**
Urine,
  acetone tests, 133
  concentration, 117
  nitroprusside test, 160

Vasopressin, resistant diabetes insipidus, **127**
Vegetable exchanges, 169
Vitamin A,
  abetalipoproteinemia, **128**
  cystic fibrosis, **127**
Vitamin B_6, (pyridoxine)
  cystathioninuria, **129**
  glutamic acid decarboxylase, deficiency, **129**
  homocystinuria, **129**
  hyperoxaluria, **129**
  hypochromic anemia, **129**
  infantile convulsions, **129**
  primary hyperoxaluria I, II, **128**
  xanthurenicaciduria, **129**
Vitamin B_{12}, (cobalamin),
  juvenile pernicious anemia, **129**
  methylmalonic acidemia, **127**
  methylmalonic aciduria, **129**
  transcobalamin II deficiency, **129**
Vitamin D,
  cystic fibrosis, **127**
  cystinosis, **127**
  pseudohypoparathyroidism, **127**
  resistant rickets, **127**
Vitamin E, PUFA ratio, 26
Vivonex,
  composition, **47**
  sources, protein, carbohydrate, fat, **49**
Vivonex HN, **47**, **49**, 55
VMA test diet, 177
von Gierke's disease, (glucose-6-phosphatase deficiency, GSD), 159, 160

Water, 84
  cystinuria, **127**
  diabetes insipidus, resistant, **127**
  endogenous, 109
  intake,
    adults, 109
    infants, 109
      retention, 109
  losses, daily, 108
    infants and children, 109
    per 100 kcal, **108**
  requirement,
    normal (all ages), 108
  weight,
    gain,
      high kilocalorie diet, 119-121
      kilocalories required, 119
    loss,
      essential carbohydrate, 122
      kilocaloric deficit required, 122
      low kilocalorie diet, 121-122
Wilson's disease, **127**